Faith in Moderation
Islamist Parties in Jordan and Yemen

Does political inclusion produce ideological moderation? Jillian Schwedler argues that examining political behavior alone provides insufficient evidence of moderation because it leaves open the possibility that political actors might act as if they are moderate while harboring radical agendas. Through a comparative study of the Islamic Action Front (IAF) party in Jordan and the Islah party in Yemen, she argues that the IAF has become more moderate through participation in pluralist political processes, while the Islah party has not. The variation is explained in part by internal group organization and decision-making processes, but particularly by the ways in which the IAF has been able to justify its new pluralist practices on Islamic terms while the Islah party has not. Based on nearly four years of field research in Jordan and Yemen, Schwedler contributes both a new theory of ideological moderation and substantial new detail about the internal workings of these two powerful Islamist political parties.

Jillian Schwedler is Assistant Professor of Government and Politics at the University of Maryland and Chair of the Middle East Research and Information Project (MERIP), publishers of *Middle East Report*. She has received awards and fellowships from the National Science Foundation, the Social Science Research Council, and the Fulbright Scholars Program, among others. Dr. Schwedler's publications include three edited volumes: *Toward Civil Society in the Middle East?* (1995), *Islamist Parties in Jordan* (1997), and the award-winning *Understanding the Contemporary Middle East*, with Deborah J. Gerner (2004). Her articles have appeared in *Comparative Politics, Journal of Democracy, SAIS Review of International Affairs, Social Movement Studies*, and *Middle East Policy*, among other journals. She is currently working on a book project on protest and policing in Jordan and a collaborative project on the repression-dissent nexus in the Middle East.

Faith in Moderation

Islamist Parties in Jordan and Yemen

JILLIAN SCHWEDLER
University of Maryland

CAMBRIDGE
UNIVERSITY PRESS

CAMBRIDGE UNIVERSITY PRESS
Cambridge, New York, Melbourne, Madrid, Cape Town, Singapore, São Paulo

Cambridge University Press
40 West 20th Street, New York, NY 10011-4211, USA

www.cambridge.org
Information on this title: www.cambridge.org/9780521851138

First published 2006
This digitally printed version 2007

A catalog record for this publication is available from the British Library.

Library of Congress Cataloging in Publication data

Schwedler, Jillian.
Faith in moderation : Islamist parties in Jordan and Yemen / Jillian Schwedler.
  p. cm.
Includes bibliographical references and index.
ISBN-13   978-0-521-85113-8 (hardback)
ISBN-10   0-521-85113-0 (hardback)
1. Political culture – Jordan.   2. Political parties – Jordan.   3. Islam and politics – Jordan.
4. Political culture – Yemen.   5. Political parties – Yemen.   6. Islam and politics –
Yemen.   I. Title.
JQ1833.A91.S39   2006
324.2533′082–dc22   2005027921

ISBN 978-0-521-85113-8 hardback
ISBN 978-0-521-04000-6 paperback

For Mom and Dad,
Wish You Were Here

Contents

List of Figures

List of Tables

Preface

Grappling with the question of the inclusion of Islamists in democratic processes has been personally challenging. As a progressive, I have frequently lent my voice to those who have argued against cultural explanations for why few Muslim societies are democratic. I am committed to encouraging democratization on a global scale, although I question whether positive change can be realized through external intervention. I believe that international standards of human rights should be applied throughout the Middle East and Muslim world (indeed, globally) and that the greatest obstacles to the realization of those norms and practices are the repressive and nondemocratic regimes that prevail in the region. It is a sad truth, as well, that many of these nondemocratic regimes came to power, have remained in power, or have been substantially strengthened by direct support from democratic nations. I am shamed and embarrassed by these ongoing practices.

An honest commitment to democratization in the Middle East and Muslim world requires recognition that Islamists are legitimate political actors with substantial constituencies. They cannot be excluded wholesale from the political arena on either normative or practical grounds. Yet I recognize that Islamist groups do not aspire to the same secular vision of freedom and equality that I embrace. They may, in fact, aspire to banish that vision from the political arena. The tension – sometimes, the open conflict – between these personal commitments is not easily resolved.

Nor, unfortunately, is it easily addressed. Most scholarship on the Middle East is haunted by what might be characterized as the Edward Said–Bernard Lewis divide: striving to understand Middle Eastern cultures and societies on their own terms (Said 1978, 1997) versus viewing Middle

Eastern and particularly Islamic culture as partly or wholly responsible for the region's failure to follow global trends of democratization (Lewis 1994, 2001, 2003). The intellectual climate, particularly since September 11, 2001, but also previously, has virtually denied a full hearing to forthright discussion of the tensions between commitments to democratization and secular liberalism. The debates are so polarized that I sometimes find myself defending Islamists alongside apologists whose willingness to overlook the regressive dimensions of many Islamist agendas makes me extremely uncomfortable.

I have contended, along with others, that not all Islamists are radical, and I believe that to be true. I have written that Islamists are unlikely to win the majorities that would enable them to overturn new democratic processes, and I also believe that to be true. But among the hundreds of "moderate" Islamists I have interviewed, I have encountered tremendous anti-Semitism (not to be confused with anti-Zionism – a legitimate political position that should be decoupled from racism). I have close friends who have lost partners and family to acts of political violence perpetrated by extremist Islamists. I am nervous when Islamists ask about my husband, as I wonder whether they will recognize his name as Jewish. I doubt that as a white, red-haired American female, I could conduct my research as easily if certain Islamist groups were successful in implementing their agendas. Nor do I not want my friends in the region to be subjected to conservative and sometimes regressive social programs – even if a majority of the citizenry supports them. But because the political climate is so polarized and the stakes are so high, progressives seldom talk about these tensions, even among ourselves. We are all worse off for that silence.

The (largely) unspoken obstacle to such frank debate is that those of us who study the Middle East recognize that our scholarship may "add evidence" to one position or the other in a public discourse full of caricatures and half-truths. Fearful of contributing to lines of reasoning that obscure complex processes and/or support undesirable policies, we sometimes frame our arguments in ways that ultimately weaken both progressive politics and our intellectual contributions. The problem is not that we hold normative commitments, but that we routinely fail to comment on these and other factors that influence the direction and shape of our scholarship.

I recognize that a great deal is at stake in the deployment of categories, such as moderate and radical, and in the characterization of Islamist participation in democratic political practices. In particular, the question of moderation in the Middle East is charged because it tends to imply that

Islamists may uniquely threaten the prospects for democratization. In this regard, encouraging moderation is often shorthand for the project of turning Islamists into democrats, if not liberals. My intention is not to limit the discussion of moderation to Islamists nor to frame the overall theoretical debate around promoting democratization per se. Rather, I hope to pose a more normatively neutral question about how groups move from a relatively closed ideology to one that is more open, tolerant, and pluralist. I take seriously the concern that we can never know what any Islamist – or any person, for that matter – believes or intends. My claims are modest and primarily theoretical, though I believe they are also highly relevant to practical debates about democratization. I hope that my transparency regarding my normative commitments will better inform readers as to my intellectual motivations and that, in turn, readers will be generous in judging the success of this effort on its own terms.

Acknowledgments

Book acknowledgments typically begin with formal thanks to institutions and granting agencies and move to more personal expressions of gratitude to friends (with veiled references to heavy drinking), family, and partner. I must start with the most personal, however, as this project spanned the loss of several lives and the introduction of several new ones. My father died as I entered graduate school and my mother died as I completed my dissertation. My dad was endlessly supportive, though I suspect he worried when his little girl decided to run off to study the Middle East. My mom saw me through most of this project and was overjoyed by the possibilities I faced compared to her own difficult and often unhappy life. They were incredible parents, and my world will never be quite right without them. My best friend from graduate school died tragically days before my first job interview, and the loss paralyzed me for months. A dear friend in Jordan who shared my commitment to progressive politics lost a devastating struggle with cancer. During those black periods, my husband and my truest love kept me alive, though I watched helplessly as he suffered when his mother died a year before my own. For twenty-one years, he has given me his undying love, steadfast support, and countless laughs. For this and more, I adore him endlessly. We started our own family, as many do, with a dog, a beautiful stray pit bull with grateful brown eyes. As I finish this manuscript, two new little people, my twin sons, happily disrupt my work with their squeals of laughter. I hope that they find life as joyous as I have, not withstanding the pain of losing loved ones. These precious lives, lost and found, have made life wonderful: Marvin Schwedler, Diana Schwedler, Janet Sherman, Aida Dabbas, John

Vantine, Joel Sherman, and my big little guys, Jake and Nick Ronin. And, of course, Ruby.

I owe special thanks to my dearest friends whose wise council, tireless support, and patient reading of various drafts are responsible for anything of value in this book: Paul Amar, Shiva Balaghi, Kathleen Cavanaugh, Janine Clark, Geoff Hartman, Marc Lynch, Pete Moore, Agnieszka Paczynska, Curt Ryan, and Lisa Wedeen. Colleagues and friends supported me at every turn, sharing precious contacts in the field and many cheap and "interesting" bottles of wine: Abla Amawi, Maha Abu Ayyash, Deborah Boardman, Marion Boulby, Laurie Brand, Bassel Burgan, Sheila Carapico, Greg Gause, Deborah "Misty" Gerner, Iris Glossimer, Lisa Hajjar, Kimberly Katz, Sa'eda Kilani, Ellen Lust-Okar, Awni Nabulsi, Scott Nilson, Dick Norton, Megan Perry, Lynne Rienner, Noha Sadek, Katri Saari Seiberg, Rajiv Sethi, Eric Thompson, Chris Toensing, Jeff Togman, Bob Vitalis, James Vreeland, Shelagh Weir, Derek Wildman, and Anna Würth. Dermot O'Brien should also be included, but I want to express special thanks to him for suggesting "Faith in Moderation" as the title of a talk I gave at New York University in the mid-1990s.

My incredible dissertation committee provided inspiration, support, and extraordinarily challenging questions: Timothy Mitchell (Chair), Stathis Kalyvas, Farhad Kazemi, Adam Przeworski, and Elisabeth Wood.

My MERIP family has been a source of inspiration and encouragement for more than a decade. In addition to those mentioned, I am particularly grateful to Joey Beinin, Joe Stork, and Michelle Woodward, who located the cover photo.

New colleagues at the University of Maryland have made my work stronger and broader, and they have become cherished friends: Charles Butterworth, Ken Conca, Christian Davenport, Virginia Haufler, Marc Morjé Howard, Karen Kaufmann, Mark Lichbach, James Riker, Shibley Telhami, and Lois Vietri. Like many scholars, I am indebted to the challenging questions of doctoral students: Cornel Ban, Diana Boros, Laryssa Chomiak, Carter Johnson, Joanne Manrique, and Shana Marshall. In particular, four students provided continual support and careful readings during the final two years of revision: Waseem El-Rayes, Samir Fayyaz, Maren Milligan, and Neha Sahgal. Participants in the DC Area Workshop on Contentious Politics provided critical readings and invaluable suggestions on many parts of this project, as did the participants of the Workshop on Contentious Politics at Columbia University and its tireless organizer, Chuck Tilly.

Financial support for research and writing was extremely generous: a Fulbright Dissertation Fellowship, the Fulbright New Century Scholars Program, the Near and Middle East Research and Training Initiative of the Social Science Research Council, the American Institute for Yemeni Studies, and the Council of American Overseas Research Centers.

Innumerable individuals in Jordan and Yemen made my work possible, but I am particularly indebted to those who generously shared their knowledge and tirelessly endured my sometimes pedantic questions. The members and leaders of the Muslim Brotherhood and IAF in Jordan and the Islah party in Yemen were extraordinarily generous in opening their libraries, archives, and homes to me. Mustafa Hamarneh, Hani Hourani, Nasr Taha Mustafa, Muhammad ʿAbd al-Malik al-Mutawakkil, Muhammad Qahtan, and Faris Saqqaf were especially generous with their time and endured long conversations about my research. ʿAbd al-Rahman Ishaq and his family welcomed me repeatedly into their home, giving me an extended family in Yemen. They have all enriched my life as well as my understanding of their countries.

Several institutions have provided additional support in a variety of forms. In the United States: New York University's Kevorkian Center for Near East Studies and Department of Politics and University of Maryland's Department of Government and Politics. In Jordan: the American Center for Oriental Research, the Jordanian-American Binational Fulbright Commission, the Arab Archives Institute, the Center for Strategic Studies at the University of Jordan, and al-Urdun al-Jadid Research Center. In Yemen: the American Institute for Yemeni Studies, the Yemeni Center for Research and Studies, the Center for Strategic Studies, and the Center for Future Studies.

My editor at Cambridge University Press, Lewis Bateman, was extraordinarily supportive and patient during the preparation of this manuscript. Christine Dunn was a terrific copy editor, and two anonymous reviewers provided detailed and substantive comments that significantly improved the manuscript.

Unconventional institutional support provided sanity through the storm that is graduate school: Stromboli Pizza on St. Marks, the Holiday Cocktail Lounge, *The Daily Show* with Jon Stewart, Mistress Formika at the Pyramid Club, Click and Drag at Mother, and New York City.

List of Abbreviations

AAIA	Aden-Abyan Islamic Army, Yemen
GID	General Intelligence Department (*mukhabarat*), Jordan
GPC	General Popular Congress party, Yemen
HAMAS	Islamic Resistance Movement, Palestine
IAF	Islamic Action Front party, Jordan
IJM	Islamic Jihad Movement, Yemen
IMF	International Monetary Fund
NCC	National Consultative Council, Jordan
NDF	National Democratic Front, South Yemen
NGO	nongovernmental organization
NSP	National Socialist Party, Jordan
PDRY	People's Democratic Republic of Yemen (South Yemen)
PELP	Popular Front for the Liberation of Palestine
PKK	Kurdish Workers Party
PLO	Palestinian Liberation Organization
ROY	Republic of Yemen (united Yemen)
SCCO	Supreme Coordination Council of the Opposition, Yemen
USAID	U.S. Agency for International Development
YAR	Yemen Arab Republic (North Yemen)
YCCSS	Yemeni Center for Cultural and Strategic Studies
YSP	Yemeni Socialist Party

Note on Transliterations and Translations

In an effort to make this work of political ethnography accessible to a non-Arabic-speaking audience, I have adopted a modified transliteration system that represents only the medial 'ayn, 'ghayn, and hamza, except in rendering proper names. Arabic terms appear in italics, often parenthetically following the English use: Council of Deputies (*majlis al-nuwab*). Because Arabic plurals take many forms, I have noted where I give the Arabic term in the singular: Islamic religious opinions (sing. *fatwa*). I have avoided pluralizing Arabic words by adding *s*. Words and names common in the English language take the familiar form (thus, "Amman" and not "'Amman") and when an individual has a preferred spelling of his name in English (thus, "Saad Eddin Ibrahim" and not "Sa'ad al-Din Ibrahim"). I have reviewed my translations and transliterations for accuracy and consistency, but if a careful Arabic reader finds fault with some of my renderings I hope he or she forgives me for erring on the side of accessibility. Unless noted, all translations are my own.

Faith in Moderation
Islamist Parties in Jordan and Yemen

I

Moderation and the Dynamics of Political Change

Do Islamist political parties threaten emerging democratic processes?[1] According to some, these groups are uncommitted to democratic norms and seek to exploit electoral processes to achieve nondemocratic ends. Others argue that the inclusion of Islamists is necessary because they represent a significant segment of their societies and because excluding them is a surefire means of promoting radicalism rather than encouraging moderation. Embedded in this latter argument is the idea that those who are included will become more moderate and tolerant as they learn to engage in democratic processes. Theoretically, we know surprisingly little about how this process might actually unfold. On a practical level, the stakes of getting political inclusion right – of deciding whom to include and whom to exclude – are extraordinarily high, particularly when pluralist institutions and practices are not yet well established.

Yet the relationship between inclusion and moderation is more complicated than typically portrayed, and two distinct propositions – that exclusion increases radicalism, and inclusion increases moderation – are frequently conflated. Inclusion and exclusion are often posited as a continuum, with moderation greatest in democratic, pluralist, and politically inclusive societies, and radicalism greatest in exclusive, repressive, and authoritarian societies. If increased inclusion means decreased radicalism, then inclusion is certainly preferable on both normative and practical

---

[1] To be sure, *inclusion* and *exclusion* do not capture the whole range of options available to state actors. Repression, when severe and comprehensive, can effectively eliminate a movement as a viable political challenger, as was the case with Syria's harsh treatment of the Muslim Brotherhood, culminating in the 1982 Hamah massacre. Various forms of accommodation and co-optation are other options, examined in Chapter 2.

I

grounds. But are these relations as strong as they are assumed to be? Even more, are the implied causal mechanisms for moderation and radicalization well established on their own, let alone as producing consistent effects with movement along a continuum?

I argue that the mechanisms that explain precisely how inclusion and exclusion produce moderation and radicalism, respectively, are poorly specified and should be unpacked and studied separately. This study explores one side of this puzzle, the implied causal relationship between inclusion and moderation, through a structured comparative study of two Islamist parties. Jordan's Islamic Action Front (*Jabhat al-'Aml al-Islami*, or IAF) and the Yemeni Congregation for Reform (*Tajamma' al-Yamani li al-Islah*, commonly called the *Islah* or reform party)[2] both participate in pluralist political processes within otherwise nondemocratic contexts. Neither Jordan nor Yemen comes close to meeting the most basic requirements for a democracy, whether in terms of the Schumpeterian minimal procedural conception emphasizing competitive elections and representation (Schumpeter 1942; Przeworski 1991) or in terms of substantive definitions of democracy in which broad participation and egalitarian distributive arrangements are emphasized (Pateman 1970; Mouffe 1992; Benhabib 1996; Cammack 1997; Shapiro 1999; Young 2000). Yet both regimes have enacted limited political openings as part of their loud and oft-repeated declarations of commitment to democracy (*dimuqratiyyah*), including the introduction of pluralist political practices (*ta'addudiyyah*) within a multiparty system, the guarantee of basic human rights (*huquq al-insan*), and fairly regular elections for national and municipal assemblies. These concepts are often left poorly defined, though they are frequently invoked.

In this chapter, I first examine the debates that inform this comparative study, including approaches to democratic transitions, the distinction between moderates and radicals, and the hypothesis that political inclusion increases moderation. After unpacking what I term the *inclusion-moderation hypothesis* in some detail, I suggest a mechanism that explains why some strongly ideological groups may become more moderate as they engage in pluralist practices, while similar groups participating in comparable processes may not. Rejecting the view that countries like Jordan

---

[2] The English word *group* is often used for the Arabic *jama'a* (*tajamma'* is a related form), but *group* fails to capture the sense of a community congregating or gathering, that is, a community "assembled." In English, the word *congregation* best captures more dimensions of the Arabic term than does *group*.

and Yemen are "stalled" along the road to democracy, I argue that in each country public political space has been significantly restructured to accommodate and even encourage pluralist practices, even though non-democratic regimes remain firmly in place and "elected" assemblies play no role in governance. Have the Islamist parties in these two cases become more moderate as a result of their participation in multiparty elections and their adoption of new practices? Both parties have changed, but not in similar let alone consistent ways. While Jordan's IAF has become more moderate over time, Yemen's Islah party has not. What explains this variation? Despite interesting cumulative effects, at a very minimum these changes cannot be characterized as movement along a single moderate-radical continuum. Even where the IAF has become more moderate on some issues, it retains conservative and sometimes even radical positions on other issues. Instead, I define *moderation* more narrowly as movement from a relatively closed and rigid worldview to one more open and tolerant of alternative perspectives. I examine multiple dimensions of change as each Islamist group begins to participate in an evolving field of pluralist political contestation and identify where moderation has occurred, where it has not, and why. Finally, I summarize my argument, explain my field research methodology, and outline the coming chapters.

THE LIMITS OF TRANSITOLOGY

While critiques of the literature on transitions to democracy, or *transitology*, have been around for years (Collier and Collier 1991; Adler and Webster 1995; Bunce 1995, 2003; Cammack 1997; Tilly 2001; Carothers 2002), a broad and often explicit "stages of democratization" framework continues to flourish in academic scholarship as well as in the policy world. As McFaul notes (2002: 6), it is difficult to argue with the transitions literature because proponents of strategic theories of democratization do not recognize a single theory despite obligatory reference to Rustow (1970) and O'Donnell and Schmitter (1986). Rustow suggests a process-oriented model to understanding transitions to democracy, while O'Donnell and Schmitter focus on the dynamics of regimes that had begun to move away from authoritarian rule. In defending his early work against critics, O'Donnell argues that he never suggested that democratization unfolded in predictable stages or along a consistent path, or even that he envisioned democracy as an end point (1996, 2002: 7). Regardless, the "paths to democracy" framework continues to dominate many studies of democratic transitions (e.g., Diamond et al. 1988–90; Higley and

Burton 1989; Przeworski 1991, 1993; Snyder 1992, 1998; Schmitter and Karl 1991, 1994; Mainwaring et al. 1993; Linz and Stepan 1996; Collier 1999; Diamond 1999, 2000; Eikert and Kubik 1999) and overwhelms policy debates.

The resilience of this framework has an obvious normative underpinning among academics as well as policy makers: the desire to see more states democratize. As Gendzier (1985), Cammack (1997), and Tilly (2001) argue, this commitment has led many scholars to fail to distinguish between *explanations* of democratization and *programs for the promotion* of democratization (e.g., O'Donnell et al. 1986; Diamond et al. 1988–90; Di Palma 1990; Linz and Stepan 1996; Diamond 1999). Others have explicitly viewed the generation of new policies as a direct measure of successful scholarly studies (e.g., Diamond 2000: 100–5; Nodia 2002: 18), even when these policies fail to produce the desired results. But if programs for the promotion of democratization have seen few successes, how have scholars fared in explaining actual processes of democratization? In fact, we do not have a model of predicable stages and identifiable processes replicated across cases.[3] Even more troubling is that few scholars explicitly acknowledge, as do Huntington (1991) and O'Donnell and Schmitter,[4] that they aim to guide political leaders in countries entering the early stages of transition. Yet the commitment to promoting democracy is near universal in the literature, leading scholars to focus on classifying various stages of transition and identifying obstacles that prevent this process from "moving forward." Many transitologists focus disproportionate attention on the role of elite actors because they play a dominant role in initiating and guiding many transitions (e.g., Rustow 1970; Karl 1986, 1990, 1997; O'Donnell et al. 1986; Share 1987; Higley and Burton 1989; Di Palma 1990; Huntington 1991; Przeworski 1991, 1993; Rueschemeyer et al. 1992; Snyder 1992, 1998; Cohen 1994; Share and Mainwaring 1996; Bratton and van de Walle 1997; Munck and Leff 1997; Hellman 1998; Higley et al. 1998; Motyl 1998; Haraszti 1999; Colomer 2000; Kalyvas 2000; Whitehead 2001a, 2001b). Some scholars (Adler and Webster 1995; Bunce 1995; Collier 1999; Eikert and Kubik 1999;

---

[3] Przeworski argues that even sophisticated statistical analyses "indicate that transitions to democracy are almost impossible to predict, even with the entire panopticum of observable factors, economic or cultural" (1998a: 137).

[4] "[W]e are providing a useful instrument – pieces of a map – for those who are today venturing, and who tomorrow will be venturing, on the uncertain path toward the construction of democratic forms of political organization" (O'Donnell and Schmitter 1986: 5).

Geddes 1999; Gill 2000; Wood 2000; Sanchez 2003) note that this has led to systematic overlooking of the role of nonelite actors, while others (Vitalis 1994; Cammack 1997) point out that most western-led pushes for democratization (including much academic scholarship) tend to prioritize the promotion of global capitalism and pro-Western regimes over democracy. More importantly, the majority of countries that had begun transitions seem to be moving less "toward" democracy than evolving into new forms of nondemocratic rule (Rose et al. 1998; Brumberg 2002; McFaul 2002: 214; Nodia 2002: 14–15). In fact, even major proponents of transitology admit that successful transitions have proved to be more the exception than the rule (O'Donnell and Schmitter 1986: 3; Diamond 1999; Carothers 2002; McFaul 2002: 212–13; O'Donnell 2002: 7), raising questions about comparability across such a wide swath of "failed" cases.[5] Nondemocratic governance certainly warrants scholarly attention, but the focus on policy implications directs attention to getting countries "back on track" toward Fukuyama's liberal and democratic "end of history" (1992).

At the same time, scholars of Middle East politics have been frustrated that transitologists tend to systematically ignore cases from the Middle East, some of which have been no less promising in their early stages than those in other parts of the world.[6] Regimes increasingly adopted the rhetoric of democracy and initiated limited political openings in the 1980s and early 1990s, and regional experts adopted the vocabulary and assumptions of models that specify paths, obstacles, and necessary, but insufficient, conditions of democratization (e.g., Niblock and Murphy 1993; Crystal 1994; Salamé 1994; Waterbury 1994; Brynen et al. 1995; Norton 1995–6; Schwedler 1995; Esposito 1997; Ghadbian 1997; Quandt 1998; Mufti 1999; Bellin 2003). Eager to dispel lingering notions of

---

[5] Bunce argues that in Schmitter and Karl's call for scholars to apply transitions theory to postcommunist contexts (1991, 1994), they fail to consider the possibility that comparing cases from Latin America with postcommunist transitions may entail comparing apples and oranges. "The key question ... is whether the differences constitute variations on a common process – that is, transitions from dictatorship to democracy – or altogether different processes – that is, democratization versus what could be termed postcommunism" (1995: 119). While she does not reject the potential for valuable comparative scholarship, her concern about applying "democratization" theories to inappropriate cases is well-founded.

[6] Among the large studies that ignore Middle East cases are O'Donnell et al. (1986), Diamond et al. (1988–90), Huntington (1991), and Linz and Stepan (1996). Michael Hudson notes that as he prepared his 1987 presidential address for the Middle East Studies Association on the question of democratization in the region, colleagues and students responded with incredulity at his choice of topic (1988: 157).

Middle Eastern exceptionalism, regional specialists published innumerable books and articles about how Algeria, Bahrain, Egypt, Iran, Jordan, Kuwait, Morocco, Tunisia, and Yemen "started down the road to" democracy, though like many incipient transitions in other regions, these "democratic openings" either "stalled" or had been "aborted" entirely.[7] Even democratic openings begun decades earlier, as in the cases of Lebanon and Turkey, were seen as stalled somewhere short of full democracy. Middle East scholars caught up to the work of transitologists and shared their focus on identifying the causes of these failed transitions.

As suggested in the preceding text, one limitation of the focus on transitions to democracy is that political change is assessed almost exclusively in terms of progress along a continuum,[8] with many processes characterized by stagnancy (in the case of stalled transitions) or a return to autocratic practices (in aborted and failed transitions). This focus often obscures the complex ways in which political institutions and practices are restructured *even in cases where political openings do not progress very far*. That is, even limited openings may produce considerable dynamic change in the public political space – the practices and locales of political struggle – and these multidimensional restructurings demand systematic analysis. Scholars should abandon the notion that the "space" between authoritarianism and democracy is characterized by a continuum of stages from primitive, traditional, or patriarchal systems of rule (authoritarianism) to modern, rational-legal systems of rule (democracy). Webs of possible political trajectories depend not only on elite-level decisions but also on popular mobilization, the particularities of each historical context, the discursive terms of political struggle, and regional and international factors. In their study of how scholars characterize these variations, Collier and Levitsky (1997) critique the often absurd ways in which ever new models are forced into a democratization framework: formal democracy, semi-democracy, electoral democracy, façade democracy, pseudodemocracy,

---

[7] Use of this language has the advantage of making Middle East politics comprehensible to nonregional specialists, particularly transitologists who see the world in terms of democracies, transitional states, and nondemocracies. In 2002 I wrote an article on the prospects for democracy in Yemen for *The Journal of Democracy*. I titled the piece "Yemen's 'Emerging Democracy'," the language favored by Yemen's nondemocratic regime, but with quotes around the words "emerging democracy" to denote irony. The journal's editors renamed the article "Yemen's Aborted Opening," placing my analysis into a "stalled" democracy framework. See Schwedler (2002).

[8] See Linz and Stepan (1996) and Diamond (2000: 95). Freedom House also posits a continuum, as its annual review of freedom in the world rates countries on a variety of issues, but the result is a continuum from 7 (least free) to 1 (most free).

weak democracy, partial democracy, illiberal democracy, and virtual democracy. As Carothers argues, "[b]y describing countries in the gray zone as types of democracies, analysts are in effect trying to apply the transition paradigm to the very countries whose political evolution is calling that paradigm into question" (2002: 10). Instead, scholars should let go of the "transitions" language and focus instead on comparative analysis of these new forms of "electoral" nondemocracies (10–14). Carothers' model of dominant-power politics, for example, better describes many Middle Eastern regimes than the language of stalled democracy: "limited but still real political space, some political contestation by opposition groups, and at least most of the basic institutional forms of democracy. Yet one political grouping – whether it is a movement, a party, an extended family, or a single leader – dominates the system in such a way that there appears to be little prospect of alternation of power in the foreseeable future" (11–12). Recent writings about this "gray zone" have advanced new typologies of nondemocracy regimes and suggest that regimes reach new equilibriums that seem to be quite durable (Lust-Okar and Jamal 2002).

But Bunce's critique of the transitions literature is more devastating than Carothers's. She argues that more is at stake than simply characterizing the type of regime accurately. "What is open for negotiation is not just the character of the regime but also the very nature of the state itself, not just citizenship but also identity, not just economic liberalization but also the foundation of a capitalist economy . . . not just amendment of the existing class structure but the creation of a new class system, not just a shift in the balance of interests . . . but something much more fundamental: the very creation of a range of new interests . . . not just modification of the state's foreign policies, but also a profound redefinition of the roles of the state in the international system" (1995: 121). In this regard, transitologists and gray-zone scholars alike have focused disproportionate attention on changes in regime and elite-level politics, to the neglect of changes in the broader public political space. While façade democracies should be subject to critique, even specious reforms typically include an expansion of political space in which diverse political groups can establish parties and put forth political agendas for public debate. These new modes of participation, though falling far short of democracy, nevertheless reshape both the political space and the routine practices of political actors. Therefore, scholars need to think systematically about the precise ways in which institutions and practices have changed in the face of the strategic deployment of limited "democratic" reforms by nondemocratic regimes.

Moderates and Radicals

With a growing body of scholarship critiquing the emphasis of elite actors, the once-common language characterizing key political actors as moderates, soft-liners, or reformers, on the one hand, and radicals, hard-liners, or stand-patters (those unwilling to undertake reforms), on the other hand, has almost disappeared among scholars of democratic transitions (e.g., Diamond 1999; Geddes 1999; Gill 2000; Angell 2001; Whitehead 2001a; Nodia 2002; O'Donnell 2002) although they continue to play prominent roles for scholars who still strive to "refine" the original transitions paradigm (Linz and Stepan 1996; Snyder 1998; McFaul 2002) or theorize the persistence of neopatrimonial regimes in the face of pressures for transition (Brownlee 2002). In the fields of Middle East and Islamic studies, however, the notions of "moderate" and "radical" are still used fairly consistently with respect to Islamist groups: moderates seek gradual reform within the existing system, while radicals seek revolutionary change often through the use of violence (Burgat 1993; Hadar 1993; Krämer 1994, 1995a, 1995b; Roy 1994; Abed-Kotob 1995; Guazzone 1995; Norton 1995; Schwedler 1995, 1998; Tal 1995; 'Ali 1996; Esposito and Voll 1996; Halliday 1996; Burgat and Dowell 1997; Esposito 1997; Ismail 1998; Kurzman 1998; Boulby 1999; Moussalli 1999, 2001; Hefner 2000; Kalyvas 2000; Kepel 2002; Hafez 2003; International Crisis Group 2003; Wedeen 2003; Wickham 2004; Lust-Okar 2005; Nasr 2005). While a few scholars view all Islamists as engaged in a common political project (the Islamization of all dimensions of state, society, and economy), the majority use the term *Islamist*[9] to describe diverse groups and practices rather than as a single category of analysis. That is, they recognize that the term *Islamist* captures, at most, a shared commitment to the implementation of Islamic Law (*shari'ah*) in all spheres,[10] but not the significant variation in tactics, strategies, or even specific objectives. Those who still favor the moderate-radical distinction argue that the terms usefully capture variation in strategies and tactics toward existing regimes: moderates work within the constraints of the existing political institutions and practices, while radicals seek to overthrow the system entirely, perhaps (though not necessarily) through the use of violence. In many ways, these labels capture a distinction between the political strategies of Islamist groups. In Jordan, Indonesia, Kuwait, Lebanon, Morocco, Pakistan, and

[9] The term *Islamicist* is sometimes used rather than *Islamist*, but the object is the same. See, for example, Wedeen (2003).
[10] The project emphasizing Islamic law is largely the domain of Sunni Islamists.

Yemen, Islamist political parties operate legally and peacefully, contesting elections, publishing newspapers, and participating in municipal councils and parliaments. In Egypt, Tunisia, and Turkey, religious parties are formally illegal, but known Islamists participate openly either as independent candidates, in alliance with legal political parties, or as a party that does not put forth an explicitly religious agenda. All of these groups can be fairly labeled moderate with respect to political participation. To be sure, our understanding of legal Islamist political parties is little advanced when we lump them in the same category with violent underground organizations such as al-Qa'ida, Islamic Jihad, or certain Salifi groups, or even with aboveground groups such as the Islamic Resistance Movement (HAMAS) in Palestine and Hizb Allah in Lebanon, which both defend the use of violence in certain circumstances while adopting pluralist practices when engaging other domestic political actors (Robinson 2004; Clark 2005b). And as the International Crisis Group notes, the notion of moderates and radicals usually boils down to "distinguishing between those with whom Western governments feel they can 'do business' (the moderates) and those with whom they cannot or will not" (International Crisis Group 2005b: 2).

Yet because all Islamists are seen as ideological actors – as embracing an ideological position that might potentially clash with the basic norms and practices of democratic governance – their participation in these pluralist (if not democratic) political processes creates no small amount of anxiety for a range of actors. Domestic regimes, capitalist economic elites, foreign donors, and secular opposition groups all express concern about the possibility of even moderate Islamists coming to power. Skeptics of Islamists' commitment to democracy often cite some Islamists' efforts to strictly impose *shari'ah*, introduce gender segregation, and place limits on acceptable forms of speech. Others point to anti-Semitism among many Islamist groups and the extent to which even some moderates defend the use of political violence under certain circumstances. Committed democrats, critics argue, should reject violence at all times. Furthermore, many "moderate" Islamists have launched harsh campaigns of intimidation and even physical attack against secular intellectuals, threatening their jobs, their marriages, and sometimes their lives. Still, most scholars and, increasingly, even U.S. government officials insist that the distinction between moderates and radicals provides a valuable means of understanding differences in the practices as well as the political agendas of various Islamist groups.

A few scholars have in recent years put forth alternative typologies. A report of the International Crisis Group, argues that the idea of Islamism as "Islam in political mode" is problematic because, first, "it presupposed that Islam per se is not political, whereas insofar as Islam is inherently interested in matters of governance, in fact it is. Secondly, it presupposes that all forms of Islamism are equally political, whereas in fact, there are significant distinctions in this regard between those forms that privilege political activism, missionary activity, or violence." The report proposes instead the notion of Islamic activism, divided into three types: political, missionary, and *jihadi* (International Crisis Group 2005b: 1, fn. 1). Alternatively, Zubaida (1993, 2001) and Ismail (1998, 2001) argue for adding to moderates and radicals a third category, conservatives, to signify groups such as the Islamic scholars of al-Azhar, who have a symbiotic relationship with the Egyptian state that often clashes not only with Egypt's radicals (such as Islamic Jihad) but also with its moderates (the Muslim Brotherhood).

Each of these alternatives, while improving on earlier models, continues to label groups wholesale and focus the debate on whether a particular group is best characterized as moderate, radical, conservative, *jihadi*, and so on. But like the binary moderate-radical categorization, applying labels to groups or movements tends to ignore variation in position across a range of issues and obscure internal party divisions. In my study with Janine Astrid Clark of women's activism within Islamist parties (2003), we illustrate the limitations of attempting to label particular groups, factions, or individuals. Looking at a spectrum of positions that various Islamists take on a range of issues, we argue that the terms *moderate* and *radical* might be applied to *some positions* on a particular issue, but hold little analytic value as wholesale *categories* of political actors. An individual Islamist, for example, may hold moderate views with respect to participation in pluralist elections, but not concerning the right of women to participate. Or, he or she[11] may hold moderate views about economic reform, but radical views about adherence to religious texts. As an alternative, we advocate the use of categories of analysis that capture positions on precise issues. For example, terms such as *accommodationist* and *nonaccommodationist* may be used with respect to political participation, while the terms *contextualist* and *legalist* may be used to capture how closely an actor adheres to literal readings of religious texts. These differences are stark among various actors and even more complex within and between

---

[11] Although the overwhelming majority of Islamist leaders are male, Islamist movements are not without female activists, though they have received little systematic attention from scholars. See Clark and Schwedler (2003) and Taraki (2003).

whole groups. This distinction between labeling political actors and label-ing particular positions is crucial for the question of moderation, as it cuts closer to the question of ideological commitments than do most studies emphasizing only whether groups seek change by working inside or out-side of the existing political system. In this study, I use a much more narrow and precise definition of moderation than any of those outlined in the preceding text. I describe this definition in detail in the following text and in Chapters 4 and 5.

THE INCLUSION-MODERATION HYPOTHESIS

The scholars and policy makers who argue in favor of including Islamists in democratic processes frequently defend their positions not on norma-tive grounds – that all voices should be included – but on practical and sometimes strategic grounds that including Islamists will both promote moderation and reduce radicalism. Inclusion is seen as a mechanism for deflating radical opposition voices, promoting tolerance and pluralism, and perhaps even advancing a democratization process. But the inclusion-moderation hypothesis is not unique to the transitions paradigm. In fact, large and varied bodies of literature deploy some version of the idea that inclusion produces moderation in behavior, practices, or beliefs. Scholars and theorists as diverse as liberals (J. S. Mill 1859) and social democrats (Habermas 1989) espouse variations of this idea in terms of promoting the vibrant public space essential for democracy. Public debate is highly val-ued in a democratic political system not only because public deliberation can be a democratic process but also because it exposes individuals and groups to the concerns, beliefs, and methods of reasoning with others. At a minimum, interaction reinforces the recognition of multiple worldviews and interpretations of how existing problems may be resolved.

The most common formulation of this argument is that institutions shape political behavior by creating constraints and opportunities, which in turn structure the choices available to political actors. If this is correct, even limited political liberalization, such as the legalization of political parties or the holding of elections, should shape the practices of those who choose to participate. The challenge is to channel dissenting voices and competing groups into state-controlled spaces of political contesta-tion by providing opposition voices with immediate incentives (e.g., legal status, the right to publish a newspaper, and the ability to put forth alter-native political agendas) and the promise of future political gains (e.g., access to political power through elections). If an opposition group agrees to "play by the rules of the game," the regime will permit increased space for the group to pursue its political agenda. These rules of the game are, of course, set and maintained by the regime, but they are also subject to public debate. Through this process opposition voices gradually become more moderate as they recognize the benefits of continued participation. Moderation is thus produced through a combination of new structural constraints and the strategic choices of political actors.[12] For example, Huntington proposes a "participation-moderation trade-off" in which radicals moderate their political agendas and agree to play by the rules of the game to become eligible to take advantage of institutional openings (1991: 165–72). The inclusion-moderation hypothesis also emerges in rational choice debates, for example, concerning credible commitments (Kalyvas 2000), co-optation (Lichbach 1995: 191–3), strategic behavior within institutional constraints (Przeworski 1985; Share 1985, 1987; Przeworski and Sprague 1986; Przeworski 1991, 1993; Roberts 1995; Share and Mainwaring 1996; Kalyvas 2000), and the conditions under which both state and nonstate actors see this trade-off as politically viable (Przeworski 1985, 1991; Cohen 1994). In the vast literature on political parties, inclusion is seen to create constraints on groups that gradually become caught up in the mechanics of building and sustaining a viable political party (Michels 1962; Keck 1992). Similarly, in debates about social movements political opportunity structures shape the behavior of political actors by making certain modes of political contestation more viable and less costly than others (Gamson 1990; McAdam et al. 1996; Giugni et al. 1998; Goodwin and Jasper 2003, 2004). Other social movement theorists have long argued that inclusion leads movements to institutionalize and deradicalize as leaders need to focus on defending their positions (Lowi 1971) or to evolve from principled opposition to engagement in formal, pragmatic politics (Piven and Cloward 1977). Certain political opportunity structures, such as those that provide legal outlets for political organization, can also decrease the likelihood of revolutionary mobilization (Zald and Ash Garner 1987: 125–6; Kriesi 1989; Goldstone 1998). These and other theories of political constraints are discussed in greater detail in Chapters 2 and 3.

   But as noted in the preceding text, arguments about inclusion and exclusion often envision a single continuum whereby more inclusion equates to more moderation *as well as* less radicalism. Conflating

---

[12] As Polletta notes, this dichotomous view of ideology and strategy has dominated much of the literature on participatory democracy as well (2002: 5).

inclusion and exclusion in this manner has a tendency to obscure complex processes and offer little in terms of precise hypotheses about the effects of inclusion and exclusion. For example, entangled in the inclusion-moderation hypothesis are several distinct propositions. Inclusion may increase moderation by a variety of methods, including:

- Turning radicals into moderates (thus reducing the number of radicals and increasing the number of moderates),
- Turning fence-sitters (those teetering between moderation and radicalism) into moderates (thus increasing the number of moderates without necessarily reducing the number of radicals),
- Leading moderates to adopt even more moderate positions than they held previously, and/or
- Providing moderates with opportunities to increase their visibility and efficacy (without necessarily changing the number of moderates or radicals).

These hypotheses about moderation, which focus on the orientation of political actors vis-à-vis the existing political system, are further entangled with questions concerning the support bases commanded by various groups. In this connection inclusion may produce an overall effect of moderation by:

- Increasing the support base for moderates while reducing the support base for radicals,
- Increasing the support base for moderates without decreasing the support base for radicals, and/or
- Decreasing the support base for radicals without increasing the support base for moderates.

In each of these cases, moderates see a relative gain in support base compared to radicals.

Any of these changes could produce the appearances of an increase in moderation when in fact very different processes or combinations of processes may be responsible. For example, changes in the number of moderates and radicals may or may not be connected to changes in the size of the support base for moderates and radicals. Or, an apparent increase in moderation may have little to do with whether political actors have actually *changed their positions on particular issues*. Instead, the outcome may be one of creating opportunities for certain political actors while disadvantaging others. That is, inclusion may not turn radicals into moderates, but rather deny radicals the support base that provides political advantage.

It may not lead political actors to change their views so much as to elevate the position of certain actors at the expense of others. Even taking the inclusion-moderation hypothesis on its own (rather than in combination with the exclusion-radicalism hypothesis), we must be very clear about unpacking both inclusion and moderation to assess precisely what has changed and why.

The diverse bodies of literature noted in the preceding text all emphasize the role of institutional constraints in shaping political behavior in ways that suggest how inclusion may increase moderation. But these formulations do not offer a theory or model for explaining ideational change, that is, precisely how a political actor may come to hold more moderate views and objectives as a result of inclusion. In particular, they are unable to deal with the question of whether an actor is sincere in her apparent acceptance of the rules of the game, or whether she is secretly waiting for the opportunity to implement a radical agenda. Rational choice theory, for example, offers much in the way of understanding institutional constraints and does acknowledge that preferences may change, but it treats preferences as relatively stable and offers no theory of preference change. As the most well-developed literature on institutional constraints, rational choice cannot as such explain ideological moderation.

Other bodies of literature come closer. In the vast literature on identity, proximity to and interaction with diverse groups are sometimes said to lead to more complex identities, therefore lessening the rigidity – and therefore the potential for violence around – particular identity divides. The literature on political learning also posits that beliefs and agendas can evolve over time as political actors engage in forms of pluralist participation. Through accumulated experience, political actors *learn*, an evolutionary process that reshapes ideas, beliefs, and political agendas (Bermeo 1992; Wickham 2004). Here, learning is treated as the mechanism for moderation. But how and what do actors learn? What if the experiences are of institutional fatigue and the inability to realize substantive reform by working within the system? Even more, what if the experiences of inclusion result in bloodshed and trauma, rather than participatory politics? Inclusion could result in this sort of outcome if a dominant actor is threatened by the inclusion of a challenger and results to extra-institutional means of competition. This happened in the case of the Yemeni Socialist Party, when its leaders and members were targeted in hundreds of assassination attempts by political challengers in the early years of unification. Indeed, actors may learn very different lessons through participation in similar processes. Even more problematic is how to explain why two political actors with comparable experiences do not necessarily learn in the same way. Asserting that some learned while others do not, skates dangerously close to description rather than explanation.

In widely diverse bodies of literature, exposure to different perspectives is seen to lead to increased levels of tolerance.[13] In the conflict resolution literature, for example, the contact hypothesis argues that intergroup contact reduces intergroup prejudice and therefore will likely facilitate conflict resolution and promote overall tolerance, including toward groups with whom one has had no contact at all (Williams 1947; Allport 1954; Pettigrew and Tropp 2003).[14] But as Mutz has argued, the empirical evidence supporting a relation between exposure to conflicting viewpoints and political tolerance is actually extremely thin (2002: 111). Some scholars of the protracted conflict in Northern Ireland reject the contact hypothesis entirely due to extensive evidence of its failure (Whyte 1991; McGarry and O'Leary 1995). And yet, policy makers and foundations seem to have bottomless reserves of funds to support intergroup contact, all in the belief that the intergroup contacts will, if not resolve conflicts, prevent them from escalating or emerging altogether (Varshney 2002). Finally, the literature on deliberative democracy, while taking the work of Habermas in various directions, tends to emphasize the positive role of substantive deliberative exchange in building or supporting democratic, pluralist processes. Poletta, for example, argues that the deliberative dimensions of participatory democracy may build meaningful relationship among participants as they recognize the legitimacy of the thinking and reasoning of others (2002: 9).

Despite the ubiquity of various incarnations of the inclusion-moderation hypothesis, however, surprisingly few scholars have conducted in-depth case studies aimed at evaluating the specific claim that inclusion leads to moderation. In many cases, "success" stories are told about actors who certainly qualify as moderate, but who were never really radical – in the sense of seeking to entirely overthrow the existing political order – in the first place (e.g., see Messara 1993; Krämer 1995a, 1995b; Norton 1995; Esposito 1997; Boulby 1999; Wiktorowicz 2001; Hafez 2003: 27–65; Wickham 2004). These scholars are not wrong to characterize these groups as moderate, but they imply (if not state explicitly) that political inclusion led these groups to *become* moderate. Furthermore, they often fail to specify that they are referring to positions on one

---

[13] Mutz provides a useful review of this literature (2002).
[14] For a critique of this literature, see Ford (1986).

particular issue (democratic participation), and instead label actors as
either moderates or radicals. In other studies, the inclusion-moderation
hypothesis is asserted as the self-evident inverse of the idea that exclusion leads to radicalism. Like the inclusion-moderation hypothesis, the
exclusion-radicalism hypothesis has seen mixed empirical evidence: some
studies support the idea that exclusion (and particularly repression) produces radicalism (Abd Allah 1983; Kepel 1986; Burgat 1993; Anderson
1997; Esposito 1997; Moussalli 1999, 2001; Fearon and Laitin 2003;
Hafez 2003; Kodmani 2005), while other scholars have found that political repression is not a reliable predictor of conflict and radicalism
(Lichbach 1987; Davenport 2000, 2005; Earl 2003; Wickham 2004).

In any case, measuring an increase in moderation *as a result of political
inclusion* has proved exceptionally difficult. In terms of the most common
definition of moderation – working within a political system rather than
trying to overthrow it – groups lacking a history of using political violence
against a regime cannot necessarily be counted among those who have
moderated as a result of their inclusion. Moderation may entail relative
increases in tolerance, but this is not the argument that is implied. Instead,
the primary normative appeal of the inclusion-moderation hypothesis is
that inclusion may deflate radicalism and turn revolutionaries into reformers, not that moderates may become more moderate. This observation
has significant import for the Middle East, where most Islamist groups
that work for change through existing political systems were never really
radical on these terms. That is, as case studies they do not necessarily
lend empirical support to the inclusion-moderation hypothesis because
most Islamist groups have sought gradual (rather than revolutionary)
political change, at least in terms of the reforming the political system.
Most branches of the Muslim Brotherhood, the movement founded in
Egypt by Hassan al-Banna (1906–49) in 1928, have long sought reform
from within the existing system, often starting with education reform
and literacy programs, but also counterposing Islamic political ideas to
Western-style democracy. Contemporary Islamist groups as diverse as
Turkey's Reform, Virtue, and Justice parties,[15] Jordan's IAF and Muslim
Brotherhood,[16] Morocco's Justice and Development Party,[17] Indonesia's

---

[15] In Turkish, *Refah Partisi, Fadila Partisi,* and *Ak Partisi,* respectively. For more information, see Göle (1995), Yavuz (1997), and White (2002).
[16] In Arabic, *Jama' at al-Ikhwan al-Muslimin.* For more information, see Adams (1996),
Milton-Edwards (1996), Robinson (1997, 1998b), Schwedler (1997), Boulby (1999),
Mufti (1999), Wiktorowicz (2001), and Moaddel (2002).
[17] In French, *Parti de la Justice et du Développement.*

Prosperous Justice Party,[18] Egypt's Muslim Brotherhood and Wasat party,[19] Lebanon's Hizbollah,[20] Yemen's Islah party,[21] Kuwait's three Islamist parties,[22] Tunisia's Islamic Renaissance Movement,[23] and Pakistan's Jamaat i-Islami[24] all might qualify as moderate because they do not seek to overthrow their regime through violent means. Here the attention to moderation on a specific issue is essential, as many of these groups support the use of political violence outside of their own country. Some have secret militant wings, though they may never have been activated. Likewise, these groups may envision dramatically different end points, many of which would entail radical political and social change even if they are to be achieved through gradual reform. Some of them have long been allied with the ruling regime, while others have worked quietly and peacefully as opposition parties. Still others have worked as moderates under certain regimes while engaging in less moderate practices under other regimes. Substantively, their agendas and political programs show considerable variation. As argued in the preceding text, these practices significantly complicate the notion of a binary moderate-radical categorization and its use for analytical purposes.

What these cases do illustrate, however, is that many regimes began including Islamists in state-controlled political processes decades before the "democratic openings" of the 1980s and 1990s. In fact, a large number of radical Islamist groups – such as Egypt's *Gama'at al-Islamiyyah*, various incarnations of *Hizb al-Tahrir*, many offshoots of Islamic Jihad, and certain *Salafi* groups – emerged as dissident movements frustrated with the integrative approaches of mainstream Islamist groups (Kepel 1986, 2002; Abu-Amr 1994; Roy 1994; Milton-Edwards 1996; Wiktorowicz 2001). Many of their members had defected from other groups, inspired by events in Iran in 1978–9 to seek revolutionary change through radical means. This distinction is crucial, as it emphasizes the notion that inclusion may be a means of isolating radicals from mainstream movements by denying them a large, popular support base, as argued in the preceding

---

[18] *Partai Keadilan Sejahtera.*
[19] In Arabic, *Jama'at al-Ikhwan al-Muslimin* and *Hizb al-Wasat*. For more information, see Mitchell (1969), Kepel (1986), Ismail (1998), Zubaida (2001), and Wickham (2004).
[20] In English, *Party of God*. For more information, see Hamzeh (1993, 1998), Jaber (1997), and Saad-Ghorayeb (2002).
[21] In addition to this book, see Dresch and Haykel (1995) and Schwedler (2003a).
[22] For more information, see Ghabra (1997).
[23] In Arabic, *Harakat al-Nahda al-Islamiyya.* For more information, see Dunn (1993), Shahin (1997), and Burgat and Dowell (1997).
[24] In English, *Islamist Group.* See Nasr (1994).

text. In this formulation, inclusion provides moderates with incentives to defect from moderate-radical alliances, to isolate radicals within their midst, and to shun radical political strategies in the first place. For groups that choose to take advantage of political openings and engage in pluralist practices, inclusion may be a mechanism for making them *more* moderate on certain issues than they had been previously. Even more complicating, some regimes seem to be as threatened by moderate groups as they are by radical groups. In Egypt, for example, Mubarak's regime has shunned the inclusion of moderate Islamists and sought instead to co-opt the clerics of al-Azhar as the regime's Islamic face while consistently excluding and repressing even the most moderate voices, such as al-Wasat (which has never received a license to operate legally as a political party).

While these various propositions need to be unpacked, at the very least there appears to be little evidence supporting the idea that inclusion – let alone democratization – will completely eliminate radicalism. Most democracies still see radical groups emerge with regularity, but these groups are widely considered fringe or extremist by popular measure and command comparatively miniscule followings. For analytical clarity, therefore, we need to be very precise about what processes are at work when making causal arguments about the connection(s) between inclusion and moderation, both in terms of particular cases as well as in building theory.

The Stakes of Moderation

In the broadest terms, then, diverse bodies of literature argue that inclusion will moderate oppositional actors either by 1) subjecting them to institutional constraints, or 2) exposing them to alternative views. In either case, the implied result is a reduction of radical challenges to the political system. In regime-led inclusion, the ruling elite win by deflating the radical opposition and gaining the ability to closely monitor legal opposition groups. Opposition groups benefit from the freedom to put forth alternative political agendas and the possibility of winning seats in parliament. Unfortunately, the possibility remains that a group may obtain power through inclusive channels without having become moderate. The "paradox of democracy," for example, is the idea that democratic processes might produce an undemocratic outcome. The concept is generally applied to the practical problem that a political group may come to power through democratic elections only to impose a nondemocratic system. In theory as well as practice, the possibility of this less-than-desirable outcome often serves to justify continued exclusion and repression. The literature on institutional constraints can neither recognize such feigned moderation, nor explain how and why moderation does sometimes take place. The literature on commitment problems recognizes that previously radical actors may have difficulty making credible commitments about participation (Kalyvas 2000), but it can only explore this puzzle of signaling and not whether – or particularly why – moderation has indeed taken place. But if a democratic system can only tolerate democrats – those who accept the legitimacy of democratic processes, either for normative reasons (Gutmann and Thompson 1996) or, minimally, as a means of processing conflict and preserving future opportunities (Przeworski 1991) – then those uncommitted to those processes and practices must be excluded to guarantee the preservation of the system.

Is it therefore possible to distinguish between moderation that is superficial, and substantive moderation characterized by truly increased tolerance and even acceptance of those with diverse views? The core issue of moderation is ideological commitments, rather than only behavior. Because we can never know what is "in the heart" of any political actor, how can we determine which political actors are playing by the rules of the game, but secretly harboring radical agendas, and which have become more tolerant, moderate, and pluralist? Those skeptical of Islamist participation in elections frequently point to the rise of the Nazi party in Weimar Germany. The analogy is powerful because the National Socialist party exploited participatory institutional channels to gain power, but it is not an example of a radical movement coming to power exclusively through electoral success.[25] The Nazi party never received an electoral majority, and its rise relied not only on weak institutional constraints but also on coersion and the intimidation of challengers (Berman 2001). Yet those most suspicious that Islamist groups harbor nondemocratic intentions often draw an analogy with the Nazi party, suggesting that democrats and democratic reformers should be cautious of Islamists because their claims of adherence to democratic norms are suspect. The possibility that any political actor may harbor a radical agenda behind a democratic façade is always a factor in democratic processes, and leaves us with the apparent puzzle of not knowing whether political actors are truly committed to democratic processes.

In his study of confessional politics through comparative analysis of the emergence of Christian democratic political parties in Europe, Kalyvas argues that the fact that groups may certainly hold antidemocratic agendas is unproblematic as long as institutions are set up in such a way as

[25] It received a high of only 37.8 percent of the vote in the July 1932 election.

to safeguard the democratic process (1996, 1998a). Even if such groups managed to come to power, the system would provide checks on their ability to reshape the system, thus preserving the integrity of the democratic processes. Like other rational choice theorists, Kalyvas rests his moderation explanation on the logic of strategic participation within institutional constraints, where ideological change follows the decision to participate (see also Przeworski and Sprague 1986). In theory, then, effectively functioning democratic institutions should process conflict as Przeworski imagines, bringing losers back to the table to try again while preventing pseudodemocrats from hijacking the system. But these formulations offer no theory of ideational change and no mechanism to explain why some political actors become moderate while others in similar circumstances do not. Thus the central problem to the inclusion-moderation hypothesis remains: how can we know with certainty whether a political actor has become more moderate in her views as a direct result of inclusion, and what mechanism(s) explain that change.

Furthermore, the logic of strategic behavior within institutional constraints provided by a democratic system offers little for understanding moderation within the gray-zone regimes characterized by weak institutions, as are common in much of the world. In this regard, analogies to Christian Democratic parties in Europe thus have limited comparative value in exploring the effects of inclusion when the political systems in question fall far short of democracy, as they do in most of the Middle East. In these cases, incipient political openings do not provide the sorts of institutional guarantees that would prevent the system from succumbing to the paradox of democracy. Indeed, regimes have proven to be among the most duplicitous and skillful actors, strategically deploying democratic rhetoric for both domestic and international audiences without producing or even intending to produce meaningful reforms. In these cases, scholarly analyses often focus on sham elections, weak civil society organizations, and the manipulation of the liberalization processes by the regime. Because the inclusion-moderation hypothesis is viewed in the context of a larger process of meaningful democratic transition, we have few analytic tools to examine moderation through inclusion in gray-zone regimes. Can we assess moderation if the liberalization process in general has not gone forward? According to the approach that views institutional constraints as the primary mechanism for encouraging continued participation, one would need to see those institutions function in a democratic manner to judge whether they actually provide the incentives to keep opposition forces engaged. When these institutions fail to provide such inducements, as in the context of stalled democratization processes, the transitions framework of analysis provides no means of testing whether inclusion is a sufficient mechanism for producing moderation in the views and practices of political actors because inclusion typically suggests inclusion *in democratic processes.*

In sum, I argue that the inclusion-exclusion hypothesis conflates a variety of hypotheses about the causal relations between repression, inclusion, radicalism, and moderation. In this book, I explore what I believe is the most challenging dimension of inclusion: the idea that inclusion in pluralist political processes may lead political actors to gradually adopt a more open and tolerant worldview than the one they held prior to such participation. Despite the importance of this question, precisely *how* moderation is produced through inclusion is seldom examined through detailed case studies. Instead, the presence of moderate groups is often correlated with the existence of pluralist processes, and the robustness of that correlation takes the force of a causal argument even though the specific (and likely numerous) mechanisms are treated together as "inclusion." To move beyond this pitfall, I seek to identify specific mechanisms that produce moderation. I wish to be clear that I do not suggest a model in which replicated processes will mechanistically produce identical results, but rather a process-tracing model in which identifying sequences of mechanisms unpacks complex processes and explains change over time (McAdam et al. 2001). My study is not exhaustive of these mechanisms, but rather seeks to begin specifying mechanisms that might be tested, expanded, and/or refuted through future comparative study.

To create an empirical base to explore this notion, I begin by assessing change *within* particular groups and then explore those changes comparatively. I avoid simply asserting that some ill-defined "moderation" has taken place or reproducing correlations that count how many included groups are moderate and how many excluded groups are radical. In this regard, identifying specific mechanisms is as crucial as observing whether moderates were in fact radicals at the outset. I use a structured comparative model to explore precisely how, and even whether, political actors become more moderate as a result of their participation in pluralist political practices, even in contexts that fall far short of meaningful democracy.

UNPACKING MODERATION

Scholarship that asserts some version of the inclusion-moderation hypothesis tends to focus on one of three phenomena: 1) the strategic behavior of moderates and radicals working within particular structural constraints; 2) attitudinal evidence about varying levels of tolerance between inclusive and exclusive political actors; or, less commonly, 3) the evolution of a political actor in terms of her actions, beliefs, and objectives before and after political inclusion. At the very least we can say that moderation entails multifaceted change. I focus on practice, not only *what* a political actor does but also the meanings she ascribes to her actions and choices within her specific (and often changing) political context. Moderation may be encouraged by changes in the broader public political space, for example through structural factors such as the legalization of new forms of political organization. And it may also be encouraged through such changing discursive constraints as the elevation of a particular vocabulary for framing political debates. I examine the internal dynamics and debates of two Islamist groups – the IAF in Jordan and the Islah party in Yemen – as well as their engagement with political actors and processes external to their group. Of particular interest is the extent to which practices and relations continue to evolve even in the context of "stalled democratization" in Jordan and Yemen. In these gray-zone regimes, the political openings have fallen far short of democratization. Consequently, we cannot assess moderation of Islamists in Jordan and Yemen as a function of participation in fully functioning democratic processes. But in each case the political space is significantly changed from what it was prior to the political openings in question, and I examine the impact of these multifaceted changes.

Jordan's IAF and Yemen's Islah party were both formed to contest multiparty elections after their regime initiated limited processes of political liberalization. Both parties have been characterized as moderate parties that lend evidence to the inclusion-moderation hypothesis, and I seek to specify a precise mechanism for moderation and test whether it has occurred in each case. My analysis focuses on three interconnected dimensions, where an initial opening in one area restructures the contours of other areas, so that these changes together may lead to the adoption of new political practices and ideological moderation. These dimensions are *political opportunity structures*, which were initially reshaped through state-managed political openings; *internal group structure* and processes of decision making; and *boundaries of justifiable action*. These three dimensions are not exhaustive, nor are they independent of each other. They do, however, illustrate the recursive relationship between various structures and practices that can begin to explain moderation. As elaborated in Chapter 4, I define moderation not as behavioral change, but as change in ideology from a rigid and closed worldview to one relatively more open and tolerant of alternative perspectives.

Shocks: Challenges to the Regime

↓

Response: Elite-Led Political Liberalization
(Channel Opposition into New Institutional Constraints)

| (Remaining Radicals Isolated)

↓

Effect: Moderation of Opposition

FIGURE 1.1. Liberalization Producing Moderation through Inclusion.

I begin by rejecting the straightforward causal argument that underpins the typical formulation of the inclusion-moderation hypothesis focusing on institutional constraints (Figure 1.1). The existing model begins by recognizing that political liberalization is often initiated as the result of a strategic decision by the ruling elites (O'Donnell and Schmitter 1986; Przeworski 1991).[26] This political opening entails the inclusion of at least some formerly excluded political actors. Once these formerly excluded actors enter the system and begin to engage in the political processes opened and maintained by the state, their members must assess whether the incentives for remaining in the system outweigh the merits of defecting (Hirshman 1970; Przeworski 1991; Lichbach 1995). When an actor chooses to continue participating, his behavior is shaped by the incentives of continued participation within state-controlled channels, and thus institutional constraints structure strategic behavior in ways that become recognizable as moderation. But is behavioral change an adequate measure of moderation? How can this model explain similar participation producing different degrees of moderation? Can it distinguish between actors who are hiding radical agendas and those whose views have substantively evolved?

Rather than focusing exclusively on the strategic behavior of political actors or the constraints and political opportunity structures created by institutional change, I examine multiple dimensions of public political space. This process-model approach, which assesses a variety of factors

[26] To be sure, not all change is initiated through structural openings as first suggested by Doug McAdam (1982) and elaborated in the social movement literature for the past two decades. Jeff Goodwin, James M. Jasper, David S. Meyer, Sidney Tarrow, Charles Tilly, and others debate the necessity of focusing on such initial openings in Goodwin and Jasper (2004), reaching no consensus. I focus here on regime-initiated openings because they are typical to processes of change that are the focus of this study: situations in which inclusion is seen as an elite-led mechanism for deflating oppositional radicalism.

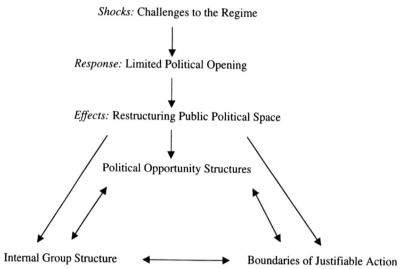

FIGURE I.2. Liberalization Producing Multiple Dimensions of Change.

and the mechanisms that connect changes along various dimensions, gives rise to a very different model of moderation (Figure 1.2) than one emphasizing strategic behavior within institutional constraints as the primary force producing moderation. In line with the transitions model of political openings, the impetus for regimes to initiate political liberalization is typically some real or perceived challenge to its power.[27] This might take the form of external pressures or threats (Robinson 1996; Whitehead 2001a), purely domestic challenges, or some combination of the two. In response, the regime may strategically choose to adopt limited political openings, gambling that limited inclusion will produce a more optimal outcome (Przeworski 1991: 51–99) than either the status quo or increased repression.[28] Likewise, all political actors are seen to behave strategically

[27] As argued in the following text, this process need not be initiated by elites. The dynamic changes explored in this book might equally be initiated through social movements, elsewhere outside of the state, or through a combination of state and nonstate forces. I focus here on elite-initiated reforms because they are characteristic of the two cases under examination in this study, and because the emphasis in the transition literature has been predominantly on elite-led openings.

[28] Of course, regimes might also opt to respond to these challenges with increased repression or the introduction of other constraints entirely unrelated to political openings. This comparative study seeks to explore contexts in which the regimes adopt political openings, but may have little intention of allowing those openings to develop into meaningful democratic institutions affecting real governance.

within institutional constraints. But while the result is a restructuring of the broader public political space, such as the introduction of new forms of political organization or new frameworks for political debate, the outcome need not represent an advance toward democratization if the regime prevents these new practices and processes from playing a meaningful role in governance. Even in such cases, however, regime-led political openings and the introduction of pluralist political practices initiate change across a number of dimensions, and it is precisely these changes outside of the formal state institutions and processes of governance that the transitions literature misses. For example, in addition to the more obvious and readily identifiable shifts in political opportunity structures (viz., the legalization of political parties and the liberalization of the media), crucial changes to the broader political field include the internal restructuring of groups, the discursive dimensions of public political debate, and the manner in which regimes justify their decisions to embark on reforms in the name of "democratization" and challengers justify their decisions to participate.

I do not suggest that political liberalization can only be initiated by the ruling elite. As I argue in Chapter 2, the impetus for such transitions typically includes bottom-up as well as top-down factors. Indeed, the "shocks" suggested here are challenges to the regime, often from nonstate actors. But I focus on elite-led openings because the inclusion-moderation hypothesis explicitly suggests a theory that causally connects elite-led inclusion to oppositional moderation as a concrete policy for incumbent regimes to deflate challenges to their rule. My alternative is a more dialectic model that unpacks complex causal processes to explain why moderation emerges in some cases, but not in others (Figure 1.2). In the contemporary global context, the discursive constraint of the democracy narrative is so powerful that even regimes that engage in abhorrent acts of repression and patently nondemocratic practices frequently deploy the rhetoric and imagery of "democratization" for a variety of purposes.[29] The fact that this practice is so widespread suggests that regimes, like all political actors, operate under ideational as well as institutional constraints, domestic as well as international. In this regard, change cannot

---

[29] Perhaps the one exception since the fall of the Soviet Union has been the rise to power of the Taliban in Afghanistan; even nondemocratic states such as Syria, Cuba, Libya, and Iraq all hold "elections" as demonstrations of regime legitimacy, while several nondemocratic states include the word *democratic* in their title, including the People's Democratic Republic of Algeria, the Federal Democratic Republic of Ethiopia, and the Democratic People's Republic of North Korea.

be adequately addressed without exploring multiple dimensions of public political space both structural and ideational, including connections between domestic political practices and the larger global context.

Even in what would be called *stalled democracies*, when regimes show little commitment toward advancing meaningful democratic reforms, the effects of this restructured public political space are considerable. New political opportunity structures create the openings necessary for the emergence of new forms of political activity and the creation of groups situated to take advantage of these openings. Structural dimensions may include 1) new spaces for political organization and debate, such as the legalization of political parties and a lessening of restrictions on the media; 2) new organizational structures, such as political parties, trade unions, and other interest groups; and 3) new narratives through which political actors debate politics and justify their practices. The connections between various dimensions of change become immediately apparent as we examine the "effects" of particular changes on political opportunity structures. For example, the emergence of new forms of political organization and innovative political practices alter the public political space within which all political actors function. A group that had quietly existed as a quasipolitical "social" organization may find it needs to clarify its objectives and revise its practices when dozens of alternative political and social organizations begin to emerge. Similarly, political actors may respond to the regime's increasing appeal to a democratic narrative by making claims in the name of democratic norms, just as the regime has done. This practice creates new constraints on both state and nonstate actors: the changing discursive field shapes political opportunity structures, and vice versa.

To be clear, I do not aim to predict moderation or to prescribe a set of reforms that will reliably produce moderation across multiple contexts. Instead, I examine what at first appear to be two similar cases in support of the inclusion-moderation argument, but in fact only one of the parties has become more moderate over time. What explains this variation?

CASE SELECTION AND EVIDENCE

The IAF and the Islah party are ideal cases for a structured comparative study of the inclusion-moderation hypothesis because despite the variations explored in this study, both have been held as examples of the successful inclusion of Islamists into the prevailing political system (Carapico 1993a; Dunn 1993; National Democratic Institute for International Affairs 1994; Adams 1996; Freij and Robinson 1996; Watkins

1996; Robinson 1997, 1998b; Boulby 1999; Mufti 1999; Saif 2001; Wiktorowicz 2001; Clark 2003). The ruling regimes in both Jordan and Yemen began processes of political liberalization in 1989 and 1990, respectively, though for different reasons. In Jordan, liberalization was initiated from above by a single actor – King Hussein – as a means of deflating the political dissent that was expected to result from additional International Monetary Fund (IMF) – mandated economic austerity measures, which he was in the process of implementing.[30] While Yemen's transition also emerged from above, it was initiated through a negotiated pact between the Yemen Arab Republic's (YAR, or North Yemen) President 'Ali 'Abd Allah Salih and the People's Democratic Republic of Yemen's (PDRY, or South Yemen) President 'Ali Salim al-Bid aimed at facilitating unification. A range of factors brought the countries together, including the loss of the Soviet Union's patronage of South Yemen, declining economic conditions in both countries, and to a lesser extent, the discovery of oil reserves on land bordering the two.[31]

By early 1993, aspects of the political openings in each country had gained popular support, if not yet institutional weight. Jordan's first full parliamentary elections since the 1967 Arab-Israeli war took place in November 1989. A large opposition bloc insured lively public debate on a range of issues from domestic policy to foreign relations. Martial law was lifted soon thereafter, opening the way for the legalization of political parties and the emergence of some two-dozen daily and weekly newspapers. A second round of elections was scheduled for November 1993. Yemen's first parliamentary elections, held in April 1993, produced a genuinely pluralist national assembly, with the ruling party of the North winning the largest share with only slightly more than a third of the seats. The coalition government that emerged, however, had been largely prenegotiated between the North and South. But the parties were joined by a third

---

[30] Vreeland demonstrates that regimes seek IMF involvement as a means of deflecting blame for economic reforms they already wish to implement (2003). In Jordan's case, King Hussein had begun such reforms, but later adopted political opening as a means of redirecting dissent into state-controlled processes.

[31] Yemini Socialist Party (YSP) leaders claim that President al-Bid insisted on immediate unification when what the politburo rulers had in mind was a more gradual unification. President al-Bid claimed that President Salih insisted on immediate unification; President Salih seems to have never been particularly committed to a democratic framework, but agreed out of certainty that the more populous North would return a strong President Salih-led government. These issues are explored in detail in subsequent chapters. I am indebted to Lisa Wedeen for sharing her insights on internal YSP debates about unification and democracy.

party, the Islah party, which had won the second largest share of seats. Like in Jordan, more than two-dozen newspapers appeared in major urban centers, and the Yemeni people utilized their long-standing tradition of spirited political debate to discuss the status of and potential for democratization in the country. No topic was taboo, with even the president lampooned in jokes told in semipublic gatherings with strangers present.[32]

In the summer of 1993, however, Jordan introduced changes to its elections law that severely restricted the ability of opposition groups to win seats in the November 1993 elections. A new press and publications law formalized the steady deterioration of freedom of speech, which most Jordanians saw as a precursor to the signing of a peace treaty with Israel. In Yemen, the pluralist outcome of the 1993 elections was overshadowed by the failure of former North and South leaders to reach agreement on several fronts, including the consolidation of the two armies, each of which remained under the control of its former ruling regime. By the spring of 1994, tensions escalated into a civil war that lasted two months and resulted in the overwhelming defeat of the southern Socialist leaders. In both Jordan and Yemen, then, the limited democratic openings of the early 1990s were virtually frozen by mid-decade, with many of the earlier gains disappearing entirely. Though both governments continue to declare their commitment to democracy, in neither case does the elected parliament play a central role in governance. Subsequent rounds of elections have been held, but few inside or outside either country see the exercise as a meaningful democratic practice. If either state were to be called a "democracy," it would require many, many qualifiers.

But even in these contexts of stalled democratization, political change continues and in particular public political space is dramatically different than it was prior to liberalization. In each case an Islamist group has emerged as a strong political party and active contester of elections. The IAF in Jordan is closely associated with the Muslim Brotherhood, an Islamist group that espouses a conservative social agenda, but seeks gradual political reform. Founded in the 1940s, the Jordanian Muslim Brotherhood has long had a symbiotic relationship with the regime of King Hussein, who allowed the group to function legally within public political space for decades during which political parties were illegal. Muslim

---

[32] In Jordan, criticizing and defaming the royal family remained consistently outside of the boundary of acceptable practice.

Brotherhood leaders have even been appointed to prominent government positions, including at the cabinet level. Similarly in Yemen, various groups that would later form the Islamist-oriented Islah party had close relations with North Yemen's ruling elite through the 1970s and 1980s. Prior to unification, the loosely organized Islamic Front fought with the northern regime in 1979 against southern-backed forces. Like Jordan's Islamists, some of these leaders held government positions as high as the cabinet level. The establishment of Islah as a political party in September 1990 saw the already eclectic Islamic Front unite with a number of tribal leaders and businessmen to form a single party with a conservative Islamic orientation.

Thus by the mid-1990s, the "democratic transitions" begun in each state had stalled or been reversed. But as the comparison of the continued participation of the IAF and the Islah party illustrates, dimensions of public political space had changed considerably, including the organization of opposition groups into political parties and the increasing practice of debating political change in terms of democracy. If we abandon transitology's focus on progress toward democracy, these "stalled" cases reveal significant changes in political structures and practices even though the same regime remains in power and democratic processes are superficial.

Several major points of similarity and difference structure this comparative study (Table 1.1). Variations in regime type and the impetus for initiating political liberalization provide a fruitful starting point. How do these points of comparison shape public political space, including opportunity structures, the organization of competing groups, and boundaries of justifiable action? What constraints do Islamist parties face concerning electoral strategy and alliances with other parties? Do publicly debated narratives about Islam, pluralism, and democracy constrain political actors? Does a party that emerges from an established and cohesive movement face different constraints than a coalition party uniting actors with diverse interests? Does the closeness of a party to the regime provide incentives for the party to conform to regime expectations or opportunities for expressing dissent with less fear of repression? What are the processes for resolving internal group conflict around specific issues? And what explains the variation in outcomes between the two cases?

In terms of research methodology, I utilize political ethnography conducted over a thirty-eight-month period (spread from January 1995 to December 2003) during which I resided in Jordan and Yemen. The primary period of the study is from the late 1980s to 2000, but in each

TABLE 1.1. *Islamists and Liberalization in Jordan and Yemen*

Point of Comparison	Jordan	Yemen
Transition type: Impetus for initiating political liberalization	Implemented by imposition of monarchy	Implemented through negotiated pact between previous regimes
Regime type and relation to field of political contestation	Monarchy, king is outside the sphere of electoral competition	Republic, president and ruling party compete in elections
Regime narratives	Arab nationalist, religious, conservative: royal family descends from the Prophet Muhammad; close relations with western regimes	*North:* Arab nationalist, republican, conservative: regime participated in revolution against hereditary monarchy, so that descending from the Prophet's family is now a liability *South:* Arab nationalist, Marxist, secular: relations with USSR
Structure and bases of Islamist party	Cohesive: Muslim Brotherhood is well-established organization; underground Salafiyya movement insignificant	*North:* Fragmented: party emerges as a coalition of disparate conservatives who share common goals *South:* Nonexistent: Islamist groups were illegal before unification, conservative trends suppressed or fled north
Relationship of Islamist party to the regime	"Loyal Opposition": long-standing relations with the regime, but with periodic conflict	"Coalition Partner": long-standing allies of the regime; some party leaders are effectively part of the ruling elite while others have had only intermittent connections
Field of political contestation before liberalization	Closed, political parties banned and martial law imposed in 1957, elections suspended in 1967	*North:* Mostly closed, regime-created national assembly included limited seats filled through elections *South:* Mostly closed, with irregular elections
Field of political contestation after liberalization	Open: political parties legal	Open: political parties legal

case I have added subsequent detail when it seemed most consequential for the analysis. (Thus, I do not give electoral results for every election after 2000, but I do discuss ongoing trends in Islamist-Leftist cooperation and Islamist activism in general.) In each country, I conducted elite interviews[33] with more than 200 political actors: leaders and members of various Islamist groups; leaders and members of other political parties, trade unions, and professional associations; university professors; independent researchers; journalists; government officials; and independent political activists. I spoke informally with hundreds more. I cite many of these interviews directly, though others remain anonymous at the request of the interviewees. I utilize such media sources as newspapers, magazines and periodicals; Internet discussion groups and Web resources; and television and radio broadcasts. At times, these sources convey a better sense of the evolution of particular public political debates than retrospective recollections of individuals. Documentation provides the core of the evidence and includes books and pamphlets prepared by each party (some for internal use, but most intended for wide distribution), official government papers and publications, official as well as informal internal party correspondence, press releases, party conference materials, and electioneering materials (including posters, pamphlets, formal election platforms, and speeches as reprinted in a variety of outlets). I also draw on video- and audiotaped lectures and symposia, videotaped sessions of parliament (plus a handful of sessions I witnessed), and video- and audiotaped sermons of Islamist leaders. Finally, a key dimension of political ethnography is to spend as much time as possible with the relevant actors to learn not only why they engage politically as they do, but how they understand those practices and processes, what they are aiming to accomplish, and how they speak of and engage with other political actors. In this regard I spent significant time with a number of Islamist activists and their families, and I attended a large number of meetings, electoral campaigns, protest activities, conferences, lectures, and discussion groups sponsored by the parties, independent research institutes, universities, newspapers, and independent activists. I spend countless hours reading in the library of the Muslim Brotherhood office in Amman and at the Islah-affiliated Yemen Center for Cultural and Strategic Studies in San'a, where I was

---

[33] "Elite interviews" does not mean interviews with the political elite (in the sense used in my analysis). As a research method, it refers to interviews with individuals deemed to have expertise on a particular topic as a result of their direct participation in particular practices or organizations.

able to observe the comings and goings of the party members and visitors and discuss my research informally with a wide range of individuals. Secondary sources are used almost exclusively for historical background for periods preceding my fieldwork as well as to locate my study within the broader field of comparative politics. In this regard, I have sought to address not only cases from the Middle East and Islamic world, but empirical material from earlier in the twentieth century and from around the globe.

OUTLINE OF THE BOOK

The following chapters explore the three aforementioned dimensions of change within the broader field of political contestation. Chapter 2 examines the changes in political opportunity structure that accompany political liberalization, even in contexts where the regime never intends the process to produce meaningful democratization. The chapter also presents a historical overview of the political scene in Jordan and Yemen and the roots of the Islamist parties that emerged after liberalization. Chapter 3 looks at each party in greater detail, with particular attention to the ways in which each has restructured itself into a political party and explored alliances among competing party factions. The chapter adds a new dimension to Chapter 2's picture of strategic participation within institutional constraints, tracing over time changes that emerge in the structure of each party as well as the broader field of competing political groups. Chapters 4 and 5 add two ideational dimensions to the dynamics illustrated in Chapters 2 and 3, with particular focus on competing narratives and changing boundaries of justifiable action. Chapter 4 presents a framework for thinking about ideational dimensions of public political space, looking in detail at narratives about democracy, Islam, and national unity. All political actors, but particularly strongly ideological groups, are constrained not only by the structure of public political space, but also by the discursive context of political struggles. For Islamist parties and regimes alike, competing reference to both Islamic and democratic norms and practices complicate interactions within each party as well as with external groups. Chapter 5 examines changing boundaries of justifiable action within each party, focusing on internal party debates and decision-making practices. The decisions and strategies of these two Islamist parties must also be located within transnational Muslim and Islamist debates about the reconciliation of Islam and democracy. This chapter also moves toward a synthesis of the dynamic model of change along multiple dimensions suggested in Figure 1.2. Each chapter builds on the previous by adding a new dimension of political contestation while considering interaction between various dimensions of political change. Chapter 6 returns the focus of the study to the larger question of moderation, emphasizing the factors and mechanisms that explain the variation between the two cases. I then briefly locate these specific parties within a broader context of Islamist politics. I conclude by raising some additional questions and possibilities for future comparative research.

2

Political Liberalization as a Mechanism of Control

The idea that authoritarian leaders can maintain their power by pretending to care about the public good has been around for thousands of years. In *The Politics*, Aristotle discusses two strategies by which a tyrant sometimes strives to preserve his rule: he may keep his subjects too preoccupied to challenge his rule (distracting them with war or with fighting each other), or he may dissuade them from conspiring against him. The second strategy requires that the tyrant publicly present a false image of himself, so that he "seems to be a steward of the public rather than a tyrant" (5.11.1314^{b}6–7). This kind of tyrant maintains his tight control of power, but pretends to work for the good of society and creates a public persona as a benevolent ruler torn by tough real-world challenges. His objectives, however, are not only to preserve his power and wealth, but to increase them as much as possible, even at the expense of the people he rules.

A contemporary correlate to Aristotle's "benevolent" tyrant is the authoritarian regime that professes a commitment to democratization while adopting only superficial reforms. The goal is to *seem* to move toward democratization while preventing the new "participatory" institutions from playing a meaningful role in governance. Political dissent and opposition movements are channeled into institutions controlled by the state as a means of managing or deflating threats to the ruling elite and preserving existing hierarchies of power. This may be accomplished by a variety of mechanisms, such as by duping the public, duping the leaders of opposition groups (including political parties), co-opting opposition voices, and so on. The twist to this story, as Aristotle recognizes, is that the falsely benevolent tyrant may unwittingly become more moderate. As a result of his efforts to represent himself as serving the interests of society, he actually *becomes* something less than a tyrant, "a man not wicked, but half wicked" (5.11.1315^{b}10). Similarly, an authoritarian leader may introduce processes of limited political liberalization for a variety of reasons unrelated to the desire for democracy, but these reforms may nevertheless increase civil and political freedoms. At the very least, implementing reforms in the name of democracy – even disingenuously – has the (perhaps unintentional) effect of emphasizing the accountability of the regime to the people, a notion which the citizenry may or may not already embrace.

In the Middle East as throughout the world, introducing limited and carefully controlled political openings has become a routine strategy for managing challenges to incumbent regimes. In many cases, processes of limited liberalization have been managed by existing regimes (Algeria, Bahrain, Egypt, Jordan, Kuwait, Morocco, and Qatar), while others have been negotiated by competing elites (unified Yemen and postwar Lebanon). Yet in the vast majority of cases, the goal of the regime is survival: leaders introduce highly limited "defensive democratization"[1] in the hope that limited political openings will serve as a mechanism to moderate or even deflate challenges to the existing political elite while making such challenges public and transparent. At the very least, it may bring opponents into the open, where their activities as legal organizations may be more easily monitored.

However, incumbent regimes risk the possibility of losing control of even superficial political openings and that challengers will exploit the new opportunities to realize their own agendas, democratic or otherwise. For their part, oppositional political actors must also consider the trade-offs of participation in these tightly controlled openings. Their question is whether the potential opportunities of working within the system are sufficient given the (usually correct) suspicions that the regime may be far less interested in pluralist politics than in bolstering its power. Studies of this bargaining between "state" and "nonstate" actors are complicated because in many cases, key opposition groups have long-established relations with the ruling elite.

As argued in Chapter 1, these dimensions of strategic behavior within institutional constraints are well established in diverse literatures. In a democracy, losers in contested elections do not opt out of the system,

---

[1] This term was coined by Robinson (1998a) with respect to Jordan, but it captures the sort of "democracy with adjectives" that Collier and Levitsky (1997) note is common in the transitions literature.

but remain engaged because they are insured of the possibility that they may prevail in the future (Przeworski 1991). While the potential payoffs are more precarious, the logic is suggested to hold in transitioning states as well. Even in less-than-democratic contexts such as Egypt, Jordan, Kuwait, Lebanon, Morocco, Pakistan, Turkey, and Yemen, for example, a diverse mix of political actors view the incentives for participation in the political system as outweighing the costs. The structural and behavioral aspects explored in this chapter are thus central to debates on both democratic transitions and the inclusion-moderation hypothesis.

In this chapter, I examine the processes of limited political liberalization introduced in Jordan and Yemen in the early 1990s. By political liberalization, I refer to an easing of centralized restrictions on civil liberties (basic individual freedoms) and political activities (organization, mobilization, public debates, and so on). I sometimes call these processes political openings to emphasize that they need not be part of a broader process of democratization but that they lead to more space for political contestation. Among these openings, changes to political opportunity structures, such as decreased repression and new channels for engaging in critical political debate, have perhaps the most immediate impact on forms of political contestation. After reviewing the debates about strategic political liberalization, I provide an overview of the context for the political openings in Jordan and Yemen, paying particular attention to changing political opportunity structures and the strategic goals of the incumbent regimes.

THE IMPETUS FOR LIBERALIZATION

What do authoritarian regimes hope to achieve by adopting processes of political liberalization? Such decisions tend to result from a combination of factors, and few such processes are initiated solely from "above" or "below." Pressures from below – grassroots and opposition movements as well as widespread general dissent – often lead political leaders to consider increased inclusion and enfranchisement as a means of countering dissent. The question of precisely what factors lead a government toward political liberalization has been central to several scholarly debates, most notably in process-oriented analyses of political transitions. In this regard, the transitions literature continues to focus attention on the contingent choices faced by elite-level actors, despite serious criticisms (as noted in Chapter 1), largely because political elites often initiate the sorts of institutional changes that are seen to mark the "beginning" of transitions.

In this view, political liberalization can be a mechanism for channeling political dissent and opposition movements into state-controlled institutions, providing elites with an alternative to repression by force (Earl 2003). Although the political elite may view this sort of inclusion strategy as a means of expanding (or at least maintaining) their power, the accompanying changes to political opportunity structures nevertheless create new space for political organization. Nonstate political actors are tolerated, for example, as long as they "play by the rules" established by state actors, who in turn adjust these rules until they produce the desired results. In such projects, commitments to democratization are typically shallow at best. As Przeworski argues, "Projects of liberalization launched by forces from within the authoritarian power establishment are invariably intended as controlled openings of political space. . . . In the light of this project, liberalization is to be continually contingent on the compatibility of its outcomes with the interests or values of the authoritarian bloc" (1991: 57). Elites implement these openings only when they face real or perceived challenges to their power. Channeling dissent into readily controllable institutions is a mechanism of political control, one that elites often view as far less costly than repression through force.[2]

As argued by many transitologists, this "first stage" of a democratic transition is broadly characterized by uncertainty. As Karl argues, "During regime transitions, all political calculations and interactions are highly uncertain. Actors find it difficult to know what their interests are, who their supporters will be, and which groups will be their allies or opponents" (1990: 6). Particularly in the transitions literature of the early 1990s, scholars focused on how reformers (also called *moderates, softliners,* or *liberalizers*) who favor political liberalization try to convince *hard-liners* (also called *stand-patters, conservatives, radicals,* or *extremists*) to invest in the new system with the promise that the latter can be sure to see their share of power preserved (O'Donnell and Schmitter 1986; Karl 1990; Przeworski 1991). The process of political change thus entails a redrawing of the rules of the game, which produces uncertainties that in turn increase the boundaries of contingent choice. "The dynamics of the transition revolve around strategic interactions and tentative arrangements between actors with uncertain power resources aimed at defining

---

[2] In Przeworski's model, the elites choose between liberalization and repression based not only on preferences but also on their expectations of their ability to repress opposition forces and the likely response of nonstate actors to state actions (e.g., repression or liberalization) (1991, especially Part II).

who will legitimately be entitled to play in the political game, what criteria will determine the winners and losers, and what limits will be placed on the issues at stake" (Karl 1990: 6). The notion of contingency emphasizes the strategic choices and political interactions of various actors. Yet it is crucial, as Karl and others correctly caution, for such an approach to be framed in terms of structural-historical constraints.

Within transitology's conceptual framework for studying political change, one of the main challenges for elite-initiated political liberalization is for the reformers to convince the *hard-liners* to get with the program. One means of accomplishing this is through the establishment of pacts, "negotiated compromises in which contending forces agree to forego their capacity to harm each other by extending guarantees not to threaten the other's vital interests" (Karl 1990: 11). A pact is often not a single agreement, but more of a series of interlocking agreements. To be effective, pacts must often extend beyond the obvious political actors to include any actor whose opposition to the reforms would threaten their success. But by insuring that the interests of a range of elite actors are preserved, the result is patently antidemocratic (Kalyvas 2000: 380). As Przeworski notes, "The ostensible purpose of such pacts is to protect embryonic democratic institutions by reducing the level of conflict about policies and personnel. Whereas institutional pacts establish the rules of the game and leave the rest to competition, these are substantive pacts intended to remove major policy issues from the competitive process" (1991: 90). In this way, many such pacts intended to "facilitate" democratic transition really do little more than guarantee, in essence, that no such transition will take place. At the very least, as Adler and Webster argue, transitologists do concede that "for a democratic transition to succeed, democracy itself must be limited" (1995: 84). Empirically, successful transitions to democracy through elite pacts may be extremely rare (Swaminathan 1999), while in many cases pacts appear to be entirely absent (Bratton and van de Walle 1997).

But instead of focusing on the extent to which transitions lead to successful democratic consolidation (to use the language of the transitions literature), thinking about political liberalization as a mechanism of political control refocuses our attention on the ways in which even limited openings can dramatically restructure public political space. By opening previously closed channels of political contestation, the regime is able to monitor challengers more closely (which is not a democratic outcome) by providing an outlet for the limited expression of political dissent (which may be a democratic outcome). At the same time, state actors need not resort to more costly physical repression, or at least not as frequently. As the process unfolds, the institutional mechanisms that regulate the new political space are adjusted to produce just the "right" amount and type of political contestation – which is to say that it falls short of threatening the regime's power. These "legal" means of control include defining and revising elections laws, adjusting restrictions on political party activities, redrawing electoral districts, and adopting legislation that broadens the range of activities considered to "threaten state security" and thus in need of state regulation. When elections are eventually held, they are frequently accompanied by restrictions on other political rights and opportunities, resulting in a sort of "electocratic rule" (Call as cited in Karl 1990: 15). And as Przeworski argues, regimes often face a trade-off between advancing economic reforms and preserving the political openings. Because the regime values its survival above all, in such cases the political reforms are usually abandoned (1991: 182). This framework provides a useful foundation for understanding elite-led processes of political liberalization in Jordan and Yemen, though I argue later that it does not provide sufficient tools for exploring inclusion and moderation or for identifying the deep changes in political practice that can result from even highly limited openings.

POLITICAL LIBERALIZATION IN JORDAN

As a nation-state, Jordan is a relatively modern creation and the direct product of European colonialism in the Middle East. In 1920, King 'Abd Allah I of the powerful Hashemite family in central Arabia headed north toward Syria with troops, intending to attack French forces there. He reportedly sought retribution for the French having forced his brother Faysal to relinquish a kingdom the latter had established on Syrian lands. When King 'Abd Allah arrived, he was persuaded by the British government, which held the mandate over Palestine as established by the Conference of San Remo in 1920, to forego the attack in exchange for heading a government in newly created Transjordan. The deal was signed and the new boundaries drawn in 1921. Transjordan was formally recognized as an independent state under British control in 1927.[3]

Following World War II, the British relinquished its mandates over Transjordan and the Hashemite Kingdom of Jordan was declared a fully

---

[3] For detailed look at this period, see Cohen (1982), Wilson (1987), and Boulby (1999: 3–72).

independent state in May 1946, with 'Abd Allah as its king. When Great
Britain's mandate over Palestine ended just two years later, Jordan joined
Syria, Egypt, Lebanon, and Iraq in opposing the establishment of an independent Jewish state in Palestine. The failure of these newly independent
Arab states in that war resulted in the first of many waves of Palestinian
refugees into Jordan, a process that had tremendous impact on Jordan's
social order. In 1949, the Jordanian-Israeli armistice left large portions
of the West Bank of the Jordan River under Jordanian control, including large waves of Palestinians that tripled Jordan's population.[4] By the
time Jordan formally annexed the West Bank in 1950, King 'Abd Allah
had already provided for equal representation of Palestinians in Jordan's
nation assembly. He was assassinated in 1951 in Jerusalem, succeeded
briefly by his son Talal, who suffered from mental illness and was removed
by a special parliamentary resolution in August 1954 (Brynen 1998: 73).
King Talal's eldest son, Hussein, took the throne in May 1953 after coming
of age, and he ruled until his death in February 1999.[5] He was succeeded
by his own eldest son, 'Abd Allah II.

Parliamentary Life

Like many Arab states, Jordan has a history of formal electoral politics
extending back seventy years (and consultative processes in which
communal elders make decisions after deliberation date several centuries
earlier). Five national assemblies were indirectly elected under British
control from 1928 to 1942, with thirteen separate chambers of deputies
directly elected since independence in 1946 (Table 2.1), at which time an
appointed upper house was introduced. Despite the routine functioning
of these assemblies, "mandate rule was autocratic in nature, reflecting
not only the protection of Britain's strategic needs in an unstable political
environment, but also the personality of 'Abdallah," who was hostile to
the introduction of parliamentary life by the British (Boulby 1999: 9–10).
The monarchy granted universal suffrage to all male citizens 19 years of
age in 1947 (this was lowered to 18 for all citizens in July 2001). The
period from 1951 to 1958 was marked by significant liberalization, and

---

[4] Boulby cites Mazur's statistics from the International Bank for Reconstruction and Development, noting that Jordan's population of 375,000 increased to 1,185,060 after annexa-
tion, of whom some 350,000 were refugees and the remainder residents of the West Bank
(1999: 14).

[5] Hussein took over control from his ill father in late 1952, but did not formally take the
throne until May 1953.

TABLE 2.1. *Jordan's Elected National Assemblies*

Mandate Assembly	Election	Comments
1st	1928	Assembly dissolved in 1931 for refusing to endorse the government budget
2nd	1931	Completes its 3-year term
3rd	1934	Completes its 3-year term
4th	1937	Term extended in 1940 to 5 years, which it completes
5th	1942	Declares independence in 1946; completes its 5-year term
Council of Deputies		
1st	1947	20 seats, doubled to 40 in 1949; assembly dissolved in 1949 in preparation of new elections and the participation of West Bank Palestinians
2nd	1950	Scheduled to serve 4 years; assembly dissolved in 1951 for refusing to endorse the state budget
3rd	1951	Opposition groups win 26 of 40 seats; assembly dissolved in 1954
4th	1954	Clashes during the elections result in 14 deaths; assembly dissolved in 1956
5th	1956	Opposition parties participate legally and win a majority; a number resign after dismissal of the government of opposition Prime Minister Suleiman al-Nabulsi
Bielections	1958	15 vacant seats are filled; assembly completes its term
6th	1961	10 additional seats bring total to 50; dissolved in 1962 for failure to cooperate with the government
7th	1962	10 additional seats bring total to 60; assembly dissolved in 1963 one day after voting no-confidence for the government of Prime Minister Samir al-Rifa'i
8th	1963	Dissolved in 1967
9th	1967	Suspended in 1967, term extended in 1971 and dissolved in 1974 (with the Arab League's recognition of the PLO as the sole representative of the Palestinian people)
10th	1984	1967 assembly reinstated; 7 vacant seats are filled in bielections; term extended in 1987; assembly dissolved in 1988; new elections postponed
11th	1989	20 additional seats bring total to 80; assembly completes its term
12th	1993	Political parties participate legally; assembly completes its term
13th	1997	Elections boycotted by opposition parties and other prominent individuals; assembly completes its term in May 2001 on schedule
14th	2003	Elections delayed from original November 2001 schedule, leaving no sitting assembly from May 2001 to June 2003; elections finally held June 17, 2003

Sources: Hourani et al. (1993b) and Baaklini et al. (1999).

opposition parties won 65 percent of the seats (26 of 40) in the third chamber of deputies. This assembly approved the new constitution in 1952, declaring the Hashemite Kingdom of Jordan a constitutional hereditary monarchy and codifying equality before the law, individual liberty, right to property, freedom of conscience and religious ceremonies, freedom of opinion, the right to hold public meetings, and the right to form political parties.[6] The constitution also designated Islam as the state religion and declared Jordan part of the global Muslim community (*ummah*). During the tenure of this assembly, King Talal was crowned in September 1951 and King Hussein was crowned in May 1953.

In June 1954, just one hour before a session during which a confidence vote was scheduled for Prime Minister 'Abd al-Huda's government, King Hussein dissolved the assembly to avoid a no-confidence vote. Elections for the fourth chamber were held in October, but widespread clashes broke out as al-Huda was accused of rigging the elections. Fourteen people died and dozens were injured, leading the opposition to declare a general strike five days later and to petition King Hussein to dissolve the new assembly. In June 1956, after more than a year of fairly regular protests and riots, he did just that. The move was accompanied by the full legalization of opposition parties, which had previously operated under considerable restrictions. Meanwhile, the king sought to respond to criticisms of the regime's reliance on the West and so ousted John Glubb, the commander of the British Arab Legion in Amman and the last remnant of direct British colonial power in Jordan. The move was popular among all political trends, from the Leftists and nationalists to more conservative regime allies such as the Muslim Brotherhood and tribal leaders. Elections for the fifth chamber were held later that year with opposition parties winning a majority, including members of the National Socialist Party (NSP), the Arab Ba'ath Socialist Party, and the National Front, all popular Leftist parties supported by Palestinians as well as East Bankers. Sulayman al-Nabulsi, an NSP member and the leader of the majority bloc, was chosen by King Hussein to form a government. The new cabinet included nine socialists. After a tenure marked by tensions with the royal family, the king asked al-Nabulsi to resign in 1957 over differences on the Eisenhower Doctrine and policies concerning Jordan's relations with other Arab countries. The resignation marked the beginning of a long period of tight state control over political activities, but also the cementing of the relationship between the monarchy and the Muslim Brotherhood, who shared the

[6] Boulby 1999: 17; see also Aruri 1972: 96–8.

desire – along with the United States – to see "communist" tendencies in the region suppressed.[7] Large-scale protests over al-Nabulsi's resignation led to the arrest of him and many of his followers, allegedly for attempting a coup. Soon thereafter, King Hussein declared martial law, banned all political parties, imposed strict censorship of the media, and purged the bureaucracy of Palestinians deemed insufficiently loyal to the regime (Boulby 1999: 21). Six socialist deputies resigned in protest and eight others lost their seats for refusing to disavow party affiliation; an additional deputy was thrown out the following year, in 1958. Five elections for the chamber were held over the next nine years, and martial law was lifted briefly in 1963 until, in 1967, King Hussein suspended the constitution and assembly in the wake of the June 1967 war (two months after the April national elections).

The Six-Day Arab-Israeli war of June 1967 had devastating consequences for Jordan, which not only lost control of portions of the West Bank and the lives of tens of thousands of its citizens, but also suffered from an influx of another 300,000 Palestinian refugees that contributed to an escalation of guerrilla activity and several coup attempts aimed at the monarchy. These attacks were mostly orchestrated by Palestinian groups emerging in the refugee camps and in the Jordan River Valley, with ideological commitments ranging from Leftist to conservative or Islamist. By February 1970, the government was effectively losing sovereignty over portions of Jordan in and around the refugee camps. The regime prohibited the carrying of arms in towns and cities, a move that resulted in numerous clashes between Palestinian militants and the army. The ban was quickly lifted, however, and the clashes subsided as the regime promised to lend full support to the struggle against the continued occupation and confiscation by Israel of Palestinian lands. For a few months, Jordan saw relative calm.

In September, however, the hijacking of three airliners by the Marxist Popular Front for the Liberation of Palestine (PFLP) set off escalating clashes in Amman. The hijackers demanded the release of Palestinian guerrillas being detained in Israel, Great Britain, West Germany, and Switzerland. In exchange, they promised to release the passengers and flight crews they held at Amman's international airport. The regime imposed a curfew over the city in an effort to stop clashes from spreading, while the army surrounded the airport to isolate the hijackers. Syria failed in its attempt

---

[7] For a detailed look at this period, see Dann 1989, Satloff 1994, and especially Massad 2001, by far the best work on the formation of the Jordanian state.

to assist the hijackers, sparking more than a week of intense fighting. Finally, the leaders of other Arab states brokered a peace between the various sides, bringing an end to the violence known as "Black September." In an accord signed in Cairo on September 27, King Hussein agreed to considerable concessions to the Palestinian guerrillas and their leader, Yasser Arafat. Tensions continued, however, until the Jordanian army destroyed the last of the guerrillas' strongholds north of Amman in 1971. In retaliation, Palestinian guerrillas assassinated Jordanian Prime Minister Wasfi al-Tal, who had spearheaded the regime's armed response to the militants, and made attempts on the lives of several Jordanian ambassadors abroad. In 1973, with the Palestinian resistance groups now relocated to Lebanon, King Hussein agreed to commute the death sentences of several Palestinian guerrillas convicted in connection with al-Tal's death. Soon thereafter, Jordan restored diplomatic relations with Syria and Egypt. The parliament briefly reconvened in 1974 when the king reasoned that with the acceptance at the Rabat Arab summit of the Palestinian Liberation Organization (PLO) as the representative of the Palestinian people, Palestinians had no place in the Jordanian assembly (Boulby 1999: 21). After the Rabat declaration, Hussein suspended the parliament altogether. The assembly was briefly reconvened in 1976 for the sole purpose of postponing national elections indefinitely (Brynen 1998: 74).

It is within this historical context that the organization and hierarchy of social forces within Jordan were gradually restructured over several decades. When the Transjordanian state was in its infancy, tribal leaders and business professionals were brought into the system through representation in the national assembly and participation in government-sponsored national conferences. In 1928, for example, "a national conference brought together 150 notables, tribal leaders, and intellectuals who adopted resolutions protesting the electoral law and the [legislative assembly's] lack of power" (Baaklini et al. 1999: 136). This formula of inviting representatives of various social forces to voice their concerns though state-sponsored channels was informally institutionalized, as similar conferences were held in 1929, 1930, 1932, and 1933. Thus from a very early stage, the political elite recognized that new regime could build a support base through limited inclusion by "providing a channel through which different constituencies – from the tribal populations of the south to the middle-class professionals living in the northern towns – could express their political demands" (Baaklini et al. 1999: 136). National conferences and the legislative assembly during the mandate period also provided mechanisms for facilitating dialogue and interaction among various powerful elites. These practices slowly altered the existing relations of power, providing increased voice and space for forces that supported the new regime. As British influence in Jordan declined with independence in 1946 and particularly with the flood of Palestinian refugees into Jordan in 1947 and 1948, the monarchy turned to conservative tribal and religious groups to support its rule. In the 1947 constitution and the accompanying new elections law, the regime established a bicameral legislature with a twenty-man elected lower house and a ten-man appointed upper house. The lower house was called the Council of Deputies (*majlis al-nuwab*) and the upper house was called the Council of Notables (*majlis al-a'yan*). As Baaklini et al. note, the regime clearly intended the electoral law to produce a lower house that was both docile and supportive of the regime, one that would bring leaders from all major social and political forces into state channels. This is evidenced, for example, in the distribution of seats in the elected assembly. Forty percent of the seats were allocated for representatives of religious and ethnic minorities, who were usually supportive of the palace (1999: 137–8). Half the seats were allocated to Palestinians, an effort by King 'Abd Allah to bring prominent Palestinians into the system and give them a stake in the system.

Formal and informal alliances proved particularly crucial for preserving the regime during the period from the 1950s through the early 1970s. With the rise of Arab nationalism and Leftist groups within Jordan as well as regionally, and particularly in light of Gamal 'Abd al-Nasser's successes in Egypt and that country's short-lived unification with Syria from 1958–61, the monarchy relied considerably on support from tribal and religious groups to sustain its authority. The flood of Palestinian refugees in 1948 also brought a more politically conscious constituency, with many Palestinians sympathetic to Leftist ideals and political movements. With the suspension of the al-Nabulsi government in 1957, then, tribal leaders and prominent members of the Islamist Muslim Brotherhood spoke out in support of the regime for dissolving a Leftist-led government and imprisoning many Leftists and Arab nationalists, including many Palestinians.[8] With the defeat of Arab forces in the 1967 war and the challenge to the regime's sovereignty in the Palestinian camps by Leftist guerilla groups over the next few years, the monarchy again relied on religious and tribal forces to support the regime. I examine the role of the Muslim

---

[8] The old headquarters of the GID (*mukhabarat*) in Amman is popularly known as Palestine Hotel (*funduk filastin*) for the large number of Palestinians known to have been detained, interrogated, and tortured there. The building was demolished in June 2002.

Brotherhood in detail in Chapter 3, but of concern here is the manner in which domestic relations of power – particularly the configuration of the ruling elite within Jordanian society – were structured by both domestic and regional political developments dating to the earliest days of state development. This history of alliances proves essential to understanding subsequent political developments as well as the alliances that emerge following the 1989 political opening.

Toward Political (Re)Liberalization

In the early 1980s, King Hussein began to ease restrictions on political activities as the country faced deteriorating economic conditions after an extremely prosperous decade.[9] Yet despite Jordan's long history of representative assemblies and electoral institutions (including the multiparty politics of the 1950s), the Jordanian people did not clamor for democracy. The absence of such activities does not mean that the suspension of the representative assembly in 1967 had been unopposed. Particularly when King Hussein dissolved parliament in 1974, even those loyal to the regime expressed concern about ending Jordan's tradition of representative governance. But debate about democracy was largely limited to the educated and urban intelligencia, and no popular demonstrations called for the reinstitution of the elected assembly or the introduction of a more democratic system in general. Rather, those who were most vocal in protesting the loss of a formal representative institution were elite-level actors seeking to protect their own positions of power and authority. Critiques of the state lessened considerably when in 1978 the king issued a royal decree establishing a new assembly called the National Consultative Council (NCC, *majlis al-shura al-watani*). This sixty-member assembly, appointed by the king, was to be dissolved upon the election of a new Council of Deputies, though no date was yet set for such elections. In practice, the NCC had virtually no power: it could not approve, amend, or reject a bill and could not pass no-confidence motions against the cabinet (Baaklini et al. 1999: 144). But it did serve to recognize the authority of a variety of social forces by bringing together prominent figures into an assembly that, however superficially, played a role in advising the regime on issues of governance. Without reopening the system to meaningful

---

[9] For details on the economic conditions, see Brynen 1992, Boulby 1999: 26–31, and Moore 2004.

political competition, the king aimed to preserve and strengthen its existing relations with powerful social forces.

King Hussein finally recalled the suspended ninth council of deputies in 1984, within a broader context of a very weak economy. Jordan had also begun multilateral talks with the PLO and Israel over the status of the West Bank, portions of which Jordan still controlled, and a possible Palestinian-Jordanian federation. Bielections were held on January 5, 1984 to replace eight deputies to the lower house who had since died or resigned, and a new upper house was appointed. The lower house enacted a new elections law in March 1986, which expanded the number of seats to 142, with designated seats for East Bankers and West Bankers (Robins 1991).[10] The law also articulated the details of the electoral system and placed a number of constraints on candidates, including a large registration fee and restrictions against affiliations with certain political groupings (Robins 1991). New districts were drawn that underrepresented urban areas where most Palestinians resided. The overall climate, therefore, was not one of increased political liberalization. The regime banned a range of routine campaign activities, including large rallies, loudspeakers on roaming trucks, placards, and posters. Political parties remained banned and the security services harassed regime critics, including Muslim Brotherhood members (discussed in the following text; also see Milton-Edwards 1993; Boulby 1999: 73–114).

King Hussein continued talks with the PLO and Israel, but he seemed much less hurried to revive the parliament through new elections than he had before the 1984 bielections. In large part, his slow pace on these fronts reflected uncertainty about the fate of the West Bank and a measure of satisfaction with the role played by the revived assembly in placating the demands of various powerful elite vis-à-vis representation in government. In late 1986, Hussein announced that the elections would not be held for at least a year, and he postponed them indefinitely after the Palestinian uprising against Israeli occupation (*intifada*)[11] broke out in the West Bank and Gaza in 1987. In July 1988, he unilaterally relinquished Jordan's formal administrative control over the West Bank. By early 1989, the apparent finality of the decision was reflected in the amendments to

---

[10] The size of the assembly was doubled in 1949, from twenty to forty, for this same purpose, but real parity based on demographics has never been achieved. The new law called for seventy-one seats for East Bankers, sixty for West Bankers, and eleven spread among the Palestinian refugee camps in the greater Amman area.

[11] Although conventionally translated as *uprising*, the term actually means to shed or slough off, as in freeing oneself (in this case, from occupation).

Jordan's elections law that abolished the seats designated for deputies from the West Bank and the Palestinian refugee camps in Jordan. The refugee camps were incorporated into other electoral districts, ending the decades-old system that had kept Palestinians from having to compete with Jordanians for seats in parliament.

Meanwhile, Jordanian leaders worked to ease the country's economic problems. The government tried to renew relations with leading business associations and the private sector, promising organized business "a greater voice in economic policymaking" (Moore 2004: 1). Debt continued to grow while the value of the dinar, despite the government's efforts, declined by two-thirds in only a few months time. By late 1988, the government had made preliminary contacts with the IMF concerning debt relief programs. Formal negotiations began early the next year.

Until that time, the renewal of parliamentary life had taken a back seat to economic reform. Because many of the traditional supporters of the regime had gained renewed voice in the NCC and in the parliament since 1984, few pressed for new national elections. The government sought to control the public debate about Jordanian identity after the monarchy relinquished its claim on the West Bank, and it forced privately owned media to sell shares to the state. As Lynch argues, "this repression and failure to achieve public consensus quickly became a major source of instability and tension in the political system, contributing directly to the uprisings of 1989" (1999: 102). Palestinians had transferred their capital out of the country (104), and "black pamphlets" circulated throughout Amman that accused public officials of corruption and demanded increased political freedoms (105). The dinar was devalued by half in late 1988, and in early 1989 Jordan negotiated a credit package from the IMF in exchange for austerity measures. But in April 1989, large-scale protests changed the political equation by bringing "from below" pressure – distinct from the nudging of elites throughout the country on the regime – to bear on the regime's political calculations. On April 16, the government of Prime Minister Zayd al-Rifa'i raised prices on fuel, cigarettes, and beverages. Two days later, Jordanians took to the streets in the southern trucking town of Ma'an in protests that spread throughout Jordan within days and claimed a dozen lives. Demonstrators demanded the resignation of al-Rifa'i and the immediate restoration of fuel subsidies. The king responded by replacing al-Rifa'i with Zayd bin Shakir and a new government and building a national dialogue (hiwar watani) with a range of actors, including business and professional associations and tribal delegations (Boulby 1999: 36). He also convened a meeting of his closest advisors,

TABLE 2.2. *Advisors to King Hussein Concerning Responses to the 1989 Riots*

Strategy	Person	Position
Hard-liners: initiate stopgap economic reforms and prosecute corrupt cabinet officials; avoid elections that could produce a Palestinian-dominated parliament and/or spiral out of control	Tariq 'Ala' al-Din Marwan Qasim	Chief of general intelligence Deputy prime minister and foreign minister
Intermediates	Zayd bin Shakir Duqan al-Hindawi 'Adnan Abu 'Odah	Prime minister Chief of the royal court Palace advisor
Reformers: initiate elections to avoid resort to further violence and provide an outlet for the legal expression of current and future dissent	Salim Masa'dah Ibrahim 'Izzidin	Deputy prime minister and interior minister Minister of state for prime minister affairs

Sources: Mufti (1999: 7–9); interviews with 'Izzidin, al-Hindawi, and Abu 'Odah, 1996–8, Amman.

including Chief of General Intelligence Department (GID, commonly called the *mukhabarat*) Tariq 'Ala' al-Din, Deputy Prime Minister and Foreign Minister Marwan Qasim, Deputy Prime Minister and Interior Minister Salim Masa'dah, Minister of State for Prime Minister Affairs Ibrahim 'Izzidin, Chief of the Royal Court Duqan al-Hindawi, and palace advisor 'Adnan Abu 'Odah (Mufti 1999: 7–9). The king listened while different sides presented their recommendations for how to respond to the riots (Table 2.2).

'Ala' al-Din and Qasim called for instituting stopgap economic reforms while making a public display of dismissing and prosecuting corrupt officials from al-Rifa'i's cabinet. The two also strongly opposed holding elections. 'Izzidin and Masa'dah pushed to hold elections as soon as possible. Only by quickly "initiating a process of political liberalization," 'Izzidin recalled arguing, could the government "hope to continue its program of economic reform without resorting to violence. We felt that more violence was simply out of the question."[12] King Hussein convened this group in an advisory capacity only; the final decision was his. He chose to adopt the strategy advocated by the reformers and immediately set a timetable for new parliamentary elections. The objective was to provide political dissent – present and future – with an outlet for legal expression as a means of preventing both further violence and the emergence of an organized opposition front that favored radical confrontation with the regime.

The extent to which elections were seen as a mechanism for political control is evidenced not only by the direct testimony of those involved in the decision, but by subsequent debates concerning the particularities of the elections, including timing, the location of district lines, district magnitudes, and the inclusion or exclusion of particular groups, such as Leftists and the Muslim Brotherhood. Of particular concern was how Palestinians, who by all but official counts constituted more than half of Jordan's population, could be prevented from gaining a majority. As then Minister of Interior Masa'dah recalled, a system of proportional representation was only briefly considered as it would have likely produced a Palestinian majority within the assembly. The objective was to produce a "fair system," but "within the context of this concern" (cited in Mufti 1999: 9). The system that was adopted preserved many of the existing electoral districts, but seats were distributed disproportionately. For example, the town of Karak, with its (East Bank) Jordanian rather than Palestinian population, was allotted nine seats, about one for approximately 10,000 citizens. All of greater Amman, by comparison, received only eighteen seats, one for every 25,000 citizens. Similar disparities existed throughout the country, with southern districts gaining the greatest proportion of seats.[13] Given that most of Jordan's Palestinian population resides in greater Amman, the objective of limiting Palestinian parliamentary representation was clear.[14]

The regime held elections in November 1989, and for the most part achieved the desired results. The assembly contained a stronger Islamist bloc than expected, though this was hardly a surprising result given that the Muslim Brotherhood had been the only national group permitted to

[12] Interview with author, April 22, 1997, Amman.
[13] Twelve seats were reserved for minority candidates: nine for Christians, two for Circassians, and one for Chechens.
[14] Many government officials, past and present, acknowledge off the record that minimizing Palestinian representation in the assembly was a primary objective behind the manipulation of the elections law. Under the new opening, this concern has been coupled with the desire to constrain the political parties, as detailed in the following text.

organize in the past thirty years, when all political parties were banned. Parties remained illegal during the new elections, but political groups were given some latitude to express in their campaigns their views and ideological ties to particular groups. As a result, a number of other opposition groups also effectively gained seats. In fact, proregime loyalists, nationalists, and tribal representatives achieved only a slim margin of victory. Furthermore, their majority depended on a number of representatives who were seen as "playing the field": siding with the loyalists but occasionally leaning toward the opposition when bargaining over issues they viewed as vital.[15] Yet even the opposition within parliament considered itself "loyal opposition," in that it never challenged the right of the regime to rule the country. The significance of this self-characterization of most political parties will be explored in subsequent chapters. Nevertheless, the king appointed mostly traditional Transjordanian elite to the upper house in a clear effort to counterbalance Muslim Brotherhood and Leftist oppositional voices who (though unorganized into a bloc) together held 60 percent of the seats in the lower house (Abu Jaber and Fathi 1990: 67–86).[16]

Most scholars agree that the expanded space for political activities and formal political contestation in Jordan was intended as a preemptive measure against future dissent.[17] However, liberalization also reestablished the formal representation of various powerful groups within a framework of state institutions. The next three years saw gradual but continued liberalizations in the spheres of civil and political rights. The king forged improved relations with a number of opposition groups, including many of the Leftists who had been jailed in the 1950s. The Muslim Brotherhood, long allied with the regime, was kept close through both official and unofficial channels, including through direct relations with the king and especially his brother, Crown Prince Hassan. The Gulf War of 1990–1 worsened the country's economic problems, however. As a result of King Hussein's decision to withhold support for the U.S.-led allied coalition, Kuwait and Saudi Arabia expelled tens of thousands of migrant workers, who returned home with their wealth, but no longer send labor remittances into the kingdom. In an effort to maintain the support of powerful social forces at home – a move that may have been necessary to prevent

[15] Interview with Ibrahim 'Izzidin, October 2, 1996, Amman.
[16] For a detailed look at the 1989 elections, see also Duclos 1990.
[17] For example, see Brand (1991), Robins (1991), Brynen (1992), Rath (1994), Hamarnah (1995), Adams (1996), Robinson (1998a, 1998b), Baaklini et al. (1999), Boulby (1999), Mufti (1999), Wiktorowicz (2001), Joffé (2002), and Moore (2004).

a resurgence of popular protest – Hussein opted for nonalliance, even at great risk of losing foreign aid. This latter fear was not unfounded, as the United States, Saudi Arabia, and Kuwait cut all aid to Jordan days after King Hussein's announcement of nonalliance.

During this tense and economically volatile period, limited political liberalization had the desired effect of lessening and refocusing dissent away from the regime. Tensions due primarily to economic conditions, for example, were attenuated through the expanded field of political contestation. On June 9, 1991, the government adopted the newly drafted National Charter (*al-mithaq al-watani*), codifying political practices and the rights of citizens to organize politically. The move was a high point in the political liberalization process, as it formalized into law the right of free political expression. The document subsequently became a principle point of reference for both the political elite and the opposition groups that challenged particular state practices and policies.

The regime legalized political parties on September 1, 1992 under the new political parties law. Twenty-two parties quickly registered, and although not all of them fielded candidates, ten won at least one seat in the 1993 assembly. Most of these parties had long existed in a variety of forms both legal and illegal, but for the most part democratic themes had not been prominent in their political agendas or publications prior to the political opening. A new press and publications law passed in May 1993 expanded press freedoms, although certain topics remained off-limits to criticism, notably the royal family as well as matters concerning "national security," a realm that state officials redefine freely and inconsistently. Nevertheless, the mood was generally positive as the 1993 elections approached.

That was, until August 1993. Three months before the scheduled November elections, the government introduced temporary amendments to the elections law that opposition parties across the political spectrum widely opposed. The 1989 elections had used a system of multiple transferable vote within multimember districts. Passed as part of the elections law of 1986, this format allowed a citizen to cast as many votes as were seats in her district and for whatever mix of candidates she wished. Parties and independent candidates put together formal and informal coalition lists, but in practice voters could pick and choose candidates as they pleased. Although the system was intended to prevent infighting among tribes (so that tribes could field multiple candidates without necessarily competing against each other), the result was that citizens could cast votes that reflected complex and multiple affiliations and interests. For example, one might cast one vote based on tribal affiliation, one based on ideological preferences, and one for a favorite local personality. This system facilitated the strong success of opposition candidates and independents in 1989.

The revised elections law of 1993 introduced a limited single nontransferable vote, whereby each citizen could cast only one vote regardless of the number of seats in his district. Opposition parties recognized that they stood to lose as a result of the revisions, but in the end they all participated (though several considered a boycott). The introduction of the new elections law, along with signals that the monarchy was moving to restore relations with Washington possibly through the establishment of a peace treaty with Israel, finally nudged Jordan's diverse political parties into cooperation. An informal coalition of the Muslim Brotherhood and other political parties together issued a statement, framed in terms of democratic practices: "The coalition of political forces aligned against surrender and capitulation is following with deep concern the implication behind the government's decision to dissolve the Parliament three months before its mandate was due to end according to provisions of the Jordanian constitution. The decision to dissolve the Lower House of Parliament coincided with a wide-scale campaign aimed at paving the ground for a new election law and coupled with signs of satisfaction over these developments displayed by certain American circles" (quoted in *The Jordan Times*, August 10, 1993).

The revised law had the desired effect from the government's point of view: although political parties had been legalized since the last poll in 1989, opposition candidates faired significantly worse. In defending the revisions, Marwan Muasher – Minister of Information from January 1996 to March 1997, and later Foreign Minister and Deputy Prime Minister – produced classified government reports based on survey research undertaken in 1991 and 1992. These documents illustrated that the system used in 1989 delivered to the opposition candidates a proportion of seats that was greatly inflated from the level of support that opposition parties actually enjoyed from the electorate. While the reforms were indeed intended to reduce these parties' share of seats, the goal, Muasher argued, was to produce an outcome that was more in line with the actual support of each group.[18]

---

[18] Interview with author, March 31, 1997, Amman. Muasher allowed me to look over the reports in his presence, but would not allow me to copy them or take notes on the survey results.

With its smaller proportion of seats in the 1993 assembly, the opposition parties began to work more closely together. In the 1989 assembly they collectively held some 60 percent of the seats, but they had not cooperated to advance reforms. The regime maintained mechanisms to make sure that even a strong opposition bloc could not pass legislation that ran counter to the wishes of the regime. For example, the lower house was constrained in its ability to enact new legislation, as legislation passed by the elected lower house also must be approved by a majority within the upper house, whose members were appointed directly by the king. Nevertheless, opposition parties increasingly began to coordinate their activities to strengthen their voice in the assembly, particularly concerning economic reforms and the regime's move toward making a peace with Israel. While some 70 percent of Jordanians supported negotiations with Israel as a means to a just and lasting resolution of the Arab-Israeli conflict (Mufti 1999: 118), most opposed the treaty because they felt that Israel had failed to fully honor the Oslo agreements (particularly the freeze in settlement construction) and had not negotiated with Lebanon and Syria in good faith. In this context, the regime began to demonstrate much less commitment to advancing political liberalization that would give voice to sizable opposition to these state initiatives.

Meanwhile, the active press was increasingly bold in its criticisms of government, particularly concerning the apparent move toward the signing of a peace treaty with Israel. The opposition disseminated their views through the weekly newspapers affiliated with the various political parties as well as in nonpartisan papers, including the partially government-owned dailies.[19] In response, the government brought charges against the journalists, editors, and owners of various newspapers, usually under statutes of the press and publications law, but increasingly under the penal code (for threatening the security of the state). Though none was convicted, the harassment, ostracization, and loss of work time and court fees produced a noticeable increase in self-censorship of the press (Kilani 1997). Direct harassment of the press increased as Jordan moved toward the October 1994 signing of a peace treaty with Israel. The treaty was

---

[19] Under the May 1993 press and publications law, the government was obligated to divest itself of ownership of the newspapers, particularly the dailies *Al-Ra'i*, *Al-Dustur*, and the English-language *Jordan Times*. Although it did sell off some of its shares in these publications, the government retained approximately 40% ownership of *Al-Ra'i* and 60% ownership of the other two. The law did not call for the government to relinquish its monopoly over radio and television, however. The broadcasting center remains under military guard and both are headed by government appointees.

wildly unpopular, and King Hussein wished to conceal this public senti-
ment from Israel and the United States as much as possible. In addition to
building ties with Israel, the king was also engaged in an ongoing effort
to restore Jordan's relations with the United States, which had suffered
considerably since 1991 as a result of Jordan's opposition to the U.S.-led
allied coalition against Iraq. In such a climate, the king did not want to
see open public debate of these issues.

Other unrest arose from time to time concerning worsening economic
problems. While the government struggled to paint a positive picture of
economic growth,[20] it resumed its IMF-designed restructuring program
including the lifting of other subsidies.[21] In August 1996, bread and fod-
der subsidies were halted, sparking a large protest in the mountain village of Karak and smaller demonstrations in parts of Amman and in
southern towns. The government grossly overreacted to the largely peaceful rally,[22] declaring a curfew in Karak and surrounding the town with
army troops while tanks drove through the streets (Andoni and Schwedler
1996).

With attention focused on the November 1997 elections, the next year
was marked by continued reversals of political and civil rights and various other measures of the liberalization process. The press engaged in
lively debate about Jordan's "retreat from democracy," while the government struggled to quiet dissent over both the Jordanian-Israeli treaty and
the economic reforms. A May 1997 amendment to the press and publications law dramatically increased restrictions on newspapers, raising
capital requirements twenty-fold and expanding the list of untouchable
"security" issues to include criticism of "friendly" governments, notably
Israel and the United States (Campagne 1997; Kilani 1997). The government also refused to consider changing the elections law, insisting that its
single nontransferable vote system was the same "one person, one vote"
system – rendered *sawt wahid*, or "one vote" – used by advanced Western
democracies.[23]

---

[20] Moore notes that the government quietly acknowledged in 1998 that it had inadvertently
"overestimated" growth rates in 1996 and 1997. Rather than 5.2% and 5.0% growth,
respectively, the figures were actually 0.8% and 2.7% (2004: 2).

[21] Vreeland (2003) argues that most states enter into agreements with the IMF not only
because they desire their assistance with economic reform but primarily to help them
push forward with reforms they already wish to undertake.

[22] The government news agency, Petra, reported that demonstrators were defacing government buildings and causing significant destruction of buildings.

[23] Interview with Marwan Muasher, March 31, 1997, Amman.

In July, an opposition bloc led by the IAF and including eight smaller opposition parties as well as two former prime ministers, Ahmad Obaydat[24] and Tahir al-Masri,[25] called for a boycott of the upcoming elections. The boycott document, signed over several days in early August, cited a number of reasons for the decision, but notably the increased restrictions on press freedoms and the refusal to revise the elections law. Both of these complaints centered on the fact that neither issue had been subject to parliamentary approval. Even with the 1993 assembly's proregime majority, the cabinet and the king were concerned that their programs would not win support. The amendments to the press and publications law, for example, were introduced by executive decree just a week after King Hussein dismissed parliament from its spring session early, a move that opened the way for reforms to be initiated without parliamentary approval. As for the economic reforms, Prime Minister 'Abd al-Karim Kabariti addressed the assembly and answered questions several times during the summer of 1996, but the specifics of the reform were never put to a vote. In the end, the boycott and the various legal reforms together produced an overwhelmingly proregime assembly in the 1997 elections.[26]

In sum, the political liberalization initiated by King Hussein in 1989 was halted by 1993, with key provisions steadily reversed. In the language of the democratization literature, Jordan's transition stalled far short of consolidation, with no advances and a few reversals characterizing the next decade. As I argue, this framework obscures the evolution of a wide range of political practices, including some that are directly relevant to the question of inclusion and moderation. Even Carother's framework of dominant power politics does not capture the extent to which opposition groups engage with each other differently, nor the impact of the regime's continued utilization both domestically and internationally of the language of democratization. The regime's strategic use of limited political openings has had a profound effect on the structure of political contestation in Jordan, allowing certain types of organization and contestation to continue while carefully controlling individual processes (e.g., electoral and press reforms) in hopes of producing desired results. I explore additional dimensions of these processes and practices in Chapters 2 through 5.

---

[24] Obaydat was Prime Minister in 1984 and 1985.
[25] Al-Masri was Prime Minister from July–November 1991.
[26] In Jordan, prior to the 1997 elections, a proregime party was formed, but it fell apart within weeks after the election and does not function at a practical level as a proregime party.

POLITICAL LIBERALIZATION IN YEMEN

Unlike Jordan, neither North Yemen nor South Yemen had a strong history of electoral politics prior to unification in 1990. The Yemen Arab Republic (YAR, or North Yemen) was established in 1962 through a military coup against the rulers of the Mutawakkilite Kingdom of Yemen, a theocratic state ruled by a hereditary line of Zaydi (*shi'i*) Imams for more than a millenium.[27] When Imam Yahya died in 1962 – he had ruled from the time of his father's death in 1948 – the revolutionary officers drove a tank into the central square of the northern plateau city of San'a and declared the establishment of a republican regime. The move started a civil war that lasted most of the decade, with Egyptian troops backing the republicans (and occupying parts of the country) and the Saudi regime supporting the royalists. The war evolved into a contest between Western-backed monarchies of the Arabian Peninsula and Arab nationalists supported by Egypt's President al-Nasser. Egypt finally withdrew its forces in early 1967. The republic survived several final pushes by the royalist forces, and a split within the republicans resulted in the defeat of the now-divided Leftist elements by tribal-backed conservatives, who led the new government.

South Yemen also underwent a revolution in the 1960s, but one of a different character. The port of Aden had been part of the British Empire since 1839. Various nationalist groups gained strength in their opposition to Great Britain following World War II, ranging from revolutionaries inspired by various Arab Socialist and Marxist ideologies, to conservative local elites. The former tended to link independence with a socialist transformation, while the latter sought to control any future independent state and its resources (Schmitz 1997: 14–15). After the North's 1962 revolution, these southern nationalists found the northern republicans to be effective allies, along with Egyptian troops eager to aid fellow Arabs in their struggle against the British. The nationalists finally won independence from Great Britain in November 1967.

The two Yemens might have moved toward unification at that time, had it not been for the fact that conservatives and tribalists emerged victorious in the North while Leftists triumphed in the South. In South Yemen, local politicians, conservative tribal leaders, and a number of merchants who had cooperated with Britain fled the country, where a socialist state

---

[27] Zaydism is a Shi'i Islamic sect that is strong throughout much of northern Yemen. The trend takes its name from Zayd bin 'Ali, the grandson of Hussayn (son of 'Ali), and was established as an Imamate in northern Yemen in 893.

was formally established as the People's Republic of South Yemen, later renamed the People's Democratic Republic of Yemen (PDRY, or South Yemen).[28] Over the next few years, relations between North and South Yemen were characterized primarily by the efforts of each to support opposition groups within the other. Leftists from the North found refuge in the South, while southern conservatives fled to the North. This antagonistic relationship flared into two separate wars between the Yemens. In 1972, southern exiles based in the North sought to overthrow the South's socialist regime, but they failed. In 1979, the northern regime was attacked by a southern-supported group of Leftists who called themselves the National Democratic Front (NDF), with fighting located primarily in the southern lands of the North. These processes of state development and the various alliances among elite-level actors will prove essential for understanding postunification politics.

The 1980s marked significant periods of change for both regimes. In the North, President Salih, who had ruled since 1978, created a national assembly called the General Popular Congress[29] (GPC, *Al-Mu'tammar al-Sha'bi al-'Amm*), which first met in 1982. The creation of the assembly did not reflect a move toward multiparty or even pluralist politics, but rather was intended to tighten relations between President Salih's regime and the powerful local elites spread throughout the country. Initially comprised of 700 elected and 300 appointed representatives, the GPC brought together virtually every prominent individual who had supported the regime, gathering in one formal assembly the elite from diverse hierarchies of power. Some of these individuals had even taken up arms to defend the regime during its ongoing struggles against the NDF in the 1970s. The establishment of the GPC set the stage for unification by institutionally linking the most powerful political forces under one umbrella organization, formalizing patronage ties and offering government positions to influential supporters. Unsurprisingly, many of the northern-based political parties emerged from the ranks of the GPC following unification, with even some members of the NDF co-opted. For the South, the 1980s were a time of struggle among a number of shifting factions. The result was considerable bloodshed, with some of the victorious leaders not surviving to see victory (Halliday 1990).

---

[28] Schmitz argues that the change in name reflected an effort by the ruling elite of the South to claim leadership over all of Yemen, while the leadership of the North claimed similar sovereignty (1997: 16, n. 5; 29–30).

[29] Often translated as General People's Congress.

Toward Unification and Liberalization

The mounting political and economic problems in both North and South Yemen led the two regimes to explore the possibility of unification. The idea was attractive because each president believed he could secure significant support among the populations of the other. Whereas Jordan's liberalization might be characterized as the restoration and expansion of earlier practice of participatory politics, the liberalization initiated through unification in Yemen, much like the unification, was entirely unprecedented (Carapico 1998: 135). In part, the leaders of the South's ruling party, the YSP, recognized that the decreasing remittances from the Soviet Union necessitated a fundamental rethinking of their economic policies, as its state-centered economy had long been reliant on external rents that were no longer forthcoming. In addition, many members of the party, particularly after the bloody in-fighting of 1986, were convinced by early 1987 that the only way for the YSP to heal its wounds would be to have a more pluralist, open system.[30] Indeed, one of the primary reasons that led to internal divisions had been the inability of the polit bureau to talk openly about the party's problems. The North's ruling elite also saw benefits in unification, not only in the possibility of gaining control of the South and the valuable port of Aden, but particularly with the discovery of oil in lands primarily in the South, but straddling a border of the two countries.

In 1989, presidents Salih and al-Bid secretly negotiated the unification of the two Yemens. They agreed on a representative democratic government for the new state, in part as a means of providing an institutional outlet to what both anticipated would be a long-standing rivalry, and in part because each believed his side could mobilize support in the other's "home" territory. The South's YSP, for example, immediately sought to build an electoral base in the North, expanding upon existing pockets of support in southern parts of the North such as in Ta'iz, a major urban center in the central region (*mantaqa wusta*) of the country. Farther north, the YSP sought to present itself as nationalist reformers and an alternative to the military rule of the North, which did not exactly enjoy widespread popular support. At the same time, the northern political elite sought to appeal to more conservative and traditional elements in the South that had been alienated and sometimes repressed during the British mandate period

---

[30] I am indebted to Lisa Wedeen for sharing this understanding of the internal debates of the YSP during this period.

and later during the period of socialist rule. Prominent tribal leaders in the North – many of whom had formal and informal alliances with the North's political elite – reached out to their southern counterparts. The South seemed considerably disadvantaged in the unification arrangement, given that it housed less than a fifth of the population of united Yemen (Republic of Yemen, ROY). In the interim government, the North's President Salih held the position of chair of the presidential council and the South's President al-Bid held the position of vice chair.

The initial period of liberalization following unification was as popular as it was remarkable. As Carapico notes, "The relaxation of security, political, financial, and legal controls, the issuance of legal-constitutional guarantees to personal, press, and political freedom, and the unleashing of pent-up desires to travel within the country, publish, organize, and hold public debates were all unprecedented" (1998: 136). In contrast to Jordan's more gradual reintroduction of political liberalization (beginning in 1984 but accelerating from 1989 to 1993), Yemen saw the whole process unfold practically overnight and did not share a similar memory of pluralist politics as did Jordan with its contests of the 1950s. Dozens of newspapers appeared in Yemen's major cities, and more than twenty political parties quickly organized even before the political parties law was passed in late 1992. Eventually forty-six parties registered prior to the 1993 elections, with twenty-two parties winning at least one seat (Mani' 1994: 227–8, 253). As in Jordan, many of these parties emerged from groups that had long existed in a variety of forms both legal and illegal, but with the exception of the YSP, few if any parties had previously invoked democratic themes prior to unification's political opening.

An interim parliament of 301 seats was formed by merging the assemblies of the North and South (159 from the YAR, 111 from the PDRY, and the rest newly appointed), with the YSP's Yasin Sa'id Nu'man serving as the interim speaker of parliament immediately after unification. The body was active immediately, debating the new constitution, a draft national charter, and a number of laws codifying the new liberalizations. The whole process culminated in the remarkable 1993 elections for the unicameral parliament, which produced a genuinely pluralist assembly. The North's GPC won the largest bloc, with 123 seats, less than a majority. The South's YSP came in third with only fifty-six seats. The "newcomer" was the conservative Islamist-oriented Islah party, a confederation party of northern tribal leaders and a mix of Islamist groups, which won sixty-two seats. Five other parties won a combined twelve seats,[31] as did a astonishing forty-eight independents. A coalition government was formed among the three largest parties, with Islah and the YSP acting as junior partners to the GPC. The three divided the portfolios (though not without considerable disagreement) and set about negotiating the final aspects of unification, notably including the merging of the armies.

The 1994 Civil War

The negotiations did not get very far. Just months after the elections, the GPC and YSP remained in fundamental disagreement on a number of issues. YSP leadership was concerned that the GPC had too quickly come to dominate the government, particularly given that leaders of the junior partner to the coalition, the Islah party, were closely tied to the North's political elite. Indeed, some of Islah's leaders were key figures in the northern elite, most notably party chair Shaykh 'Abd Allah ibn Hussayn al-Ahmar, the head of the large Hashid tribal confederation from which President Salih hailed.[32] President Salih secured de facto political authority in large part through patronage, the granting of economic favors, and the allocation of prominent government positions, resources, and salaries to tribal shaykhs and other clients. In short, his political authority rests in part on the consent of local elites and their support in bringing their constituencies to respect government authority in certain spaces.[33] In this connection, the President Salih–Shaykh 'Abd Allah connection is significant.

[31] The twelve were the Ba'ath Arab Socialist Party (7); the Zaydi Islamist party, Hizb al-Haqq (2); the socialist Nasirist Unionist Party (1); the socialist Nasirist Democratic Party (1); and al-Tashih (1).

[32] Salih and Shaykh 'Abd Allah both belong to the Sanhan tribe of the Hashid confederation, though they are members of different families (both named al-Ahmar). The Hashid tribal confederation is smaller in size than Yemen's second major confederation, the Bakil, which is also located in the North. But the Hashid are more powerful, largely due to a relative lack of intratribal conflict about lines of authority. Whereas Hashid tribes all recognize Shaykh 'Abd Allah as the top figure, Bakil tribes have reached no such consensus. See Dresch (1989, 2000) and Dresch and Haykel (1995).

[33] This was evident during the 1994 violence, which was more of a confrontation between President Salih and Vice President al-Bid than a civil war in the conventional sense of reaching 1,000 battle deaths, a common threshold in the literature on civil wars. There is considerable evidence that during the conflict, few tribal groups became involved, leaving the two armies to fight it out. Carapico (1998) has argued that Salih accomplished this feat through bribes and promises to various tribal leaders, and through the considerable mediation efforts of Shaykh 'Abd Allah.

Meanwhile, YSP leaders were targets of assassination, and more than a hundred YSP leaders and members were killed over a three-year period from 1990 to 1994. YSP leaders were likely right in their claim that the GPC and its militant Islamist allies were responsible for the attacks. Other points of contention included specifics about the role of law in governance, the role of women in public (and particularly political) life, and the unification of the militaries. To some extent, the North had already absorbed the South's military, but YSP leaders were concerned about the final integration of the forces because they disagreed about specifics of joint command. In a context of continued assassinations, the political and military rivalry between the YSP and the GPC escalated, with southern leaders reluctant to proceed in the face of what was the rapidly emerging northern dominance in a nondemocratic direction. The conflict escalated into military conflict that lasted from May to July 1994. After a failed secession attempt, the southern leadership fled the country, with only mid-level YSP leaders remaining in Yemen.[34] The now northern-dominated government tried many of them for treason in absentia.

Since then, the northern-based regime has sought to maintain the formal trappings and appearance of democratic governance, but in practice it never really evolved from being a military autocracy under the leadership of President Salih, who continues to head the military. When national elections for Yemen's second parliament were held as scheduled in April 1997, the GPC emerged with 188 of 301 seats. According to a number of GPC officials, this was at least twenty seats more than the party had wanted, as it wished to gain an absolute majority while preserving the appearance that the elections were a site of real political contestation.[35] To further maintain this appearance, President Salih scheduled presidential elections for 1999, which he easily "won" in large part by eliminating all competition. A YSP candidate was disqualified by the GPC-Islah-dominated parliament, leaving only an "alternative" GPC candidate, who was paid by the regime, on the slate against President Salih (Wedeen 2003: 682–92).

At that time, the constitution limited a president to two five-year terms in office. Since Yemen's first presidential election was held nearly a decade

---

[34] Those who remained behind maintained the YSP as a legal entity, though the party boycotted the 1997 elections. The YSP did field candidates in the 2003 elections, but won only seven seats.

[35] These officials, interviewed in September and October 1997, have asked to remain anonymous; they include three cabinet members and two other high party officials. The idea that the GPC went overboard in its manipulation of the elections has been so widely expressed and debated that it is, for all practical purposes, public knowledge.

after unification, President Salih would have been limited to "only" ten more years in that office. In February 2001, a national referendum was introduced by GPC deputies in parliament to extend the term for presidency to seven years and the term for parliament from four to six years. The parliamentary elections scheduled for April 2001 were thus delayed until 2003, and President Salih was left eligible to remain in office until 2013 (two seven-year terms), meaning that he could "democratically" lead united Yemen for a total of twenty-three years, in addition to his twelve years leading North Yemen. President Salih's son Ahmad, who won a parliamentary seat in the 1997 elections, has in recent years become an increasingly visible public figure, and public speculation has already begun about Yemen's new "hereditary presidency."[36] The referendum also authorized the creation of a new 111-person consultative council (*majlis ishtishari*), to be appointed by the president, which "activists charge will allow the President to offset the role of the elected parliament and promote indirect executive control of legislation" (Wedeen 2003: 691).[37] Meanwhile, Yemenis remain subject to deteriorating economic conditions, not to mention arbitrary arrests, summary judgments (often without formal charges having been filed), and torture (Human Rights Watch 2001). With these reversals of the political openings begun in the early 1990s, what President Salih and others have taken to calling Yemen's "emerging democracy"[38] is anything but.

This overview of regime dynamics in Jordan and united Yemen has been brief because aspects of these processes will be explored in detail in subsequent chapters. Even a quick examination, however, illustrates that each of these regimes – Jordan's monarchy and Yemen's military regime (though not the YSP leadership at the time of unification) – have used liberalization reforms for instrumental reasons. In Jordan, the regime sought to consolidate authority and power at the earliest stages of state development by reaching out to certain powerful social actors, the elite within various social spaces – tribal, religious, ethnic, regional, and economic. In Yemen, the northern regime of President Salih operated similarly, though the breadth of his power in Yemen was not as comprehensive as it was for

---

[36] Al-Ayyam, November 14, 1997.
[37] Wedeen reports that forty persons died and hundreds more were injured in violence related to the elections, which included not only the referendum but also elections for local councils (2003: 691).
[38] Salih picked up this phrase from a conference organized by the National Democratic Institute and convened in Yemen in June 1999 on the topic of emerging democracies in the Arab world. Fifteen countries attended the gathering.

Jordan's monarchy. Nevertheless, President Salih entered into the democratic transition accompanying the unification process in large part to consolidate and expand his power. Leaders of the YSP, in contrast, appeared
to be much more committed to promoting democratic reform in a united
Yemen. Thus for each country, the context in which the political openings
were initiated in 1989 and 1990 was characterized by elite-level alliances
and power relations that had been constructed through processes of state
development and during periods of crisis for the regime. All sides of the
political elite sought to preserve their existing bases of power, although
with varying commitments to the promotion of meaningful democratic
reforms.

The comparison of processes in Jordan and Yemen highlights a key
variation in the structure of relations of power and the political elite's
position vis-à-vis the new institutions. In Jordan, King Hussein introduced limited political openings in 1989 to deflate current and future
dissent toward state policies, particularly concerning economic reforms
and the move toward normalization with Israel. Although he had been
very successful in maintaining relations with a variety of powerful social
actors and in bringing many of the ruling elite into the new process, this
strategy was strained with the emergence of popular collective protests
against the IMF-mandated economic reforms in the south, the regime's
traditional base of support. Like Jordan, Yemen's liberalization was initiated at the elite-level, but not for the immediate purpose of deflating
popular dissent. Rather, the processes resulted from an elite-level pact –
conducted secretly between President Salih and President al-Bid – to unify
the north and south. The process was quickly embraced at the popular
level, but unlike in Jordan, popular mobilization or demands for greater
political representation played little if any role in the direction of change.

ISLAMISTS AND THE REGIMES

How did the IAF and the Islah party fit into these processes? Even before
the 1990s brought these political openings, the groups from which both
the IAF and Islah emerged were already prominent players on their respec-
tive political scenes. Neither had a history of opposing the authority of
the regime, while many of the individual leaders had played a direct role
in supporting the regime. In this respect, the "emergence" of these political parties might better be described as an organizational transformation of allies of the political elite to best take advantage of new institutional opportunities. In Jordan, the Muslim Brotherhood's goal was

to strengthen its influence and support base without challenging existing relations of power or antagonizing the monarchy. In Yemen, the northern-based Islamists also sought to preserve its alliances with the northern ruling elite, but for the express purpose of defeating the YSP and its progressive socialist agenda. Neither the Islamists in Jordan nor those in Yemen, therefore, should be mistaken for political opposition brought into the system as a result of democratic political openings. Chapter 3 explores the emergence and evolution of these parties in detail, focusing on internal organization, decision-making practices, and alliances with other political actors. In the following sections, I briefly examine each party's relationship to the regime, though further details appear in subsequent chapters.

Jordan: The Islamic Action Front

The IAF party emerged primarily because the Muslim Brotherhood decided to create an inclusive Islamist party to contest elections after the regime legalized political parties in 1992. The Muslim Brotherhood had long been a prominent actor on Jordan's social and political scene, with its influence due in large part to the group's long-standing and close relationship with the monarchy.[39] In 1945, a group of merchants who supported a religious struggle (*jihad*) against Zionists in Palestine founded the Muslim Brotherhood in Jordan.[40] From this beginning the group, under the leadership of loyalist Hajj 'Abd al-Latif Abu Qurah, gained the support of King 'Abd Allah I, who established close relations with the Islamists as a means of buttressing the weak support base of the regime as well as to avoid the risk that the group might emerge as a strong opposition force,[41]

---

[39] On the history of the Muslim Brotherhood and the IAF in Jordan, see Hourani et al. (1993a), Schwedler (1997), Cohen (1982), and especially Boulby (1999), by far the best single study from the group's founding until 1993. For views from Muslim Brotherhood and IAF members, see Akailah (1993), Ma'aytah (1994), and Gharaybah (1997a, 1997b).

[40] The Jordanian Muslim Brotherhood is formally a branch under the overall leadership of the Egyptian Muslim Brotherhood, but in practice the group functions autonomously. The Jordanian Muslim Brotherhood leaders have periodically sought council from the Egyptian group, but these instances are rare and should not be interpreted to mean that the group is functionally subordinate.

[41] According to several authors, the origins of the Muslim Brotherhood in Jordan date to the mid-1930s, though the group was not formally established until just before Jordan received its independence; see Kilani (1994: 9–20) and Dabbas (1995: 15–16). These references seem likely to refer to the Abu Qurah's initial support of the Palestinian strike in 1936, which the Egyptian Muslim Brotherhood supported. Boulby notes that Abu

though at the time the Muslim Brotherhood had no political objectives outside of the liberation of Palestine (Cohen 1982; 'Ubaydi 1991; Boulby 1999: 37).[42] The monarchy was also concerned with the growing strength of the country's other political alternative, the NSP headed by al-Nabulsi, which like the Muslim Brotherhood attracted a new generation of politically conscious Jordanians (Boulby 1999: 12–13). Thus on November 19, 1945, the king personally inaugurated the opening of the Muslim Brotherhood office in downtown Amman, welcoming the group as a religious charitable society, with understood limits on political activities.[43] Since at least the 1950s, the Muslim Brotherhood leadership has been comprised primarily of professionals (Boulby 1999), a trend that continues to be reflected in the IAF's leadership (Hourani et al. 1993a: 36). Many hold graduate degrees from Western universities, speak English or French, and travel routinely to Western nations including the United States. Though they have consistently opposed Western imperialism in the Muslim world, Jordan's mainstream Islamists have never been a militant or radical movement, have never challenged the authority of the monarchy, and have

Qurah's presence in Palestine at the time is undocumented and seems suspiciously coincidental (1999: 41). Gharaybah's study of the organization begins his narrative rather abruptly in 1946 with Jordanian independence (1997a: 45).

    Some Muslim Brotherhood members date the founding of the organization not to the inauguration of its Amman headquarters, but to several months later, in 1946, when the group adopted a formal internal structure and bureaucratic assemblies.

[42] Boulby notes, "A brief survey of *Al-Kifah al-Islami*, the weekly Muslim Brotherhood publication that appeared briefly in 1954 and again in 1957, demonstrates both a superficiality of political analysis and a tendency to resort to bombastic rhetoric which have characterized the movement's few publications" (1999: 39).

[43] Following government approval of the group's registration as a religious organization under the Ottoman Law of Associations, Abu Qurah was elected to lead the group's general bureau in 1947. Upon Abu Qurah's resignation in 1953, Muhammad 'Abd al-Rahman Khalifah assumed the position of overseer-general (*al-muraqib al-'amm*), a title not used during Qurah's tenure. Khalifah was considered the most influential member of the group throughout the middle part of the century, holding the group's highest office for more years than all others combined. According to Kazem (1997: 17), Khalifah demanded he be given the role for life, though in principle the position was to be elected every two to four years. Khalifah is generally said to have held the position of overseer-general of the group until his death in 1994, but in practice the title was given to a number of leaders: Khalifah 1952–4; Sa'id Ramadan, 1954–5 (at which time he was deported to his native Egypt); Khalifah, 1954–63; Yusef al-'Azm, 1963; Ramadan, 1964; Khalifah, 1964–94; 'Abd al-Majid Thunaybat, 1994 – present. Ramadan's position seems to be as head of the Palestinian Muslim Brotherhood, rather than the Jordanian branch, but their activities, membership, and leadership overlapped significantly during the 1950s through 1967, when Jordan controlled the West Bank.

sought to promote their social reform program within the boundaries of regime-defined constaints.[44]

As argued in the preceding text, the Hashemite monarchy relied for support in its infancy on a range of conservative social actors, including tribal leaders, minorities, and religious groups. The Muslim Brotherhood emerged as the most powerful of the latter, playing an essential role in supporting the regime as waves of Palestinian refugees brought a more politically active constituency into Jordanian politics, many of who embraced Leftist ideologies. The Muslim Brotherhood expanded its social bases of support among Palestinians and attracted many Palestinians into its ranks, largely due to its unwavering anti-Zionist position and its message of Muslim unity in the face of continued foreign intervention into the politics of the region. In the late 1950s and 1960s, at a time when members of Jordan's socialist and communist parties were subject to repression and imprisonment for their support of the Arab nationalist movement, the king gave the Muslim Brotherhood considerable latitude in pursuing its conservative social reform agenda. When in 1957 Hussein dissolved al-Nabulsi's government and suspended civil and political liberties, Muslim Brotherhood leaders defended the regime for its decisions.

Among the events that illustrate this strong regime–Muslim Brotherhood relationship, none stands out as much as the Islamists' support for the regime in its stand against Palestinian guerrillas during the events of Black September in the early 1970s. Despite the Muslim Brotherhood's strong position in support of an exclusively Arab Palestine, its leaders did not back the Palestinian guerrillas in their confrontations with the regime to maintain their bases in the East Bank. The decision did cause discord among Muslim Brotherhood ranks, but those who favored strong-regime relations prevailed. In fact, regime–Muslim Brotherhood relations have been so strong that from its founding, but increasingly in the 1960s and 1970s, a number of prominent Muslim Brotherhood leaders have even held formal positions within the government. King ʿAbd Allah I gave ʿAbd al-Hakim Abdin, the founding secretary of the Muslim Brotherhood in 1946, a cabinet position the same year he inaugurated the Muslim Brotherhood offices (Hourani et al. 1993a: 9).

Born in a West Bank village in Palestine, Ishaq Ahmad Farhan joined the Muslim Brotherhood in 1948 and has periodically been a member

---

[44] In Chapter 6, I explore the relationship of Muslim Brotherhood and IAF leaders with militants in other countries, notably HAMAS.

of its consultative council (*majlis al-shura*). He was IAF secretary-general from 1992–8 and chair of the IAF's own consultative council from 1998–2002. Farhan is an example of a Muslim Brotherhood member with long-standing connections to formal channels of political power. He served as head of curricula at the Ministry of Education from 1964–70 and was Minister of Religious Affairs and Endowments and Minister of Education for overlapping periods from 1970–3.[45] Similarly, 'Abd al-Latif 'Arabiyyat – a periodic member of the Muslim Brotherhood consultative council, IAF secretary-general from 1998–2002, and chair of the IAF consultative council from 1992–8 and again in 2002–4 – served as director of the Department of Vocational Education throughout the 1960s, head of curricula at the Ministry of Education from 1971–3, Director General of the Amman Education Department from 1981–2, and secretary-general of the Ministry of Education from 1982–5 (Riedel 1993). Hamzeh Mansur, IAF Secretary-General since 2002, served a prominent position in the Ministry of Education as director of a special section on combating illiteracy (Hourani et al. 1993a: 64). Numerous other prominent Muslim Brotherhood (and later IAF) leaders have also served government agencies in various capacities.[46]

While the relationship between the Muslim Brotherhood and the regime has been symbiotic for decades, the Muslim Brotherhood has not been fully co-opted by the regime. The group was granted space to pursue its own agenda only as long as those activities did not challenge the regime's sovereignty. Muslim Brotherhood members have been arrested and imprisoned from time to time – including since the 1989 political opening – often for boldly criticizing government practices.[47] In the late 1950s, for example, the Muslim Brotherhood was at the forefront of

---

[45] Because the Muslim Brotherhood was permitted to function as a charitable society, but not in a formal political capacity, Farhan formally suspended his membership in the group during this period. Some Muslim Brotherhood members protested his acceptance of the post. Farhan reactivated his membership in 1980 (Hourani et al. 1993a: 60), but had remained close to high circles in the Muslim Brotherhood during the intervening period.

[46] In prominent positions as division directors of various ministries, these included Muhammad Awaydah, 'Abd al-Rahim Muhammad Akur, and Ahmad Kufahi.

[47] For example, Yusef al-'Azm, editor-in-chief of the Muslim Brotherhood publication *Al-Kifah al-Islami* (which appeared intermittently in 1954 and again in 1957), was several times arrested for publishing articles that strongly condemned corruption in the government. Interview with author, July 12, 1995, Amman. More recently, 'Arabiyyat sustained a slight injury to one finger in a clash with police during a protest in May 2001. Interview with author, November 3, 2003, Amman.

criticizing the regime for its ongoing relations with Great Britain, and particularly the latter's role in advising the Jordanian regime on military and security issues. On the whole, however, the close relations between Muslim Brotherhood leaders and kings 'Abd Allah I and Hussein enabled the regime to draw on the power bases of the Muslim Brotherhood in times of need. While the king may not have supported all aspects of the group's reform proposals, he did appoint a number of Muslim Brotherhood members to powerful government positions, particularly related to education reform. Given that eliminating illiteracy and improving the kingdom's education system was one of King Hussein's stated primary objectives – and one of his successes, due to the dramatic decreases in illiteracy from 67.6 percent in 1961 (UNESCO 1980: 50) to 10 percent in 2005[48] – the extent to which he placed Muslim Brotherhood members at the center of these projects offers strong evidence that they shared many ideals. Indeed, strong Muslim Brotherhood presence in the Ministry of Education continued through the 1990s (Hourani et al. 1993a: 13). Furthermore, following Syrian President Hafiz al-Asad's brutal crackdown of a merchant-Islamist revolt in Hamah, Syria, in February 1982, King Hussein allowed a number of leaders of the Syrian Muslim Brotherhood to take refuge in the kingdom. When King Hussein began to rebuild relations with al-Asad in the mid-1980s, however, he put a stop to the Muslim Brotherhood – organized military attacks against Syria that he had previously encouraged.

It is within the context of this historical relationship between the Muslim Brotherhood and the regime – a relationship that had allowed the group to function since the 1950s while other movements and all political parties were banned – that Muslim Brotherhood candidates won a large bloc of seats in the 1989 parliamentary elections. The IAF was formed just a few months after martial law was lifted and political parties were legalized in late 1992. Since then, the IAF has been widely recognized as the Muslim Brotherhood's political wing, though as Chapter 3 illustrates, it functions largely independently of its sister organization.

Yemen: The Islah Party

The Islah party was formed on September 13, 1990, just months after the unification of North and South Yemen. But unlike the IAF in Jordan,

---

[48] In 2005, the male illiteracy was 5% and female illiteracy 15% UNDP (2005: 20).

Islah did not emerge out of a single cohesive movement, rendering the party's internal dynamics quite distinct from those of the IAF. Prior to the 1962 revolution in North Yemen, a number of Yemenis claimed membership in the banned Muslim Brotherhood. Although the group has roots in Yemen dating to the 1930s and 1940s, it did not play a prominent role on the political scene, as had the Muslim Brotherhood in Jordan, nor was it well organized (Sa'id 1995: 13–27).[49] After the 1962 revolution, Muslim Brotherhood leaders formed the group's first formal consultative council under the leadership of Shaykh 'Abd al-Majid al-Zindani, a radical and (many say) charismatic speaker who had strong Islamist credentials and a modest personal following. The group later joined other conservative trends in supporting the new republican leadership against the more Left-leaning members of the revolutionary guard. Thus from the earliest days of the YAR, the Muslim Brotherhood had close relations with the political elite.

In the late 1970s, after more than a decade under al-Zindani's guidance, a number of younger Muslim Brotherhood members felt it was time for a change in leadership and mounted what several of them describe as an internal coup against al-Zindani.[50] Several expressed concern that al-Zindani was developing his own cult of personality at the expense of group's broader vision shaped by the teachings of Hassan al-Banna, the Egyptian who founded the Muslim Brotherhood in 1928.[51] Shaykh Yasin 'Abd al-'Aziz al-Qubati became the new head of the Muslim Brotherhood, a position he continues to hold.[52] Al-Zindani went to Saudi Arabia, reportedly in a fit of anger at having been ousted. During his self-imposed exile from Yemen, he strengthened his ties with Saudi Arabia's Wahhabi government and conservative Salafi movement. He also became secretary-general of a powerful Islamic scientific institute in that kingdom.

In 1979, the southern-based NDF launched border skirmishes with the northern regime, in part with widespread, if secret, support of northerners,

---

[49] For a history of the Muslim Brotherhood in Yemen, see Sa'id 1995. For the role of early Muslim Brotherhood members in the Free Yemeni Movement (which challenged the Imamate in the 1930s and 1940s), see Douglas 1987.

[50] Interviews with Yasin 'Abd al-'Aziz, Muhammad al-Yadumi, Faris Saqqaf, Zayd Shami, Nasr Taha Mustafa, and Muhammad al-Afandi, 1995 to 1998, San'a. See also Sa'id (1995).

[51] For a general history of the Muslim Brotherhood through the 1960s, see Mitchell (1969).

[52] Al-Qubati continues to lead the Muslim Brotherhood since Yemeni unification in an unofficial (but well-recognized) capacity; he is also the vice-chair (to al-Zindani) of Islah's consultative council.

including (*sunni*) Shafi'i[53] sharecroppers, (*shi'i*) Zaydi villagers, workers, and students from the southern regions of the North (Carapico 1998: 36). The northern army defeated the NDF, however, in part due to the support of an informal group of conservatives and Islamists known as the Islamic Front. This group included members of the Muslim Brotherhood, conservative tribal leaders, and a few smaller Islamist groups. The willingness of Islamic Front members to fight for the regime cemented their relationship with North's President Salih, who had taken power in 1978. When President Salih inaugurated the GPC in 1982, Islamic Front members were prominent among their numbers, as were a few co-opted NDF members.

Following unification, the core members of the Islamic Front joined with others who shared highly conservative and sometimes radical social visions to collectively form the Islah party. The party is often said to consist of two primary wings, one religious and one tribal, along with a small number of business leaders and intellectuals. While this picture does broadly reflect the party's social bases, the labels "tribal" and "religious" wrongly suggest a level of cohesiveness among the various branches that obscures complex relationships and does not reflect the group's internal dynamics. In practice, tribal leaders are also religious, and many Islamists have tribal ties. The most powerful and prominent member of Islah, for example, is Shaykh 'Abd Allah, head of the Hashid tribal confederation and Sanhan tribe from which President Salih hails. Shaykh 'Abd Allah was a supporter of the republican government of the North from the time of the 1962 revolution and a strong defender of the government against dissenters throughout the 1970s and 1980s. He has served as speaker of North Yemen's national assembly, a position he has held under three parliaments in unified Yemen, and also has strong ties to the Saudi government. At the same time, he has long-standing ties to strong Islamist trends and, by many counts, has been increasingly influenced by Wahhabi ideology since the mid-1990s. Thus while Shaykh 'Abd Allah is by all counts a major tribal leader in Yemen, he cannot be characterized as *not* Islamist and therefore illustrates the limits of suggesting a clear tribal-Islamist divide within Islah. Likewise, Shaykh 'Abd Allah is not the party's sole tribal leader. Another is Shaykh Naji 'Abd al-'Aziz al-Sha'if, a prominent leader of the Bakil tribal confederation. He and Shaykh 'Abd Allah have not consistently presented a united "tribal" front within the party.

---

[53] Shafi'ism is a school of Sunni Islamic thought, with followers in parts of both northern and southern Yemen and major centers of learning in Tarim, a small town in the eastern part of the Hadramawt.

Nevertheless, Shaykh ʿAbd Allah is widely recognized as one of the most powerful individuals in all of Yemen and, as such, he is in large part responsible for Islah's strength as a party through his ability to mobilize a large constituency in the North and ensure a role for the party in elite decision making.

What has been called the religious or ideological wing of Islah may be more accurately described as a collection of somewhat diverse actors: members of the Muslim Brotherhood; followers of al-Zindani and his radical (now Salafi) teachings; and Salafi Wahhabis who do not follow al-Zindani, to name only the most prominent. Islah also includes a small number of Zaydis among its ranks, though many complain of a "glass ceiling" that prevents Shiʿa from holding prominent or influential positions in the party.[54] As noted, al-Zindani was based in Saudi Arabia from 1979 until unification, and much of his power today is derived not only from his personal following, ties to Saudi Arabia, and control of a network of thousands of Islamist institutes,[55] but also from his lucrative business investments. The latter were the cause of some scandal when they were reported in the press in early 1997, just prior to the second parliamentary elections, given al-Zindani's self-portrayal as a pious Muslim unconcerned with material wealth.[56] Like Shaykh ʿAbd Allah, President Salih, and many powerful individuals in Yemen, al-Zindani has found close ties with the Saudi government to be both a political and economic resource. Muhammad al-Yadumi, a Muslim Brotherhood leader and Secretary-General of the Islah party since 1994, likewise has ties to Saudi Arabia. As a former prominent head of political security in North Yemen, al-Yadumi also brings considerable resources beyond his Muslim Brotherhood ties to his position as head of the party's administrative bureau. And ʿAbd al-Wahhab al-Anisi, a party leader with diverse credentials that cross tribal, Islamic, and Leftist lines, brings his own resources and constituency to the party's elite relations and support base. Thus Islah is not, despite initial appearances, comprised of a cohesive tribal wing and a cohesive ideological wing; as subsequent chapters illustrate, it is far from a cohesive party at all.

---

[54] Interviews with author, 1995–8, Sanʿa, names withheld by request. Yemen has a small Zaydi Islamist political party, Hizb al-Haqq, but its influence has been extremely limited though it routinely fields candidates in parliamentary elections.

[55] The number of these scientific institutes (sing. *maʿhid ʿilmiyyah*) increased throughout the 1990s, but began to decline in the early twenty-first century in part as President Salih sought to strengthen relations with Washington.

[56] Al-Zindani brought charges of slander against the journalists and editors of the articles.

To be sure, Islah leaders readily acknowledge the party's internal divisions, and some have even sought to put forth a democratic spin when news of internal contentions reaches the public. Al-Yadumi, for example, frames internal party divisions as a strength of the party, and as democratic: "Of course there are different views within the party, but it would be a mistake to say the group is divided. Is it not a natural and healthy characteristic of democracy to have disagreements and debates among members? We encourage members to express their opinions, then through debate we come to a decision based on consensus (*ijma*'). This practice is Islamic first, but it is also central to democratic politics."[57] Commenting on al-Zindani's frequent contradictions of formal Islah positions, Shaykh 'Abd Allah has argued, "As far as Shaykh Zindani is concerned, he is a leading member of our party but he cannot commit to anything beyond the prescribed party decisions. In general, these rumors [about divisions within Islah] are intended to discredit us internationally, especially in the West."[58] This line of defense illustrates the extent to which party leaders have sought to downplay its internal divisions and portray the party, at least to outsiders, in terms of democratic practices. From a comparative perspective, Islah significantly varies from the IAF in Jordan in that it did not emerge from a single, coherent movement. This factor, which will be examined in detail in subsequent chapters, shapes the ways in which party leaders have sought to adapt to the changing political environment of postunification Yemen.

SUMMARY

In this chapter, I have examined the recent political openings in Jordan and Yemen as mechanisms for the political elite to maintain power, whether in the context of a stable, unchanging regime (Jordan) or in a transitional regime (Yemen undergoing unification). Each country initially adopted a number of similar measures, including the establishment of a nationally elected assembly, an easing of restrictions on the press, the legalization of political parties, and the drafting of a national document codifying these changes. In Jordan, King Hussein sought to use the political openings to lessen popular opposition to state policies, particularly IMF-led economic reform. As widespread dissent began to take the form of popular collective protest, the carefully controlled political openings effectively channeled

---

[57] Interview with author, April 6, 1995, San'a.
[58] Interview in *The Yemen Times*, June 10, 1992.

dissent into state-regulated institutions. In Yemen, political opening was an integral part of a North-South pact that accompanied unification. Yemen's two presidents agreed to merge their countries by adopting an institutional framework that would provide each with a means of protecting its power during the initial stages of the transition, although northern leaders proved far less committed than their southern counterparts to the eventual goal of meaningful democratization.

The transitions literature provides some guidance for understanding certain dimensions of elite-initiated transitions. For example, elite-level models focus on the structure of power distribution and the strategy of different political actors, and these cases vary in terms of the impetus behind the political openings. In Jordan, King Hussein initiated political liberalization after suspending pluralist politics some thirty years earlier. Though he consulted a number of other powerful actors at various points in time, they served only an advisory function while he alone took the decision. In contrast, the presidents of North and South Yemen agreed on unification in secret, announcing that power would be shared between the political elites of the North and South during the transition period, but that the eventual goal was democratization.

These sorts of largely structural differences have been approached in the transitions literature as variations of "top-down" liberalization. Drawing on her work in Latin America, for example, Karl (1990) focuses on two broad types of elite ascendant liberalization. The first type, "pact," results from compromise among the ruling elite. The second type, "imposition," is implemented through force. In both cases, the objective is to initiate reforms to achieve some specific objective without ushering the incumbent elite out of power. This type of framework highlights some of the differences between Jordan and Yemen in terms of the composition and relative strength of the various actors. In Jordan's monarchical regime, power is concentrated in the hands of the royal family, indeed in the hands of a single actor, the king. Particularly in the early days of state development, powerful actors from other spheres were essential for the consolidation of the regime. Yet in 1989, the decision to liberalize was the king's alone: a transition by force, through imposition. In Yemen, by contrast, power was shared by the northern and southern political elite at the time of unification, with a number of tribal, economic, and religious elites intimately involved in negotiating the details. The actual decision to unify was made in secret between the two presidents: a transition by pact, which engaged existing powerful elite to insure that all major actors supported the transition.

In addition to highlighting various modes by which elites initiate political openings, the transitions literature also draws attention to the likelihood that certain models of democratic openings will achieve meaningful transitions. Przeworski's typology of the forms of institutions adopted for the transition suggests that each model has advantages and disadvantages in terms of realizing democracy (1991: 82–4). Jordan fits the model in which the relations of forces are known and uneven. One actor overwhelmingly initiates and controls the openings, and the institutions are carefully designed to reproduce existing power relations. Most political actors, including opposition groups, are ensured a sufficient minority to keep them participating within the system even though they are unlikely to ever gain a majority or obtain a meaningful role in governance. This type of transition is usually stable as far as it goes, which is not likely very far. Yemen best fits a second model, in which the relation of forces are known and balanced, at least at the outset. The political elite reach an initial agreement on the openings, but new processes raise such uncertainties that elite actors continuously question their relative strength and consider alternative strategies and alliances. This type of transition is more likely to break down, particularly given the precarious nature of the balance of forces, but it is also more likely to progress toward democracy if it survives the initial period of uncertainty and instability.

A similar point of comparison between Jordan and Yemen concerns the relationship of the elite to the processes of political contestation. In Jordan, the king controls the process from a position external to the field of party contestation; in Yemen the ruling elite is part of that field, competing in elections as a political party (the GPC). This position vis-à-vis political competition structures the possibilities for other political actors, particularly opposition groups. When the ruling elite must share power (e.g., using a pact) and compete in electoral contests, they often utilize "agreements among leaders of political parties (or proto-parties) to (1) divide government offices among themselves independent of election results, (2) fix basic policy orientations, and (3) exclude and, if need be, repress outsiders" (Przeworski 1991: 90). This type of pact has had a long tradition in Venezuela, Italy, Spain, and Uruguay (90) and shares certain characteristics with Yemen's political opening. In addition to the initial agreement between the leaders of the North and South, the collection of political actors who later formed Islah was effectively a partner to the northern political elite at the expense of the southern elite. By comparison, Jordan's imposed transition saw all political groups channeled into a field of political contestation in which the ruling family was not a participant.

For the Islamists there, the process meant that their previously privileged position was put into jeopardy as other political actors emerged, but no group needed to formally ally with a ruling party (there was none) to insure success at the polls. These dynamics will be explored in detail in Chapter 3.

In this connection, one of the more interesting comparative characteristics of the political openings in Jordan and Yemen is the relationship of each Islamist party to the broader opposition bloc in each state. These regime-Islamist and opposition-Islamist relationships will be examined in detail in Chapter 3. Here it is sufficient to recognize that the relationship of the regime to public political space – particularly whether the ruling elite are subject to periodic electoral validation – structures the field of political competition by creating opportunities and obstacles for proregime and opposition political actors alike (Herb 1999; Lust-Okar 2005).

The models from the field of transitology seem appropriate for exploring certain dimensions of the transitions in Jordan and Yemen because both were top-down processes and in neither country had the general citizenry been clamoring for democratization. This literature helps to illustrate structural differences between the cases and to identify the strategic actions of various political actors given the broader political opportunity structures. These sorts of political openings "work" for regimes precisely because they can be used for control rather than for regime-level change. These processes can take many forms, including the co-optation of opposition, the production of a narrative of democratic legitimacy for the regime, and by duping both the public and opposition political actors into thinking that the regime is undergoing meaningful changes. Overall, however, the transitions literature has little if anything to say about the continued evolution of democratic practices under stalled transitions, and even less to say about whether political inclusion under such specious circumstances can nevertheless produce moderation.

3

Public Political Space

How do limited political openings restructure public political space, even when transition processes seem to have stalled? As argued in Chapter 2, regimes use highly controlled political openings to undermine the power of political challengers by steering them toward particular modes and channels of contestation. This form of political coercion may be accomplished through a variety of mechanisms, most obviously through such state-regulated apparatuses as legal channels of political participation and the judicial system. For example, state actors may prohibit certain targeted groups from adopting legal institutional forms (e.g., Islamist groups in Egypt, Tunisia, and Turkey, which are not permitted to form political parties) or render certain modes of political contestation illegal (e.g., publicly questioning state policy in Syria or Saddam's Iraq, or criticizing "friendly" governments in Jordan). Regimes may erect administrative obstacles such as elaborate processes to obtain required permits, or they may fail to process such permits in a timely manner. Political elite may even deem certain ideas subversive and seek to quash those debates entirely. The governments of Egypt and Syria, for example, have at times rendered political opposition organized on the basis of Islamic principles outside the boundaries of acceptable issues for public political debate (Moaddell 2002). Likewise, Leftist narratives historically have been repressed through a variety of mechanisms in countries as diverse as Jordan, Iran, Mexico, Northern Ireland, Saudi Arabia, the United States, and Yemen.

This form of exclusion through the careful organization of "inclusive" processes (institutional as well as discursive) exists in every state, even the most advanced democracies. Because direct repression is typically most effective in controlling or crushing dissent when it is very high or very low (an inverted U curve), channeling may prove the most effective form of coercion in "middle" contexts of so-called gray-zone transitions. Selective inclusion and exclusion are tried and true mechanisms for regime preservation, whether to protect democratic institutions or to entrench authoritarian regimes. Therefore, one of the most powerful mechanisms for structuring public political space is drawing the boundary between inclusion and exclusion, a practice dominated by state elites. Their goal is to structure participatory institutions and processes in ways that allow for participation only on certain terms. In Turkey, for example, political parties overtly based on ethnicity are expressly forbidden, a restriction that prevents the country's sizable Kurdish population from advancing its interests through a legal political party organized around Kurdish identity. Instead, Turkey's Kurds have sought to pursue their interests through illegally constituted political parties (notably the Kurdish Workers Party, or PKK) and by joining other political parties. Interestingly, this form of exclusion has led Turkey's Kurds to work with various incarnations of Islamist parties, despite the predominantly socialist orientation of the country's Kurdish population.[1] As a result, the Kurdish population has obtained a small but significant voice in parliament.[2] At the same time, the illegal Marxist PKK engaged for years in armed confrontation with the military and the police, demanding that Kurds be allowed both to express ethnic identity and to organize politically and socially along those lines. Turkey's example illustrates how political elites seek to control political dissent through practices ranging from the careful structuring of institutions and legal provisions to direct and physical repression; it also demonstrates how opposition groups strive to navigate these constraints to advance their own agendas and interests.

In countries such as Jordan and Yemen, the introduction of political openings examined in Chapter 2 effectively restructured public political space: political actors who choose to participate within these legal channels adopted new practices and organizational structures appropriate to the changing environment. But how can we theorize structural openings and their effect on political actors? The literature on social movements and contentious politics provides a starting point for thinking about such

---

[1] In 1997, the Welfare Party was declared illegal, in accordance with the constitutional ban on parties organized around religion; the Virtue Party emerged in 1998 with many of the Welfare Party's members and leaders and was replaced a few years later with the Justice Party, which won the largest bloc in the 2003 parliamentary elections. See White (2002).

[2] In 1995, one Kurd elected to parliament as a Welfare Party candidate caused a scandal by reciting the oath of office in a Kurdish language before repeating it in Turkish.

controlled political liberalization, particularly the institutional constraints that shape political contestation. Synthesizing the vast literature on social movements, McAdam, McCarthy, and Zald argue that the broad political environment in which social actors function "constitutes a powerful set of constraints/opportunities" affecting social actors (1996: 12). The very structure of state institutions renders certain forms of political organization and contestation more effective than others, with direct participation in state institutions limited to elite-proscribed modes of contestation. A tribe, for example, may not be able to participate within the institutional framework of liberal participatory politics qua tribe, though its members may form a group that meets the specific requirements for forming a political party (which may include, among other things, restrictions on asserting tribal identity). The parameters of participation are again determined by the state, which stipulates in what capacity tribes or their members are eligible to participate. One may always participate as an individual, though in practice that might mean performing as a party of one and adopting strategies similar to those of political parties: fund raising, formulation and dissemination of an identifiable platform, mobilization of a wide support base, expansion of membership, and so on. Forms of political contestation are often most effective not only when they are sanctioned by the state, but when a given state institution is explicitly structured to engage particular organizations. A nationally elected assembly, for example, anticipates and encourages the formation of national political parties. Przeworski argues in this vein that in a democratic society, "unions have a place to go: industrial relations institutions have the state; [political] parties have parliaments; and lobbies have bureaus" (1991: 11, n. 4). Organizations that have no state agency to which they may direct themselves tend to require more creative efforts on the part of members and leadership. They are also often more costly to form and maintain and less effective in realizing their goals. In this way, political elites can shape forms of political contestation by establishing state agencies that encourage nonstate actors to adopt particular institutional forms.

In this chapter, I explore the impact of regime-led openings on the ways in which the IAF and the Islah party have adapted their organizational structure and their strategies to new opportunities. In my effort to discern whether these groups have substantively evolved in terms of their ideological commitments or merely adapted to new opportunities without becoming more moderate in the process, I examine shifts in the broader field of political contestation and the ways in which political actors structure and are structured by the emergence and adoption of new political practices. First, I outline in greater detail what I mean by public space, public political space, and practice, and then I explore how identifying these dimensions provides a richer understanding of the IAF and the Islah party. In each case, recent developments point to the emergence of new modes of political contestation, although each also remains relatively unchanged in certain, though not identical, dimensions.

SPACE AND PRACTICE

The inclusion-moderation hypothesis suggests the evolution of political actors as they maneuver within a public political space characterized by particular practices, competing ideologies, and systems of symbols and meanings generally comprehensible to other actors. I will begin by defining what I mean by the concept of *public space*, a notion central to a wide range of social theory. While scholars have reached little definitional agreement, in the broadest terms a "public" is a space of social activity distinct from private space, which is personal and often familial.[3] Many discussions of public space stem from liberal conceptions of a "private sphere" that limits the control of both state and nonstate social forces over the individual. In this view, public space is the realm of social interactions that are outside of the private sphere. The normative dimensions of this divide, particularly nonintervention of the public into the private, echo debates about public space in general: state activities are commonly differentiated from nonstate activities, with consensus that the state possess disproportionate power over society but that its power should be limited.

Theorists disagree, however, on whether state and nonstate dimensions of public space can be separated conceptually, let alone empirically. Contract theorists as diverse as Hobbes, Locke, and Rousseau, for example,

---

[3] Debates about the divide between public and private space are old and complex. Contract theorists typically located economic activity in the private sphere (thus the term *privatization* to refer to economic activity free of state intervention), though contemporary scholarship tends to treat economic exchange as a public activity. Similarly, scholars increasingly locate families within private space, though a comparative look at legal systems illustrates that this boundary is also not so clear. As Wendy Brown has illustrated, these issues are extremely relevant to Western democratic systems (1995; also see Pateman 1983). These debates about familial units and extended family networks are of particular relevance to the cases of Jordan and Yemen, both of which are characterized by the presence in some areas of tribal structures that traverse conventional public-private divides. They are not essential for this study, however, as the focus of the analysis is on public political contestation.

all examine public space when they discuss how civil society might bring
an end to the warring behavior of men that characterizes the condition
of nature. They treat civil society as virtually synonymous with the state
and relegate economic activities to the private sphere. In contrast, Hegel
and Marx, despite their many differences, treat the state as distinct from
civil society, which they see as a sphere of primarily economic relations
and interactions. In these formulations, the state effectively serves to protect and promote the interests of the economic elite. These debates are
expanded and developed in the neo-marxian literature as well as in other
philosophical traditions. Gramsci's discussions of civil society, for example, conceptualize a public space that is both separate from but complexly
connected to the state. His notion of the state includes the formal apparatuses of domination (from legislation to coercion), while the seemingly
private (nonstate) sphere of civil society actually reproduces state domination through civil, ideological hegemony, the manufacture of sponta-
neous "popular consensus" over the social, cultural, and moral values of
the elite.

By comparison, Habermas's "public sphere" is a public characterized
by an "ideal speech situation" in which a bourgeois class of individual
participants engage in uncoerced, rational, and critical debate on issues of
shared public concern, a practice that (if realized) could allow enlighten-
ment values to reach their fullest emancipatory potential.[4] In *The Structural Transformation of the Public Sphere*, he examines the historic emergence and decline of the "bourgeois public sphere" in modern Europe,
focusing on two central requirements of a public sphere: citizens' engagement in critical discussion, and the mediated, reflexive role that such mini-
publics, in tandem with other mini-publics, play in helping to produce
the impersonal, audience-oriented broader public of anonymous citizens
(Wedeen 2005).[5] Like Habermas, Gellner also envisions civil society as a
liberal and secular space, but he emphasizes the autonomy of its pluralist

---

4 Habermas's first articulation of the public sphere was *The Structural Transformation of
the Public Sphere*, published in 1963 and translated into English only in 1989. The notion
of the public sphere was also central to his exploration of the speech-act in his post-
1970 theory of communicative action (see especially 1984). For discussions of Habermas's
conception as relates to Jordan, see Lynch (1999); as relates to Yemen, see Wedeen (2005).
5 As Wedeen notes, Habermas's "public sphere" entails three dimensions: 1) a set of places
(coffeehouses and salons) where bourgeois citizens historically met to argue about literary
and political matters; 2) the substantive activity of private persons coming together as a
public for the purposes of rational-critical debate; and 3) the mediated, reflexive ways
in which these critical conversations in public places referred to, and actually influenced,
events and arguments appearing in print (2005).

and self-regulating institutions from state influence. Nonstate institutions are protected by the state while also constraining the power of the state over the public, and the realization of this sort of public space is largely responsible for the emergence of a capitalist economy and society (1994).

Like Gramsci, other scholars have sought to theorize the more nefarious dimensions of state control over nonstate actors (within both public and private space). In Foucault's examinations of how power produces the individual subject, he highlights the evolution of forms and practices of exclusion, including (but not limited to) modes of state domination (1977, 1991). Exclusion, for example of the insane or the criminal, is one mechanism through which a modern state and society is constructed (1967, 1977).[6] Scott (1985, 1992) and Wedeen (1999) examine some of the ways in which the subaltern contest the seemingly hegemonic control of the elite over public practices. Exploring these complex relations between state and nonstate actors, Mitchell points out the theoretical as well as empirical difficulty in identifying precisely where the state ends and society begins. The elusiveness of this boundary, he argues, should be taken as a clue to the nature of state power rather than an empirical puzzle to be solved (1991, 2002b). The boundary between the two – a notion also central to the vast contemporary literature on civil society – initially seems obvious precisely because the appearance of such a boundary facilitates the exercise of power by the state. Mitchell does not see the state as indistinguishable from society, but he suggests that we should dedicate attention to exploring the processes and practices that obscure the divide, asking whom the appearance of a clear divide actually benefits (1991, 1992).

Clearly, the idea that states exert some influence over publics (including various conceptualizations of society, civil society, the public sphere, public space, and so on) has a long scholarly tradition, one that does not need further rehearsing. These scholarly debates are not of ancillary interest to practical questions of inclusion and moderation, because they explore the role that spheres of public activity play in political change, particularly the role of the state in structuring public political space. In short, political elites dominate many public spaces through mechanisms ranging from legislation to channeling to coercion to the use of violence. Many

---

[6] However, Foucault cautions, "We must cease once and for all to describe the effects of power in negative terms: it 'excludes,' it 'represses,' it 'censors,' it 'abstracts,' it 'masks,' it 'conceals.' In fact, power produces; it produces reality; it produces domains of objects and rituals of truth" (1977: 24).

political actors work within these constraints, limited by state control, but working to find room to meaningfully contest state power. Others entirely reject the rules and practices proscribed by the state, but they still engage these constraints in their efforts to overthrow them.

The transitions literature tends to take the dominating role of the state as given, and many transitologists even argue that such state control is essential to successful democratic transitions. Instead, I adopt an approach that follows Gramsci, Mitchell, and Wedeen in exploring the complex ways in which the state exercises power over a field of political contestation, but does not control it absolutely. To elucidate the mechanisms at work in the inclusion-moderation hypothesis, I focus on modes of political contestation within contexts of elite-led openings. If "moderation" is an effect of political inclusion, understanding precisely which mechanisms are at work will require identifying not only how state actors utilize political openings as a means of control, but also how the structure of public political space(s) shapes various modes of contestation, and how these practices likewise reshape public political space. I will first define key terms and then examine these changing structures and practices in Jordan and Yemen.

I use the concepts of *public* and *public space* interchangeably and in an ordinary language formulation as a sphere of human social activity, including (but not limited to) noncoercive relations and practices such as collaboration, cooperation, and contestation among social actors. These interactions take place among nonstate actors as well as between state and nonstate actors. Indeed, the Islamist parties examined here illustrate that the distinction between state and nonstate actors is not always clear. In addition, a society may be characterized by the presence of multiple publics. Spheres of political contestation, social exchange, communal practices, and extended kinship ties and associated obligations, for example, may be distinct from one another or overlapping, in tension or mutually supportive.

Each public is characterized by particular kinds of interactions among actors that are meaningful to its participants. A public is not a bounded unit whose contents can be easily mapped, but more of a sphere of social activity characterized by sets of practices and relations familiar to and understood by actors in that space, even if not shared by them equally, and concerning a clear set of interests (e.g., politics, economics, social status, etc.) (Somers 1994). As Lynch argues, "instead of conceptualizing the public sphere as a single, unified arena in which a unified public debates the affairs of a single state, it is possible to think about public sphere structure as a network of overlapping and competing publics, which are not necessarily bounded by state borders" (1999: 47). Among these diverse and overlapping publics, this study is most interested in spaces of political contestation, that is, the relations and practices related to the contest of state power. I call this space the public political sphere.

Within these publics, the actions of actors are treated as practices, that is, "practical activity shot through by willful action, power relations, struggle, contradiction, and change" (Sewell 1999: 44). "Cultural" aspects of political participation are therefore not separate from institutional or behavioral dimensions of politics, but integral to them. As Sewell argues, "human practice, in all social conexts or institutional spheres, is structured simultaneously both by meanings and by other aspects of the environment in which they occur – by, for example, power relations or spatiality or resource distributions" (1999: 48). As Wedeen (2002) argues, practices are not merely behavior, but meaningful actions that are repeated over time; they are learned, reproduced, and subject to risks through social interaction. Practices are also unique to human beings: they involve "freedom, choice, and responsibility, meaning and sense, conventions, norms and rules" (Pitkin 1993: 242). They may be self-consciously executed, but they need not be. They also tend to be intelligible to others in context dependent ways. As Pitkin argues, practices are ultimately "dual," composed both of what "the outside observer can see and of the actors' understandings of what they are doing" (Pitkin 1993: 261; also see Wedeen 2002). In this chapter, I wish to emphasize the interactive ways in which structure and action reshape public political space, whose form and practices in turn inform actors' choices.

Thinking in terms of practice draws our attention to the ways in which the intentional and meaningful actions of political actors contribute to the ongoing reconstruction of the public political space of which those actors are part. We can identify which modes of political contestation are routine and which are innovations that might, if repeated, become routinized into practices. In Tilly's terms, the range of perceptions and responses of political actors within a particular context constitute a collective historical memory in which familiar modes of contestation form repertoires of contention (1986). Actors' choices among particular forms of contention are shaped by those modes that are currently being used, how effective they have been historically, and how effective they are perceived to be at the time. The idea of tried and true practices, for example, illustrates how past experiences and perceptions affect what choices actors make. At the same time, as political struggles play out, they in turn shape and reshape public political space, informing what practices might be adopted by actors in the future. In short, political actors adopt particular modes of political contestation based on their perceptions of what is possible given available resources (including known repertoires).

The point I wish to emphasize here is that efforts to organize politically are shaped by a variety of relations and practices, including repertoires of contention, the efforts of the political elite to manage participation, the structure of oppositional groups, and the ideological commitments and resources of all political actors. Do the opportunity structures of controlled inclusion produce shifts in practice in predictable ways? What sorts of shifts in practice would we consider evidence of increasing moderation? I explore the cultural dimensions of practice in detail in Chapters 4 and 5, and there propose a specific mechanism for explaining ideological moderation. In this chapter I examine the ways in which groups that participate under even limited political openings adapt by choosing among new and old practices. I turn now to the evolving practices of Islamist political parties that seek to take advantage of limited and controlled political openings.

ISLAMIST PARTIES AND THE NEGOTIATION OF PUBLIC POLITICAL SPACE

When the ruling elite of Jordan and Yemen introduced limited political liberalization and called for national elections, a range of existing political actors began exploring the new opportunities for political organization and contestation. Political actors who sought to fashion themselves into political parties adopted similar practices to prepare for upcoming parliamentary elections, to position themselves to accept cabinet portfolios, and to broaden their support bases by establishing or increasing their presence in local communities. To explore the inclusion-moderation hypothesis, I am particularly interested in the ways in which the organizational structure and practices of each group have evolved (or not) in response to shifting opportunities associated with limited political openings. In this next section, I explore the ways in which Jordan's IAF and Yemen's Islah party each took advantage of the new political opportunities that emerged with the introduction of liberalization in 1989 and 1990, respectively. I focus on three dimensions of organization and contestation to illustrate the breadth of the impact: the institutionalization of formal party structures, practices, and decision making; formal participation within state institutions; and old and new alliances with a range of political actors.

Political Organization and the Institutionalization of a Party

Often the first visible evidence of the impact of political liberalization on actors is the emergence of new ways of organizing. With the introduction of limited political openings in the early 1990s, both Jordan and Yemen witnessed a rapid proliferation of political parties, special-interest groups, nongovernmental organizations (NGOs), and research institutes. As outlined in Chapter 2, the IAF and Islah both emerged from existing social movements: the IAF from an established organization and the Islah party from a collection of conservative and radical groups and individuals with common interests. Even some well-established groups adopted structural changes before registering with the appropriate government agency. These included the establishment of a formal office or headquarters, the adoption of an administrative structure, and efforts at increasing visibility nationwide through regional offices.

In Jordan, where political parties were not legalized until 1992,[7] the Muslim Brotherhood had a strong advantage over other political groups. In addition to having a license to operate openly (as a social organization) after political parties were outlawed in 1957, the group also enjoyed a well-established network of regional offices. Mobilization and recruitment within the Muslim Brotherhood has been organized since the group's founding around the family or kinship cell (*usrah*).[8] Intermarriage and close personal connections ensure tight networks of supporters and members. These small, localized groups were used by the Muslim Brotherhood during the 1989 elections to generate support for its candidates and subsequently to mobilize its members around the creation of a formal political party in 1992. The group also commands a well-established network of Islamic charitable institutions and a series of mosques and schools throughout the kingdom (Dabbas 1997; Wiktorowicz 2001: 83–110; Clark 2003). While the Muslim Brotherhood did not restructure immediately following the opening of 1989, the group's use of membership networks intensified and the existing leadership structure worked to field candidates in many of the country's districts.

---

[7] Many of these research institutes, women's rights groups, environmental protection advocates, and human rights organizations have emerged largely as a result of the availability of large grants offered by foreign agencies. See Brand (1995b); on Yemen, see Carapico (1998, esp. ch. 2). As Ryan notes, a number of books analyzing the range of Jordanian political parties and their ideologies appeared in Jordan well before parties were legalized in late 1992 (1998: 394, n. 35).

[8] For a detailed discussion of these cells and other dimensions of the group's grassroots social bases, see Boulby (1999: 74–80).

The Muslim Brotherhood chose not to refashion itself into a political party, however. This decision was largely due to necessity, as the new law legalizing parties forbid parties with ties outside of Jordan. But the leadership also decided that the Muslim Brotherhood should retain its character as a charitable social organization concerned primarily with issues of education, health care, and the spread of Islamic values. Prominent Muslim Brotherhood members were nevertheless at the center of the formation of Jordan's first Islamist political party, the IAF. In September 1992, a twenty-person preparatory committee undertook initial procedures to register the IAF with the government. The law required that each new party provide a list of founding members, so the group presented 353 individuals (including 11 women) as its founding committee when the party submitted registration on October 8, 1992 (a week after the parties law was issued). The party was issued a license two months later, on December 8. The formal registration of names marked a significant shift for the Muslim Brotherhood, which has never been legally required to disclose the names of its member rosters. Indeed, Muslim Brotherhood officials state that no such rosters even exist.[9] The internal structure of the new party also included mechanisms for accountability and structures of representation and authority. The membership at large, open to individuals twenty-five years and older, directly elects the committees and the executive. The founding committee plus all subsequent new members make up the general committee,[10] which meets annually and elects a 120-person consultative council.[11] Members of the consultative council serve a four-year term, meeting every six months and exceptionally by decision from the executive bureau. The consultative council is responsible for setting party policy as well as electing the chair of the consultative council, the secretary-general of the party, and the members of the executive bureau for two-year terms (Hourani 1993a: 34–58). This organizational structure is similar to that of the Muslim Brotherhood, with two critical exceptions: the overseer-general (*al-muraqib al-'amm*) within the Muslim Brotherhood, the highest ranking office,[12] holds authority over the

---

[9] 'Abd al-Majid Thunaybat, interview with author, November 15, 1996, Amman.
[10] When the number of members of the general committee exceeds 1,000, a general assembly – consisting of the consultative council, members of administrative committees, and a portion of the general committee – takes over the general committee's functions.
[11] The Muslim Brotherhood's consultative council has thirty members.
[12] The overseer-general of the Muslim Brotherhood theoretically must be reelected but in practice he may hold the position indefinitely, whereas the secretary-general of the IAF is limited to two two-year terms (or four years).

organization's executive bureau (called the "general bureau") as well as over the consultative council. In the IAF, the party's highest office is that of secretary-general, who is elected by that assembly and does not head the consultative council. Control of the party is less concentrated as no one person may simultaneously hold the party's offices of secretary-general and chair of the consultative council (Awad 1997: 84).

The IAF established a central party headquarters not far from the Muslim Brotherhood offices and the Islamic Hospital in Amman, initially with twenty-two regional branches throughout the country, most linked closely with Muslim Brotherhood offices (and many sharing the same physical space). Although the Muslim Brotherhood and the IAF are widely considered branches of the same group, they maintain formal separation. In fact, the IAF was originally conceived to bring together a wide range of Islamists in Jordan, of which the Muslim Brotherhood would be but one (albeit principal) part. The list of founding party members reflects these efforts, though that diversity was not sustained. When the IAF's first consultative council – a one-year temporary and transitional body – was elected on December 25, 1992, many of the independent Islamists who originally joined the Muslim Brotherhood in forming the IAF protested that their representation on the council was negligible. Twenty-two original non–Muslim Brotherhood party members, including five former ministers, resigned in a letter to the party's temporary secretary-general, in large part due to Muslim Brotherhood dominance. They wrote, "The consultative council elections on December 25, 1992, proved our fears and put an end to the doubt that the Muslim Brotherhood wants the party to represent them. ... Since the [Muslim Brotherhood] did not carry out its commitment to the great goal of uniting the Islamist trends in this country, and since the actions did not meet the words [promising that the party would be inclusive], we find that this party will not be able to attract new faithful elements or even keep the present members who are not Muslim Brotherhood. ..."[13]

According to Ra'if Nijm, one of the signatories, independents had been promised that Muslim Brotherhood members would account for no more than 60 percent of the council, with the remaining going to independents (Hourani et al. 1993a: 34–58). Ishaq Farhan, IAF Secretary-General from 1992–8, insists that no such agreement existed and that the election was carried out fairly and through secret ballot. "Some people rejected the

---

[13] "Risalat ila al-akh al-amin al-a'am al-muwaqqat li Hizb al-Jabhat al-'Amal al-Islami," December 28, 1992.

process when they did not like the results. But the elections were fair and democratic, and this is how we function internally."[14] The letter, however, names Farhan as one who had lent his reassurances that the party would be inclusive. Of those who resigned, a few later rejoined the IAF, which quickly became known as the political wing of the Muslim Brotherhood.

Despite these complaints, few observers were really surprised that the first leaders of the IAF emerged from the elite ranks of the Muslim Brotherhood. Many Muslim Brotherhood and IAF leaders are closely related, often through marriage and extended families. Farhan and 'Arabiyyat, for example, are brothers-in-law married to sisters of a third family, while many of the prominent members belong to families that if not related have long-established relations. Likewise, most of the women active in the party are wives, sisters, and daughters of prominent party members (Clark and Schwedler 2003). These sorts of connections underline the central role of kinship networks in the organization of a range of social, economic, and political activities, a practice of which nonconnected Muslim Brotherhood members complain bitterly.[15] Many IAF leaders also had long-standing and close relations with members of the royal family, including King Hussein and particularly Crown Prince Hassan. As noted in Chapter 2, several Muslim Brotherhood and later IAF leaders had held government positions as high as the cabinet level. In fact, at the time of his election as IAF Secretary-General on January 8, 1993, former Minister of Education Farhan was serving as a senator of Jordan's appointed upper house of parliament. 'Arabiyyat, who had worked in several government ministries since the early 1970s, was elected as the first chair of the party's consultative council.

When the Islah party was founded in Yemen on September 13, 1990, it did not enjoy an organizational foundation as developed as that of the Muslim Brotherhood in Jordan. Although the Islamic Front, one of the main groups that emerged under the umbrella of Islah, had begun to gain cohesion as an entity in the 1980s, it lacked an institutional structure and relied instead on the resources and connections of prominent individuals within the group. The new party immediately set out to create a centralized administration, establishing its national headquarters next

---

[14] Interview with author, June 12, 1997, Amman.
[15] Interviews with student activists at Jordan University, 1996–7, and with a former reporter for the Islamist *Al-Sabil* weekly, June 14, 2002, Amman. Several university students and self-identified Islamists expressed frustration with the fact that even the more prominent student leaders were the sons, daughters, nieces, and nephews of prominent Muslim Brotherhood and IAF leaders.

to the police academy in San'a,[16] with eight separate bureaus to handle economic, political, social, educational, information, religious, judicial, and women's affairs.[17] The party established regional offices throughout Yemen, some by exploiting the existing but loose network of Muslim Brotherhood offices. It expanded the network of regional offices in just a few years from a handful to several dozen, including neighborhood sub-offices in the larger urban centers. Many of these offices were located in spaces formerly occupied by the YSP and awarded to Islah by President Salih as political "booty" following the 1994 conflict in recognition of Islah support for the regime. The move of Islah offices into former YSP spaces was imbued with tremendous symbolic meaning not lost on local communities, a marking of the defeat of socialism in Yemen by a northern-based conservative Islamism. The practical objective of this expansion was to establish a presence in communities to build support for Islah and to more easily identify areas in which the party might contribute to community development.[18]

The new party adopted a formal internal party structure based on the structure of Muslim Brotherhood organizations in other countries.[19] In addition to the eight administrative divisions of the headquarters office, the party created an executive committee and a consultative council, both of which were to be filled through elections. The founding members elected 'Abd al-Wahab al-Anisi, a moderate ideologue with tribal ties, to serve as the party's first secretary-general. Shaykh 'Abd Allah, the powerful Hashid tribal leader, became the chair of the party, an outcome that was a foregone conclusion. Like the IAF leadership, prominent leaders within Islah were close with the highest government powers. But in many ways, some of Islah's leaders were more directly integrated into the highest levels of social, economic, and political power.

For both the IAF and Islah, the next step was the organization of public events to expand their visibility and preparation for upcoming national elections. In Yemen, the Islah party began holding a series of

---

[16] The unification agreement originally provided for San'a to serve as Yemen's capital during summer months, and Aden to serve as capital during winter months. This arrangement proved logistically difficult, with the northern city dominating.

[17] The women's section was later moved outside of the central office: the party created parallel women's offices for each of the remaining seven sections. In practice, this has further marginalized input from Islah women although Islah leaders argue that it enables women to have an equal role in the party. See Clark (1997: 13–15) and Clark and Schwedler (2003).

[18] Interview with Muhammad al-Yadumi, April 6, 1995, San'a.

[19] Interview with Muhammad al-Yadumi, April 6, 1995, San'a.

meetings and conferences, some organized around current issues (e.g., proposed constitutional amendments) and others as regular gatherings of party committees. The practice of holding such gatherings had quickly spread in unified Yemen, with tribes as well as political parties organizing large conferences on a wide range of themes. From December 27–30, 1992, for example, Islah organized a "Unity and Peace Conference" in San'a under the slogan of "The Qur'an and the Sunna supercede the constitution and [secular] law" (*Al-Qur'an wa al-sunna fowk al-dustur wa al-qanun*, a theme I discuss in greater detail in Chapter 5). In Shaykh 'Abd Allah's keynote address to an audience of more than 4,000, he criticized the organizers of similar gatherings throughout Yemen, accusing them of fomenting national fragmentation by holding partisan meetings. Curiously, he did not consider Islah's own gatherings as similarly partisan.

Islah initiated a process of convening broad member gatherings at two-year intervals. The party's first general congress was held in San'a from September 20–2, 1994, during which the party elected its leadership[20] and adopted the weekly *Al-Sahwah* newspaper, a Muslim Brotherhood publication, as its official mouthpiece. In September and November 1996, Islah held its second general congress, during which the activities of the party since 1994 were reported and discussed.[21] Following the November session of that meeting, Islah issued a statement that summarized the conference's proceedings and outlined the party's views on a number of local, regional, and international issues.[22] The meeting was fully open to

[20] Shaykh 'Allah was elected chair of the party and of the fifteen-man executive council; Shaykh Yasin 'Abd al-'Aziz al-Qubati, the chair of the formally dissolved Muslim Brotherhood consultative council, was elected vice-chair; al-Zindani was chosen to lead the 100-man consultative council, the central committee of the party; 'Abd al-Wahhab al-Daylami was elected chair of the judicial council; Muhammad al-Yadumi was elected secretary-general; 'Abd al-Wahab al-Anisi moved from secretary-general to assistant secretary-general; and Faris Saqqaf was elected director of information and public relations.

[21] The official programs and documentation from both the 1994 and 1996 conferences describe each gathering as Islah's "first" general congress. For clarity, I call the 1994 meeting the first general congress and the 1996 meeting, held in two sessions, the second general congress. Subsequent meetings were held in November 1998, December 2000, December 2002, and December 2004.

[22] "Bayan li Tajammu 'al-Yamani lil-Islah," n.d., circa November 1994. Members are urged to pay their dues and to contribute to the party as generously as possible. The statement also demands that the constitution and the law be implemented fully and routinely, and that the distribution of authority between the executive, legislative, and judicial be formalized to insure order and law (*nizam wa qanun*), a phrase they share with Leftist parties, including the YSP.

the press, who were given folders with conference agendas and statements on various issues to be discussed.

The IAF held similar gatherings in Jordan, assuming in 1992 the role of organizing political activities initiated by the Muslim Brotherhood in 1989. These included political protests and rallies (e.g., the large-scale protests organized against the U.S.-led allied coalition during the Gulf War of 1990–1), general assemblies of party members (e.g., in 1993 and 1997), and public as well as member-only gatherings to debate party policies and current events. Like Islah, certain prominent leaders within IAF took every opportunity to declare the party's adherence to democratic procedures and its commitment to contributing to the country's democratic transition. Each of these parties also has prominent and often highly popular individuals who have consistently criticized the party's participation in democratic processes, its periodic cooperation with other (particularly non-Islamist) individuals and groups, and even the willingness of some party leaders to meet with foreign researchers. These more extremist voices are frequently downplayed by each party, particularly when party leaders are trying to put forth their most democratic image (for domestic as well as international audiences), but they are vital to maintaining the support bases of the group. In the IAF, figures like Muhammad Abu Faris and 'Abd al-Munim Abu Zant each command sizable followings through their passionate sermons and sharp political rhetoric. In Islah, al-Zindani plays this role most prominently. IAF Secretary-General Mansur acknowledged to me in June 2003 that the party's support base is largely disinterested in, if not opposed to, the party's commitment to democratic processes. Its constituency is more moved, he argued, by its advocacy for conservative social programs, Islamic education reforms, and criticisms of official foreign-policy positions (notably opposition to Jordan's peace treaty with Israel and the normalization of Jordanian-Israeli relations).

An additional aspect of the routine party operation is the formulation of official positions on a variety of issues. Party officials and their decision-making bodies debate specific policies and publish the outcomes; they issue numerous statements to the press in response to specific social, political, and economic developments; and they prepare electoral programs prior to each national election. Members and nonmembers alike may debate the party's political program or weigh its performance against its declared goals and principles, but in the end the party takes a single position (although with varying implications for doing so). On occasion, the articulation of official policies may even constrain the group by pressuring the leadership to act in accordance with the party's stated principles. In Yemen, by comparison, the Islah party formally issues similar statements, programs, and policy papers, but its leaders are not equally committed to honoring those positions. These debates and their consequences will be examined in detail in Chapter 5.

The media have been loci for the dissemination of party policies and the debate of public issues. Both Jordan and Yemen have a lively and relatively free press, particularly compared to other Middle Eastern and Third World countries.[23] Many of the weekly papers, in particular, are associated formally or informally with various political parties and perspectives. The Muslim Brotherhood weekly newspaper *Al-Sahwah* was made the official mouthpiece of Islah in Yemen, though the group has been associated with a number of other publications that publish irregularly, including *Al-Islah* and *Al-Balagh*. Similarly in Jordan, a number of newspapers have been closely associated in recent years with the Muslim Brotherhood and the IAF.[24] One such paper, *Al-Ribat*, was licensed in Jordan in 1991 as a foreign paper to enable its publication under martial law restrictions, though the government occasionally censored its articles. *Al-Ribat* was closed and replaced with the new weekly *Al-Sabil* when the press and publications law of 1993 allowed for the functioning of a relatively free press within the country. Although *Al-Sabil* is not formally the mouthpiece of either the Muslim Brotherhood or the IAF, it is widely understood to reflect Muslim Brotherhood policies and perspectives, with many Muslim Brotherhood and IAF leaders regularly contributing to its pages.[25] Both the IAF and Islah produce a number of regional periodicals as well, distributed (sometimes irregularly) in urban centers outside of each country's capital, including the monthlies *Al-Ummah* and *Al-Liwa*.

In addition to newspapers, magazines, press releases, and formal party platforms, both parties occasionally publish books and pamphlets on topics of economic, political, and social concern. A number of these publications appear in English as well as Arabic, underlining the extent to which both parties seek to insure the availability of first-hand information about

---

[23] Each country has a few dailies and more than a dozen weeklies, with exact numbers changing as new publications emerge and others close or temporarily suspend publication.

[24] The first newspaper of the Jordanian Muslim Brotherhood, *Al-Kifah al-Islami*, was published in Amman in 1954 and again in 1957.

[25] Many IAF and Muslim Brotherhood leaders contribute regularly to a wide range of publications, including the partially government-owned dailies *Al-Ra'i* and *Al-Dustur*.

their activities and agendas to a foreign readership. In Jordan, the IAF has a small library, although at least as of the late 1990s most party documents were housed in the more extensive Muslim Brotherhood library at that group's headquarters. In Yemen, Islah has taken an additional step of forming a research institute, the Yemeni Center for Cultural and Strategic Studies (YCCSS), inaugurated on July 28, 1996 by Prime Minister 'Abd al-'Aziz 'Abd al-Ghani. The inaugural director of the institute was then Islah member Nasr Taha Mustafa, who resigned as editor of the official weekly *Al-Wahdah* to take the position.[26] Although the YCCSS is not formally linked to Islah, Mustafa acknowledged that the institute has close relations with the party.[27] The YCCSS houses a small library open to the public in which a number of Islah documents are archived, including conference programs, official statements by Islah leaders, and Islah publications.

A final aspect of party organization includes the establishment of mechanisms to respond quickly to pressing social, economic, and political developments and to challenge specific government policies. Both parties have organized rallies, demonstrations, and local gatherings to mobilize citizens and party members around particular issues, though these practices were not new under the political openings. In Jordan, Islamists have organized peaceful rallies and demonstrations since the late 1940s.[28] In Yemen, a range of public gatherings, including tribal conferences, increased in popularity during the 1980s (Carapico 1998). However, such large-scale gatherings were restricted in Yemen, and had been outright prohibited in Jordan since the establishment of martial law in 1967. In this regard, the liberalization of the political system in 1989 in Jordan and 1990 in Yemen did facilitate the reemergence of these forms of political contestation. In Jordan, the promulgation of the National Charter in 1991 and the lifting of martial law in August 1992 formalized the right to free speech and assembly, although in practice the government has selectively limited the exercise of this right. In October 1990, the

[26] Mustafa has since resigned from the institute to accept a position as official spokesperson for the government and with Saba, the government news agency. He appears frequently in this capacity on the Qatar-based satellite station, Al-Jazeera.

[27] The YCCSS's first event was a three-day seminar held from July 29–31, 1996 at Taj Sheba hotel in San'a under the theme, "Administrative Reforms in the Republic of Yemen," the proceedings of which were published in book form by the institute. The YCCSS also publishes a journal, *Shu'un al-'Asr*, which was launched in 1997.

[28] For example, the Muslim Brotherhood organized several antiwestern rallies and pro-Palestinian demonstrations in the 1940s and 1950s.

Muslim Brotherhood organized a rally to protest U.S. intervention in the region and the massive U.S. arms buildup in preparation for an attack on Iraq. Approximately 100,000 Jordanians attended the rally, which was tolerated if not supported by the government. In Yemen, at least 25,000 citizens attended an Islah-sponsored rally prior to the 1993 parliamentary elections, with thousands more attending similar gatherings sponsored by President Salih's GPC and the South's YSP (Carapico 1998).

A final note about the relationship between the Jordanian Muslim Brotherhood and the IAF illustrates some additional effects of having internal decision-making mechanisms separate to each group. As noted, the IAF is routinely characterized as the political arm of the Muslim Brotherhood, and in many ways this characterization is accurate. But the two organizations have increasingly come to function independently and do not see eye to eye on all issues. In June 1997, for example, the Muslim Brotherhood took a decision to boycott the upcoming parliamentary elections. The decision underlined the continued role of the Muslim Brotherhood in Jordanian politics, particularly since the group is legally a charitable society rather than a political party. The IAF was expected to honor the decision, but when it did not quickly do so, tensions between the two groups ensued. A preliminary but unofficial list of IAF candidates was published in the press, suggesting that the IAF was moving ahead with electoral preparations. Several weekly papers reported that Secretary-General Farhan resigned in protest, though he immediately denied that claim.[29] In the following days, the two sides reconciled and together denied that the conflicts ever happened. Farhan explained that the IAF did not immediately follow the Muslim Brotherhood decision because the question of the boycott had to be put before its own consultative council, as neither he nor any other member of the executive committee could take that decision without deliberation. Likely the hesitance was also due to disagreement among both organizations' leadership about the best course of action. When a vote of the IAF consultative council was taken, the party joined the Muslim Brotherhood decision to boycott. Farhan honored that outcome, even though he personally felt it was the wrong move.[30]

After just a few years in existence, the IAF and the Muslim Brotherhood can no longer be assumed to automatically adopt the same position on issues. A compelling indicator of this growing division is that in July 1998,

[29] Interview with author, June 22, 1997, Amman.
[30] Interview with author, June 19, 1997, Amman.

IAF leaders Farhan and 'Arabiyyat both failed in their reelection bid for seats on the Muslim Brotherhood consultative council.[31] Their defeat was part of a broader defeat of what party members call their "doves" (hama'im, as opposed to the "hawks," suqur) with a centrist coalition bringing to power a new generation of Muslim Brotherhood members. That the two most powerful IAF leaders lost their seats on the Muslim Brotherhood's 120-person consultative council underlines the extent to which the institutional division of two groups may be extending to other areas.

These internal processes for reaching decisions on particularly contentious issues are a significant point of variation between the IAF and Islah. Both parties have similar internal decision-making processes, but whereas IAF leaders almost uniformly adhere to those practices and honor outcomes they might have opposed, Islah leaders frequently do not. Structurally, the Islah party is not cohesive and its power is not centralized in the formal party bureaus. In particular, Shaykh 'Abd Allah and al-Zindani appear to align themselves closely with the party when it suits their purposes, but take positions that fundamentally contradict formal party positions almost casually and with frequency. As examined in Chapter 5, the potential for ideological moderation in these cases hinges in part on the manner in which party leaders reach decisions on contentious issues and the extent to which those positions are honored.

Electoral, Parliamentary, and Cabinet Participation

As noted, the groups that formed the IAF and Islah had been active on the political scene for years, with an intensification of activity beginning in the 1970s in Jordan and the 1980s in Yemen. These included roles as cabinet ministers and seats in other appointed government bodies, influential positions of employment within various ministries, and popularly elected members of the lower house. In Jordan, this also included Muslim Brotherhood members appointed by the king to the senate. The Muslim Brotherhood began contesting parliamentary elections soon after King Hussein assumed the throne in 1953. In the 1954 parliamentary elections, for example, Muslim Brotherhood members won 10 percent of the

---

[31] From 1992–8, Farhan served as the secretary-general of the IAF and 'Arabiyyat as the chair of the consultative council; the 1998 party elections saw them switch those positions, effectively keeping leadership in the hands of these brothers-in-law until 2002, when Hamzeh Mansur became secretary-general and 'Arabiyyat reclaimed the position as chair of the consultative council.

seats (4 of 40).[32] When Hussein recalled the long-suspended parliament in 1984, he scheduled bielections to replace eight deputies who had died or resigned since the last poll was held, in 1967.[33] Though only a few seats were at stake, the bielections were seen as a gauge to the political climate. Women had the opportunity to vote for the first time since suffrage was extended to them in 1974, as did the many Jordanians who had come of age during the intervening seventeen years. Of the eight seats open to contest, two were quota seats for Christian candidates. When the results were in, Islamists took three of the six remaining seats: Muslim Brother Ahmad al-Kufahi won more than 30 percent of the vote in the northern city of Irbid; Muslim Brother 'Abd Allah 'Akaylah won in Tafilah; and independent Islamist Layth Shubaylat was a surprise success against thirty-five other candidates in the upscale neighborhood of Amman's third electoral district (Robins 1991: 191). Clearly, Islamists had gained considerable support outside of the Palestinian refugee camps, which many observers had suggested were the group's only significant base of support, developed with the exile of the Leftist Palestinian guerrilla groups after the Black September events in 1970. This support base seemed to make the regime nervous, and Muslim Brotherhood members were frequently harassed and closely monitored by the GID. 'Akaylah was even forced to resign his position as deputy when, in 1988, he was outspoken in his criticism of the intelligence agency's campaign against the Muslim Brotherhood (Boulby 1999: 101). These hostilities abated by the spring of 1989 when the deteriorating economic situation brought increased dissent and the regime reconsidered its campaign of alienating a key ally.

With the political opening of 1989 and the elections on November 8 of that year, Muslim Brotherhood members did extremely well, winning twenty-two of eighty seats, a share of 27.5 percent. Only four of the group's candidates were unsuccessful. Together with the twelve independent Islamists who won seats, the Islamist bloc controlled 40 percent of the house with its combined thirty-four seats.[34] Leftists, liberals,

---

[32] Khalifah and al-'Azm were two; the names of the other two Muslim Brotherhood deputies have been lost. See Boulby (1999: 62).

[33] The 1967 parliament was suspended following the 1967 war with Israel and dissolved in 1974. However, it was this group of representatives that the king recalled in 1984. See Table 2.1 in Chapter 2.

[34] Boulby places the numbers at twenty Muslim Brotherhood seats and fourteen independent (1999: 103). The discrepancy concerns whether two members connected to Muslim Brotherhood circles were Muslim Brotherhood candidates or independent Islamists; after the elections, the two identified with the group. But because parties were illegal, whether a candidate belonged to one group or another is open to interpretation.

reformers, and nationalists held thirteen seats. They formed the Democratic Bloc in an attempt to counterbalance the Islamists' strength. Although together these opposition parties held a combined 60 percent of the assembly, they did not cooperate or coordinate, even on issues of common concern (e.g., opposing the U.S.-led allied invasion of Iraq). In fact, the Muslim Brotherhood had been successful in part because it was able to utilize its regional and local networks to organize rallies and support for its own candidates and was uninterested in any sort of cooperation. Islamist candidates who were readily identifiable not only by reputation but also because they collectively campaigned under the slogan, "Islam is the solution" (*Islam huwa al-hall*).

Nevertheless, the king was able to limit the influence of the Islamist bloc in government in several ways. First, he appointed only Farhan from the Muslim Brotherhood ranks to the forty-person upper house of parliament. The remaining members were, on the whole, Transjordanians loyal to the regime (Abu Jaber 1990: 62–83). As for cabinet positions, Muslim Brotherhood leaders were frustrated that the only portfolio they were offered in Prime Minister Mudar Badran's first cabinet was the Ministry of Higher Education, which has no say in shaping the national curriculum – an area of central interest to the group. Muslim Brotherhood leaders lobbied for the Ministry of Education and the Ministry of Religious Affairs and Endowments, the latter of which is responsible for appointing *imams* (who give sermons and lead prayers) to every mosque in the country. In the early 1970s, Farhan had controlled these two powerful portfolios. In the end, the Muslim Brotherhood refused to accept only the cabinet position for the Ministry of Higher Education as the sole offering, though the party did give a vote of confidence to the government (Milton-Edwards 1991). Despite its sizable bloc in the lower house, the Muslim Brotherhood–led Islamists in parliament had virtually no influence in the upper house and cabinet.

In November 1990, as the Gulf War approached, 'Arabiyyat was elected speaker of the lower house of parliament. The Muslim Brotherhood initially criticized Iraq for the invasion, but eventually lent its support to Iraq and Saddam Hussein as the U.S.-led allied coalition positioned for invasion. Some party members even visited Baghdad during the massive troop buildup of Operation Desert Shield. With the Muslim Brotherhood enjoying considerable popularity at a time when the United States and key Arab allies cut their foreign aid to the kindom, King Hussein decided to bring the group into the cabinet, a move that would expose the Muslim Brotherhood to public scrutiny and potentially deflate its popular support.

On December 31, 1990, the Muslim Brotherhood was given five portfolios in a cabinet reshuffle: Social Development, Religious Affairs and Endowments, Health, Justice, and Education.[35] The media dissected the Muslim Brotherhood ministers' every move. Widespread public outcry followed the proposal of a total ban on alcohol in the kingdom and the implementation of sex segregation in some government offices and a ban against fathers watching young women (and hence their daughters as well as strangers) compete in athletic competitions. In the press, a range of voices opposed to the Islamists' role in government were quick to criticize the ministers, describing them as ineffective and no different from other corrupt politicians. Many Jordanian observers argue that this inclusion of Islamists at a high level of government was intended to deflate that popularity by placing them in a position in which they would be subject to public scrutiny and criticism. That criticism did emerge and in the end few of the measures introduced by the five ministers actually endured.[36] The second Badran government, along with its five Islamist ministers, was dismissed after six months, in June 1991.

In the wake of the Gulf War of 1990–1, the United States, Saudi Arabia, and Kuwait punished Jordan for its stand against the U.S.-led allied coalition by cutting all their aid to Jordan. Coupled with the return to Jordan of some half-million migrant laborers who were forced to leave Kuwait and Saudi Arabia, the Jordanian economy again came under considerable strain. King Hussein set out to repair relations with the United States and other nations that had been damaged as a result of Jordan's opposition to the Gulf War. The new Prime Minister, Tahir al-Masri, supported working toward a peace settlement with Israel. The choice to follow Badran with al-Masri sent a strong message to the Muslim Brotherhood about its place in government, particularly in light of the group's stance against Israel. Informal contacts between al-Masri and Muslim Brotherhood leaders suggested that the Islamists might be offered a few minor cabinet portfolios, but al-Masri knew that the positions were of such low stature that the group would not accept.[37] The group countered by organizing a failed effort to bring a vote of no confidence against al-Masri's government.

---

[35] Yusef al-'Azm was named Minister of Social Development; Ibrahim Zayd al-Kilani, Minister of Religious Affairs and Endowments; Adnan al-Jaljuli, Minister of Health; Majid al-Khalifah, Minister of Justice; and 'Abd Allah 'Akaylah, Minister of Education.

[36] The effort to ban the serving of alcohol on Royal Jordanian flights was partly successful: the airline no longer serves alcoholic beverages on flights between Muslim countries.

[37] Interview with author, March 13, 1997, Amman.

However, al-Masri did resign less than six months later, when another, potentially successful no-confidence vote was pending.

The regime took other measures to constrain the Islamist bloc in parliament and the Muslim Brotherhood in general. In June 1991, for example, the Ministry of the Interior banned the organization of group prayers in open fields and in March 1992 refused to allow the Muslim Brotherhood to organize a large gathering to celebrate Islamic poetry. Neither group prayers nor the poetry festival were expressly political events, but the government was searching for ways to limit the power and support base of the Muslim Brotherhood without apparently targeting the group. Brotherhood leaders protested that similar large gatherings organized by other groups were routinely approved, and in June 1992 they launched an unsuccessful attempt to have the Minister of the Interior removed from his office.[38] According to another minister at that time, the government was self-consciously striving to restrict the Muslim Brotherhood's ability to mobilize supporters.[39]

The National Charter introduced an executive veto as well as an upper-house veto over decisions passed by the elected lower house, which ensured that the lower house would remain effectively powerless.[40] Previously, the parliament had the ability to override even a royal veto by two-thirds vote. The government intelligence agency also closely monitored Muslim Brotherhood leaders and deputies, and the king sought to further reduce the Muslim Brotherhood's strength through additional legal reforms. With the establishment of the political parties law of 1992, political parties were prohibited from engaging in political activities in mosques, schools, and religious institutions, with extremely loose criteria for what constitutes a "political activity." As one minister during that period noted, "It was clear from the beginning that the measure was intended to check the political strength of the Islamists. We are an Islamic country, but it is unfair to the other parties that the Islamists should be able to use [their power] in the mosques to increase their political strength."[41] Farhan argued that although he and his colleagues felt that they had been unfairly targeted by the government, they chose to not challenge the new law to demonstrate their commitment to pressing for reform only through

---

[38] Document of the legal case filed with the High Court of Justice, June 13, 1992.
[39] Interview with author, July 1995, Amman, name withheld by request.
[40] As Boulby notes, "many of the legal provisions limiting the power of parliament were inherited from the constitution of 1928, although some reforms were introduced in this regard in 1952. The constitution was designed by the British to produce a powerless legislature" (1999: 139).
[41] Interview with author, June 1995, Amman, name withheld by request.

democratic channels.[42] In fact, Muslim Brotherhood deputies sought to improve their relations with the regime by voting in January 1993 to support the government's budget – which was structured by its agreement with the IMF – despite strong opposition within the movement concerning the IMF's condoning of usury and strong western ties. As the next round of elections approached, the government sought ways to reduce the strength of the Islamist bloc in the next lower house, temporarily amending the 1988 elections law on August 13, 1993. The regime introduced the "one vote" system, discussed in Chapter 2, just months before Jordan's first multiparty contest. With the revisions, voters could select only one candidate in their multiseat constituencies, regardless of the number of seats being contested. In what would emerge as a pattern, the king dismissed parliament in early August, freeing the executive to alter the existing law without submitting the amendments to parliament for debate.

The executive bureau of the IAF carefully considered how to respond. The possibility of a boycott gained considerable support in view of further government efforts to block IAF campaign efforts. As the elections approached, the party found that the Ministry of Interior, which issues licenses for large gatherings such as campaign rallies, was not processing IAF requests. Muslim Brotherhood Overseer-General (*al-muraqib al-'amm*) 'Abd al-Majid Thunaybat, a lawyer by profession, pressed a case against the Ministry of Interior, arguing that the office was intentionally failing to process IAF requests to organize campaign activities as a means of weakening Islamist candidates in the coming elections.[43] Just a few weeks before the November polling, a high court found in favor of the IAF and ordered the ministry to process IAF requests promptly,[44] which it subsequently did. In the end, the IAF did not boycott the elections. On November 8, 1993, polling for Jordan's first multiparty elections returned seventeen seats for the IAF, and few dispute that the loss of seats is directly attributable to the amendments to the electoral law (Charillon and Mouftard 1994).[45] In the senate, the IAF retained its one seat, with 'Arabiyyat appointed in place of Farhan. The IAF was not offered any portfolios following the elections, and the IAF deputies withheld their

---

[42] Interview with author, June 19, 1997, Amman.
[43] Interview with author, May 8, 1997, Amman.
[44] "Al-Qarar, #20," Mahkamah al-'Adl al-'Alia al-Urdunniyyah, Wazirat al-'Adl, October 20, 1993.
[45] The IAF won sixteen seats, with Muslim Brotherhood member Dib 'Abd Allah giving the bloc a seventeenth seat. 'Abd Allah and Ahmad Kasasbah resigned from the IAF in January 1996, reducing its bloc to fifteen seats.

vote of confidence for the new government of 'Abd al-Salam al-Majali.[46] Less than a year later, al-Majali's cabinet pushed forward the Israel-Jordan peace treaty, which was signed in October 1994. Since then, the IAF has consistently refused to accept cabinet positions, arguing that to do so would be equivalent to supporting the peace treaty and thus recognizing Israel.

Public debate about the electoral law continued, and the IAF presented to the government several possible alternatives, none of which were adopted.[47] The biggest demand was that the amendments should be subject to public debate and parliamentary review, particularly because they had been introduced when parliament was not in session (having been rather conveniently dismissed by royal decree). The IAF and all of the opposition parties objected not only to the one-person one-vote system, but also to the lopsided distribution of seats among the districts. As noted in Chapter 2, the uneven population-to-seat ratio across districts prevents the lower house from being dominated by Palestinians, who reside predominantly in the greater Amman region and who most scholars believe comprise more than 50 percent of the citizenry. Government officials stated that although they welcomed input from the parties concerning the formation of a new electoral law, there would be no changes to either the districting or the general distribution of seats.

Thus by the mid-1990s, Jordan's political opening had by conventional counts stalled. In March 1997, parliament was again dismissed months before completing its full term, with the cabinet of 'Abd al-Karim al-Kabariti (who had replaced al-Majali in January 1996) replaced by a second al-Majali government. That May, in a reminder of the manner in which the electoral law had been amended nearly four years earlier, the government promulgated amendments to the press and publication law, a move that led to the almost immediate closing of one weekly newspaper and the suspension of thirteen others three months later, just as the campaign period for the November parliamentary elections was getting underway. The amendments were widely criticized, and in July the IAF declared that in light of the content of the electoral law and press amendments, and particularly considering the undemocratic manner in which they were promulgated, the group would boycott the elections.

---

[46] Dib 'Abd Allah, a Muslim Brotherhood deputy but at that time not a member of the IAF, was not present for the vote.

[47] "Proposal to Prime Minister 'Abd al-Salam al-Majali: Alternatives to the Electoral Law," IAF document, June 19, 1997.

Significantly, the boycott argued that this series of extraparliamentary procedures were unconstitutional.[48] The IAF did, however, participate in the next round of elections, which were originally scheduled for November 2001 but were delayed for a variety of reasons including the outbreak of the second Palestinian *intifada* in fall 2000, uncertainty about the repercussions of the September 11, 2001 attacks, and concern about whether the first elections under King 'Abd Allah II would return a sufficiently proregime assembly. When the elections were finally held in June 2003, the IAF participated and won seventeen seats. As detailed in the following text, the changing dynamics of the political scene and particularly the relations between the regime and the IAF led to the emergence of cooperative practices among opposition groups that were unprecedented in Jordan.

Like the IAF in Jordan, the Islah party has been active in Yemen's political scene through its direct participation in state institutions, such as the presidential council, the cabinet, parliament, and the consultative council.[49] Because many Islah leaders emerged from within the ranks of the GPC in preunification North Yemen, the new Islamist party held a number of seats of the newly unified parliament (combining the assemblies of the North and South for a total of 301 seats) from the time of unification until the first postunification elections were held on April 27, 1993. In that contest, Islah won 62 seats of 301, less than the GPC's 122, but more than the YSP's 57. Shaykh 'Abd Allah was elected by the new assembly to the position of speaker of the assembly with 223 votes. The GPC, the YSP, and Islah formed a coalition government, with the YSP and Islah as junior partners. When YSP Prime Minister Haydar Abu Bakr al-'Attas announced his new government, Islah was given six portfolios: Legal Affairs; Local Governance; Health, Religious Affairs and Endowments; Supply and Trade; and Deputy Prime Minister. [50] The

---

[48] The press and publication amendments were indeed found to be unconstitutional by the country's high court on January 26, 1998. According to the constitution, the government cannot enact temporary laws by executive degree except in situations involving national security (in which case there would be a state of emergency in effect). Judge Faruq al-Kilani wrote a majority opinion arguing that because such conditions were not present, the law was unconstitutional. He was removed from his post three weeks later. In June 1998 a new draft press law was submitted to both houses of parliament for debate, causing outrage among representatives, who called the draft even more restrictive than the May 1997 temporary law. See Kilani (2002).

[49] The Consultative Council was established only in May 1997. It is not part of parliament, but a separate advisory body whose members are appointed by the president.

[50] 'Abd al-Salam Karman was named Minister of Legal Affairs; 'Abd al-Wahab al-Anisi, Deputy Prime Minister; Muhammad al-Dammaj, Minister of Local Governance; Najib al-Ghanim, Minister of Health; Ghalib 'Abd al-Kafi al-Qurashi, Minister of Religious

ministries opened direct formal channels for Islah to influence public policy, although the new Islah ministers – like the YSP ministers – soon
learned that the government bureaucracies were so overstaffed due to
patronage that efforts to implement change were difficult at best. In October 1993, Islah also gained a seat on the five-person presidential council
in the appointment of al-Zindani.

Following the 1994 civil war and decline of the YSP on the political
scene,[51] the new cabinet of GPC-member 'Abd al-'Aziz 'Abd al-Ghani gave
nine posts to Islah members.[52] Al-Anisi was promoted to First Deputy
Prime Minister, Islah's highest executive position in the government.
With Islah's expanded role in the cabinet, newspapers and public opinion
focused on the implications of the party's rise to power – particularly the
extent to which it would implement a highly conservative Islamist agenda.
As with the IAF in Jordan, Islah sparked concern particularly among more
progressive- and secular-minded Yemenis. For its part, Islah leaders did
not fail to notice that they had been given primarily service ministries,
including Health, Supply and Trade, Electricity and Water, and Education.
Party leaders and media outlets alike speculated that Islah had been set
up to fail. Indeed, for both Jordan and Yemen reform in the service indus-
tries would prove both exceptionally difficult and economically painful,
and thus unpopular with the citizenry. In a sense, these practices suggest precisely how a "political opening" may in effect represent a closing

Affairs and Endowments; and 'Abd al-Rahman BaFadl, Minister of Supply and Trade.
Islah complained when it was initially offered only four portfolios compared to the YSP's
eight, despite Islah's greater electoral victory. Two additional portfolios brought Islah's
total to six, including one that went to al-Anisi (Carapico 1993a: 39). In a statement to
the proregime *Al-Wahdah* newspaper, Karman said that he was not a member of Islah.
Islah Secretary-General al-Yadumi refuted this in a statement to *26 September* newspaper,
(called *Sitta Ashrin Uliyu* in Arabic) September 13, 1993, saying that Karman had not
expressed himself well.

[51] The influence of the YSP declined significantly from 1994, particularly with the exile of
many of the party's leaders. But the YSP never disappeared, and it fielded candidates in
the 2003 parliamentary elections. The party faired poorly at the polls, but there were
signs (discussed in subsequent chapters) that the YSP might regain some of its political
strength, particularly as deputy director Jar Allah 'Umar led a move to improve relations
with moderate Islah leaders.

[52] New Islah appointments included Muhammad al-Jubari, Minister of Supply and Trade;
'Abd al-Wahhab al-Daylami, Minister of Justice; Abdu 'Ali al-Qubati, Minister of Education; and 'Abd Allah al-Akwa, Minister of Electricity and Water. Al-Ghanim, al-Dammaj,
and al-Qurashi retained their portfolios of Health, Local Governance, and Religious
Affairs and Endowments, respectively. BaFadl was later given the portfolio for the
newly revived Ministry of Fisheries, charged with reforming and reviving Yemen's fishing
sector.

of political space as the regime channels participatory practices into highly constrained spheres.

Meanwhile, a number of disputes arose between Islah and GPC ministers. One widely debated issue concerned the level of corruption within the ministries and the extent to which reform was virtually impossible without a fundamental overhaul of the staff.[53] The GPC and Islah accused each other of trying to staff the ministries with their own party members. One Islah minister reported that members of his own party came to him for employment and complained to the central Islah office when their requests were not accommodated.[54] Another dispute, over budgetary issues, emerged when several Islah ministers argued about the exchange rate at which currency was transferred among ministries before the rial was floated in 1996.[55] And several Islah ministers complained that their every move was branded as "Islamist" not only in the media but by GPC leaders in an attempt to mobilize partisan opposition to their attempts to reduce corruption or introduce much-needed reforms. Islah Secretary-General al-Yadumi further complained that President Salih tended not to send Islah ministers abroad and never appointed them as ambassadors because Yemen was striving to improve relations with a number of western and secular nations and Islamist ambassadors might not be well received.[56] More than ten years after unification, no Islah member has served as ambassador.[57]

Islah ministers quickly realized that they would not be able to affect much change. Beginning in 1995, several of them resigned their posts: Muhammad al-Jubari resigned as Minister of Supply and Trade, but was

---

[53] Within Yemen's government bureaucracy, corruption is facilitated not only by ministers wishing to gain their share, but by the vast number of positions that, though unnecessary, cannot be eliminated for patronage reasons. Ministers from all political trends complain of the inability to fire employees, despite the fact that many never show up to work and of those who do, many are not needed. On one visit to the Ministry of Health, for example, I was told that the minister's secretary alone had seven assistants: one to sort incoming mail, one to handle outgoing mail, one to screen appointments, two to fetch coffee and tea, one for general errands, and one to inform the minister's driver when the minister is on his way.

[54] Interview with 'Abd Allah al-Akwa, September 14, 1997.

[55] At the time, the exchange rate was eleven rials to the U.S. dollar, while the black market yielded around ten times that rate. BaFadl reported that as Minister of Supply and Trade in 1993, he was pressured to accept highly unfavorable rates and was not free to explore alternate means of exchange, such as purchasing currency on the open market. Interviews with author, October 9–10, 1997, San'a. Other Islah and GPC ministers have recounted similar stories, noting the head of the central bank is a political appointment.

[56] Interview with author, October 13, 1997, San'a.

[57] As of this writing in spring 2005.

replaced by Islah member Muhammad al-Afandi. In December 1995, however, al-Afandi also resigned, as did 'Abd Allah al-Akwa, Minister of Water and Electricity. Both complained that they were unable to do their jobs and were prevented from taking steps to reduce corruption within their ministries. Each was replaced by GPC a member.[58] Al-Akwa felt he had been personally targeted, evidenced by a series of cartoons lampooning him that appeared in a GCP-affiliated newspaper over the course of several weeks that summer.[59] 'Abdu 'Ali al-Qubati resigned as Minister of Education in October 1996, replaced by Islah member 'Abd al-Majid al-Mikhlafi.[60]

One of the most interesting aspects of Islah's role within the ministries concerns its choice of members to accept the cabinet posts. With the exception of 'Abd al-Wahhab al-Daylami, who served as Minister of Justice after the 1994 civil war until 1997, all of the Islah ministers were relative moderates compared to al-Zindani. Most had long-standing, but sometimes informal, ties with the Muslim Brotherhood since the 1970s. About half were educated in western institutions and spoke English, French, or both. 'Abd al-Rahman BaFadl, for example, was educated in Paris and speaks French at home with his family. As he tells it, he was living in Jeddah as a businessman in 1993 when an Islah official called to tell him that he would be announced as Minister of Supply and Trade the next morning. He returned to Yemen to take up the position.[61] Al-Akwa states that he was not close to the Muslim Brotherhood until his campaign for a parliamentary seat in 1988 in preunification North Yemen (when political parties were illegal). The Muslim Brotherhood supported his candidacy, he recalls, because he called for social reforms similar to those advocated by Muslim Brotherhood leaders. Following unification, he formally joined the Islah party.[62] The Islah party's selection of moderates to fill

---

[58] Various interviews with author, 1997.

[59] Interview with author, October 5, 1997, San'a.

[60] BaFadl resigned from his post on January 27, 1997, but for a different reason. Ministers who wish to stand in the elections must resign three months prior to the polling. BaFadl was successful in the May 1997 elections and took up the position of heading the Islah bloc in parliament.

[61] Interview with author, October 9, 1997, San'a.

[62] Interview with author, October 5, 1997, San'a. Akwa's case is particularly interesting in that he has, on occasion, publicly opposed Islah positions. For example, he voted against accepting the new constitution, a move that was popularly seen as a vote against unification. Islah leaders did not share his view that it was the act of voting, and not the content of his vote, that substantively supported democratic participation and, thus, support of unified Yemen's new democratic orientation.

ministerial positions is meaningful in that it suggests the leadership's realization that to maximize the party's influence, it needed to present ministers that would receive both wide government support as well as popular acceptance.[63] Within the party, some leaders see these moves as motivated by President Salih and the GPC to divide Islah leaders among themselves, or at least prevent them from forming a more cohesive and thus powerful party. By 1996, Islah had witnessed a considerable decrease in its power as a party. President Salih was appointing fewer and fewer Islah members to cabinet positions even as Islah ministers continued to resign. At the same time, certain prominent Islah leaders remained close to the president, notably Shaykh 'Abd Allah. Several Islah leaders and former ministers expressed that their biggest mistake was to try to implement reforms too quickly, particularly in challenging corruption.[64]

As the April 1997 elections approached, an agreement between the GPC and Islah concerning who would campaign for particular seats fell apart. The GPC no longer needed Islah's support to win a majority of the 301 seats, with the logic of bringing Islah into a coalition government proving more tactical than strategic.[65] While Islah did retain fifty-three seats, the GPC increased its share to 187, giving it majority control of the assembly. Islah candidates from the party's ideological trend faired particularly poorly as compared to the party's more tribally connected candidates.[66] With its dramatic victory in the 1997 elections, the GPC had no need to form a coalition government, and no Islah members were offered cabinet portfolios under the leadership of Prime Minister Faraj ibn Sa'id ibn Ghanim. Shaykh 'Abd Allah was reelected speaker of the lower house, an outcome that clearly has less to do with his leadership of Islah than with his position as a prominent tribal leader and his close personal relationship with the president. President Salih did finally follow

---

[63] Although in theory the prime minister makes all ministry appointments, in practice they are selected by Salih.

[64] This view was repeatedly expressed to the author from July through November 1997 during interviews conducted in San'a with al-Yadumi, al-Anisi, al-Afandi, al-Akwa, BaFadl, Muhammad al-Qahtan (head of Islah's political bureau), Zayd al-Shami (head of Islah's education section), and others.

[65] Interview with a GPC minister and a GPC party official, August and November 1997, names withheld by request.

[66] Prominent ideologues within Islah who were unsuccessful in the elections included Muhammad 'Ali Ajlan, Mansur al-Zindani (brother of 'Abd al-Majid al-Zindani), former minister Muhammad al-Afandi, 'Abd Allah al-Maqalih, and Muhammad al-Sadiq 'Abd Allah. Most of these are closely associated with the relatively moderate Muslim Brotherhood trend in the party (as compared to al-Zindani and other Salafi trends). Every predominantly tribal candidate fielded by Islah was successful.

through on his promise to create an appointed consultative council in May 1997, though this body is not an upper house of parliament and serves only in an advisory capacity. Islah members were given about ten seats, including three to former cabinet members.[67] One GPC minister in the Ghanim cabinet described this move as a concession to Islah, a means of keeping the party from joining an opposition bloc with other weak political parties following its own striking electoral losses, a move that Islah party leaders had informally threatened.[68]

The experiences of the IAF and Islah in these formal channels of political participation led to shifting political opportunities from the initial period of political opening to those that emerged by the mid-1990s. In Jordan, regime efforts to limit the power and appeal of the Islamists was due in large part to the monarchy's desire to rebuild relations with Washington and forge a peace treaty with Israel. In Yemen, the relationship between the regime and the Islah party deteriorated rapidly following the demise of the YSP on the political scene. In both cases, the role of the Islamists in formal government processes was in large part structured by other factors relating to broader regime interests.

Alliances and Cooperative Agreements

One of the most interesting developments under a multiparty system is the formation of coalitions among seemingly unlikely partners and across ideological lines. As argued in Chapters 1 and 2, the notion that institutional constraints structure behavior is one of the key propositions of the inclusion-moderation hypothesis. According to this logic, groups will begin to cooperate with even former enemies when the incentives are strong enough. The IAF and the Islah party have both explored such agreements, sometimes even with groups that have been long-time adversaries. But only with the IAF has cooperation become normalized through practice over time. Islah, by comparison, has flirted with such cooperation, but instead prioritized maintaining relations with the regime. In this section I explore the experiences of the IAF and Islah in two types of cooperative political action: the participation of actors from diverse political backgrounds and ideological perspectives in formal state processes, and cooperative activities among groups within the larger field of political contestation (i.e., activities that extend beyond the party infrastructure

---

[67] They were al-Anisi, al-Dammaj, and al-Afandi.
[68] Interview with author, September 1997, San'a, name withheld by request.

and parliament) to directly challenge the dominant power in a given situation.

As detailed in the preceding text, the Muslim Brotherhood and the IAF have worked directly and cooperatively with other political actors in Jordan in a range of institutions, including in the upper and lower houses of parliament, the Badran cabinet, and numerous government committees. One example not yet mentioned is the National Charter Commission that met in 1991. The National Charter is the primary document of reference in terms of political freedoms and rights, and its creation marked a significant political break with the previous twenty years of martial law rule. King Hussein issued personal invitations to political actors with diverse orientations to insure through the pluralist body that all political trends would be invested in the process. Prominent Muslim Brotherhood members Farhan, 'Akaylah, and Yusef al-'Azm were all invited to join the commission alongside Leftists, liberals, nationalists, and more traditional elites, notably leaders of powerful tribal units.

Cooperative agreements of other sorts have enabled the Muslim Brotherhood and IAF to position themselves politically. The Muslim Brotherhood constructed coalitions with certain conservative local elites in the 1989 parliamentary elections because each voter in that contest could cast as many votes as were seats in her district. Because political parties were at that time illegal, the aim was to tap into various allegiance networks to gain support beyond those of the group. The strategy linked the Muslim Brotherhood and other conservative elites: Muslim Brotherhood members would vote for certain non-Islamist candidates, and the supporters of prominent locals would cast their remaining votes for Muslim Brotherhood candidates. IAF deputies also forged an alliance among opposition parties leading up to the 1993 elections, particularly as the reforms in the elections law seriously disadvantaged all political parties. Although the Islamist deputies had shunned cooperation with other parties in the 1989 assembly, the new law hurt the prospects of electoral success for all the parties. Farhan joined several leaders from smaller parties in a press conference condemning the new law, marking one of the first instances of highly public cooperation with formal rivals around an issue of common concern. Following the 1993 elections and as the regime moved toward a peace treaty with Israel, the IAF joined several other parties in coordinating an opposition block in parliament to offset the majority bloc of regime loyalists. This opposition bloc began to meet monthly at the IAF headquarters in Amman, a site selected primarily because it has a large a conference room. Within the lower house, the opposition bloc has learned that coordination and vote pooling are effective strategies under a system in which decisions are taken by majority vote. The parties span the ideological spectrum, from various communist and socialist parties, to liberal and national parties, to the socially conservative IAF. Jordan's opposition bloc has evolved over the years, but Islamist and Leftist parties have consistently joined its ranks since 1993. The groups that enter into such coalitions need not agree on all issues or share a common ideology, but they must recognize that strategic bargaining and cooperative agreements are among the most efficient and effective means of political contestation. The opposition bloc was eventually formalized among thirteen parties as the Higher Committee for the Coordination of National Opposition Parties.

In 2000, particularly with the outbreak of the second *intifada* and the looming delay of the polls scheduled for November 2001, the Higher Committee formed a leadership committee among the six major parties, with a rotating chair who sets the agenda and leads the meetings (Clark 2005a: 10). With frequent protest activities by the opposition to the delayed elections and numerous temporary laws, the new leadership committee undertook coordination of a wide range of opposition activities. The level of cooperation, unheard of in 1989 but increasing since 1993, has been remarkable (11).

Jordan has also witnessed a number of cooperative efforts outside the realm of electoral competition and parliamentary blocs. When particular issues arise around which a range of political organizations share a common view, such as opposition to Jordan's peace treaty with Israel, coordinating efforts can mean the difference between being heard and being ignored. On January 8, 1997, for example, a large rally was organized outside of an Israeli trade fair in Marj al-Hammam, west of Amman. Many different civil society groups and political parties were opposed to the normalization of economic relations with Israel, some because they felt that the much-touted "economic benefits of peace" had not materialized and others because they rejected Israel's right to exist at all. The idea for a protest to the Israeli trade fair was the topic of a lively debate on an Internet discussion group organized by NETS, a local Internet service provider. Those discussions led to the formation of a temporary group, the Committee to Protest the Israeli Trade Fair in Marj al-Hammam, led by former Prime Minister Obaydat and his son Tamir, a Harvard-educated lawyer. A wide range of groups within various publics were mobilized for the event, which was organized as a rally to promote the Jordanian economy and national pride rather than as an anti-Israeli forum. The Muslim

Brotherhood, the IAF, prominent personalities, former government officials, and every political party were represented at the demonstration,
which lasted three days. Speakers alternately took the microphone to
criticize Israeli roads into the Jordanian economy, particularly given that
Jordan has not seen the promised economic gains from the 1994 treaty.
Citizens who could not attend the rally were encouraged to post Jordanian
flags in the windows of their cars, apartments, and places of business. In
the end, the event was perhaps the widest mobilization of Jordanians since
the 1989 bread riots that sparked the liberalization process (Schwedler
2005). Perhaps more remarkably, the police did not respond with violence.[69]

Later in 1997, a number of political parties from the opposition bloc
including the IAF joined prominent independent politicians and Muslim
Brotherhood leaders to boycott the parliamentary elections. As argued in
Chapter 2, signatories included not only familiar members of the opposition bloc, but former prime ministers Obaydat and al-Masri, neither one
of whom was considered a "friend" of opposition parties or, in particular,
Islamists. Obaydat had also been a prominent figure in the secret police
since the 1960s and was director of that organization from 1974 to 1982
(Riedel 1993: 106). As such, he was frequently at odds with members
of the Muslim Brotherhood as well as various opposition groups. Yet
Obaydat was the first to sign the boycott document, and al-Masri, whose
cabinet in 1991 followed the one in which the Muslim Brotherhood held
five portfolios, signed second. The range of individuals who signed the
petition, some eighty in all, not only illustrates the extent to which a wide
segment of the political spectrum had become frustrated with what they
saw as a façade democracy, but highlights the ways in which opposed
groups may come to cooperate around issues of common interest. As the
November 1997 elections approached, many of the parties honoring the
boycott organized loosely into what they describe as a national coalition
intended not as a formal opposition bloc, but to facilitate the coordination of oppositional activities of the groups that found themselves without

---

[69] A large police contingent dressed in riot gear pressed the crowd of 2,000 to 4,000 back
from the exhibition hall, theoretically to allow people to attend the trade fair. At one
point water cannons were employed to press the demonstrators back, but there was no
resort to the violent repression of the 1989 bread riots, the 1996 bread riots, or the 1998
demonstrations against the UN sanctions against Iraq (which left one dead). In each
of these instances, dozens, sometimes hundreds of demonstrators were imprisoned for
weeks or months, though many were never charged. See Andoni and Schwedler (1996)
and Schwedler (2003b).

parliamentary representation as a result of their boycott. This group evolved into the Conference for National Reform, a group formally launched in June 1998 that brings together political parties, civil society organizations, and professional associations.[70] Many of the members of this group organized a Twenty-fifth National Congress that convened on July 25, 1998, coinciding with the anniversary of the First Jordanian National Congress held in 1928. The preparatory committee – which included Obaydat, al-Masri, Muslim Brotherhood leader Thunaybat, IAF leaders Farhan and 'Arabiyyat, and the heads of most other political parties – met at the IAF headquarters to draft the political program. These cooperative practices have since the mid-1990s occurred with considerable frequency, and for the most part are so unexceptional that they fail to attract much attention at all. Compared to the tactical alliances of the late 1980s and early 1990s formed primarily with conservative groups whose political and social agendas largely overlapped with those of the Muslim Brotherhood, by the mid-to-late 1990s the IAF was working regularly with groups that had previously been serious political and even ideological rivals, notably Leftist parties, liberals, and former state security officials.

In Yemen, the Islah party also explored a number of formal and informal agreements with other parties and political trends, though its position as "partner" of the GPC in Yemen's coalition precluded the emergence of sustained alliances with opposition parties until the late 1990s. As the former ruling parties of North and South Yemen, the GPC and the YSP by the time of unification already had agreed to rule as a coalition. When Islah had won more seats (62) than the YSP (57) in the 1993 elections, YSP leaders had little choice but to agree to GPC demands to include Islah in the coalition as a junior partner. Islah leaders have been much more antagonistic toward the YSP than the IAF toward Jordan's Leftist parties. Whereas the IAF supported a parliamentary vote in Jordan declaring the right of all groups to organize political parties, some Islah leaders have been outspoken against the YSP and the "evils" of socialism even as the party formally adopted a position in support of political pluralism. In fact, numerous Islah members participated on attacks and assassination attempts against YSP members both before and after unification. And while the Islah party has formally accepted the right of socialists to organize (so long as they do not advocate atheism, which South Yemen's socialists have never done), Islah leaders have criticized Leftist groups

---

[70] "Al-Tariq ila al-Islah al-Watani," founding document of the Conference for National Reform, June 13, 1998.

on the basis that they oppose the central tenets of Islam. Al-Zindani has most consistently and strongly criticized the YSP on ideological grounds, arguing that as Muslims, Yemenis are called upon by God to fight against communists and socialists. These debates are examined in detail in Chapter 5.

The 1994 postwar GPC-Islah coalition signaled the expansion of northern dominance following the YSP's defeat, but the outcome ironically led to a decline in Islah's power. To be sure, the Yemeni state is a fragile political entity, and President Salih's autocratic regime does not come even close to exercising full authority over the whole of unified Yemen. Saudi Arabia has considerable influence in certain border regions, while powerful and well-armed tribes entirely control certain regions, particularly but not only in the northeast. Islah leaders such as Shaykh 'Abd Allah remained central to the highest circles of power even as Islah's influence decreased when the GPC no longer needed Islah to help offset the influence of the YSP. As Islah ministers increasingly resigned from their posts, the party saw fewer and fewer overtures from the GPC and the relationship deteriorated.

In light of this deteriorating relationship, Islah became concerned with its prospects for the 1997 parliamentary elections. When the GPC announced in June 1996 that it would strive to obtain a majority of seats, a number of columns and articles in *Al-Sahwah*, Islah's official newspaper, criticized the GPC for seeking to undermine Yemen's multiparty system. Members of the YSP remaining in Yemen or having returned from abroad were already discussing a boycott, and a number of Islah members from the Muslim Brotherhood trend expressed interest in supporting such a boycott. Islah leaders struggled to reach an agreement with the GPC that would ensure that prominent candidates from each party did not run against each other. By August, however, the GPC-Islah negotiations had not moved forward and party leaders began exploring possibilities of cooperation with opposition parties. Islah representatives held several meetings with Yemen's organized opposition bloc, the Supreme Coordination Council of the Opposition (SCCO). They discussed their common concerns that the GPC had been manipulating electoral laws and other legal measures in an attempt to dominate the next elections. Members of the SCCO at the time included seven parties, including the socialist Nasir and Ba'ath parties as well as two smaller Islamist parties that have traditionally opposed Islah.[71] Yet as Islah saw its role in the "coalition"

---

[71] The seven parties are Hizb al-Haqq, Al-Hizb al-Wahdawi al-Sha'bi al-Nasiri, Ittihad al-Qiwah al-Sha'biyyah, Al-Tajammu' al-Wahdawi al-Yamani, Hizb al-Ahrar al-Dusturi, Hizb al-Ba'ath al-Arabi al-Ishtiraki, and Ittihad al-Qiwah al-Wataniyyah.

government decline to almost nothing, the political expediency of cooperation began to outweigh other differences. On August 27, 1996, Islah
and the SCCO jointly issued a statement of cooperation, which was published in several newspapers. The document expressed "grave concern for
the direction of democratic development in Yemen," and particularly the
role of the regime in fragmenting the political opposition. It is notable
that neither President Salih nor the GPC were named in the statement,
which criticized only abuses by the regime (*sulta*). In October, Muhammad Alawi, a member of Islah's consultative council and a representative
to the talks with the SCCO, spoke of regret over Islah's years of isolation from the opposition parties. "Lack of dialogue with other parties
was a gross error. Islah has now taken an historical step by talking to
other parties. . . . It is rumored that Islah has started talking to the opposition for political gains. I say this is not so. Islah has a democratic aim
especially after the Islamist movement in Yemen changed its attitudes and
mechanisms."[72]

Yet Islah members had not abandoned hope of reaching an agreement of the coordination of candidates for the April 1997 elections. On
October 24, 1996, its consultative council issued a statement in which
it expressed the desire to maintain a strong relationship with the GPC,
noting that their coalition had been established on "basic national foundations unstained by any narrow interests." The language of the document
lacked the harsh criticism that characterized the articles published in *Al-
Sahwah*, or the broad criticism of the regime in the Islah-SCCO statement
from August. Still, tensions between the parties continued to escalate.
On December 4, the remaining Islah ministers walked out of a cabinet
meeting following heated discussions concerning the 1997 budget.[73] By
January 1997, however, the GPC and Islah agreed that GPC candidates
would run uncontested by Islah candidates in 100 constituencies, and
Islah would run uncontested by the GPC in fifty. In the remaining 151
constituencies, the parties would freely compete. Within weeks both GPC
and Islah spokespersons accused the other party of violating the agreement
by supporting third-party candidates and by secretly running candidates
as "independents" in districts from which they had agreed to withdraw
their candidates. It is difficult to know how much of the agreement held in

---

[72] *The Yemen Times*, October 7, 1997.
[73] *The Yemen Times*, December 9, 1996. The disagreement revolved around an ongoing
debate concerning the operation of a network of "scientific institutes" controlled by al-
Zindani. The GPC and others had long argued that they should fall under the domain of
the Ministry of Education.

the end, but considerable evidence suggests that in broad terms, it simply fell apart because it no longer served the interests of the GPC.[74]

SUMMARY

The limits of the transition framework come into sharper focus through the systematic exploration of these changes in party organization, practice, and cooperation with other parties. Both Jordan and Yemen are undoubtedly stalled transitions, but the single-minded focus on progress toward democracy obscures the multifaceted changes that these two political fields have undergone. In Jordan, the IAF emerged from a cohesive movement; in Yemen, the Islah party was fashioned as multiple groups came together to aid the northern regime in offsetting the potential influence of the YSP following unification. Both parties adopted organizational strategies and practices aimed at best competing in a formally pluralist system while initially shunning cooperation with political parties of alternative ideological orientations. Formal pluralist bodies put Islamists in regular contact with their longtime rivals, however. When the transition failed to move forward – in Jordan due to the desire to rebuild relations with Washington and sign a peace treaty with Israel, and in Yemen with the defeat of the YSP – each party saw its share of power gradually decline, albeit for very different reasons. Much of the public political debate in each country has revolved around government interference in national elections, even though all political trends recognize that the popularly elected assemblies have little to do with governance. Newly formed alliances and periodic cooperation among former adversaries also continued, even as the incentives for bargaining and cooperation were not realized through the functioning of democratic institutions.

This chapter therefore provides a significant empirical basis for the claim that the notion of stalled democracy tends to obscure a wide array of changes that continue to unfold within public political space. Attention

---

[74] There are signs that the dispute went to the highest level, between President Salih and Shaykh 'Abd Allah. A short news article in the London-based *Al-Hayat* daily newspaper reported that Shaykh 'Abd Allah was considering withdrawing his candidacy for a seat in the April elections. Then editor of *Al-Hayat*, Khairallah Khairallah, is widely acknowledged as close to both President Salih and Shaykh 'Abd Allah and has occasionally served as a conduit through which the two would send delicate messages to each other. Several former ministers told me they believe that Shaykh 'Abd Allah leaked the story to Khairallah to push President Salih to honor the GPC-Islah agreement on candidates. In the end, Shaykh 'Abd Allah did not withdraw his candidacy. See *Al-Hayat*, March 16, 1997.

to the changing structure of various publics, however, illustrates a striking evolution of political space even in the initial five years since each state's political opening. In particular, the IAF and Islah both sought to take advantage of the new opportunities of the evolving political space. As each adopted a new organizational structure and engaged in new practices, they directly contributed to the reshaping of public political space. The transitions paradigm fails to capture this dynamic change, and particularly the extent to which those practices continue to reshape political spaces even as the transitions failed to progress.

What do these dimensions contribute to unpacking the inclusion-moderation hypothesis? The factors explored in this chapter offer a partial explanation by highlighting elite alliances, the relation of the ruling regime to public political space, and the evolving structure and practices of the IAF and Islah. In terms of Yemen in particular, the complex GPC-Islah relation and the fragmented nature of the Islah party together presented conditions that have prevented the party from evolving significantly over time in ways that might be recognized as moderation. The ideational dimensions of these structures and processes will be examined in Chapter 4. In terms of Jordan, however, these factors offer a rich explanation of why the IAF has evolved from shunning cooperation with ideologically rival parties in the early years of the openings, to engaging in sustained cooperative bodies with Leftists and liberals in particular. The structure and content of the practices that make up these comparative political publics do, therefore, explain a considerable portion of the variation between the two cases. But as argued in the preceding text, a practice-oriented approach moves well beyond the conventional focus on how institutional constraints structure the behavior of political actors. If practices are understood as repeated actions inscribed with meaning, how can we know what actors understand themselves to be doing as they engage in various practices? In terms of the inclusion-moderation hypothesis, how can we know if these internal restructurings, the adoption of new practices, and the forging of alliances with ideological rivals are merely tactical, or whether each party has become more tolerant and pluralist? To answer these questions, I examine ideational dimensions of public political space.

4

Cultural Dimensions of Political Contestation

In the preceding chapters, I have explored in detail two dimensions of change in Jordan and Yemen that resulted from regime-led political openings: political opportunity structure and internal group practices (organization, decision-making processes, and willingness to forge alliances with rival political actors). Changes in each of these dimensions of public political space have significantly impacted the other. The comparison between the IAF in Jordan and the Islah party in Yemen thus far has highlighted structural dimensions, such as the role and position of the regime in the transition process, whether the regime competes as a party or sits above the field of pluralist political contestation, and the structure of competing factions and level of cohesion within each party. In this chapter, I begin to explore a third component of change, the cultural dimensions of political contestation, focusing on three dominant narratives central to public political debate in both countries: Islam, democracy, and national unity. I examine the ways in which these narratives have created opportunities and constraints for all political actors, but I focus my attention on regimes and Islamist parties. This chapter is devoted to identifying these cultural dimensions of political contestation in Jordan and Yemen and examining how insights from these cases can contribute to a theory that might explain precisely how moderation can take place. Chapter 5 identifies one mechanism for ideological moderation and then examines whether this mechanism was at work within the IAF and the Islah party to explain varying degrees of moderation between the parties.

CULTURAL FIELD, NARRATIVE, AND WORLDVIEW

As detailed in Chapter 3, scholars have suggested numerous ways of conceptualizing public political space. I have focused on practice-oriented
approaches, which emphasize not only actions – what actors do – but
also the meanings attached to, and created by, these very actions. The
ideational dimensions of practice are reflected in Bourdieu's *habitus*, in
which actions are socially intelligible because they are inscribed with
shared meaning. For Bourdieu, *habitus* is "the subjective but not individual system of internalized structures, schemes of perception, conception, and action common to all members of the same group or class and
constituting the precondition for all objectification and apperception"
(Bourdieu 1977: 86).[1] Practice is meaningful action and is intelligible to
others because it takes place within a shared cultural field, which may be
public or private. Every society is characterized by a variety of overlapping
cultural fields, so unpacking practice entails, in part, the identification of
the relevant cultural fields that make the actions in question meaningful as well as comprehensible to others. Each cultural field is characterized, among other things, by institutional arrangements (conceptualized
as processes and not as a fixed system), relations, practices, signifiers, and
narratives that cannot be reduced to a closed or fixed set of signs and relations. Political actors do not simply move within and among cultural fields
as if navigating a forest in which they encounter trees, but remain fundamentally apart from them. Instead, the meaningful practices adopted
by political actors both structure and are structured by the cultural field
within which they take place. Culture is thus a constitutive social process
that actively creates different ways of life (Williams 1977). Comaroff and
Comaroff build on Bourdieu's work on fields to define a cultural field as
"the space of signifying practice, the semantic ground on which human
beings seek to construct and represent themselves and others – and, hence,
society and history. As this suggests, it is not merely a pot of messages,
a repertoire of signs to be flashed across a neutral mental screen. It has
form as well as content; is born in action as well as thought; is a product
of human creativity as well as mimesis; and, above all, is empowered"
(1991: 21–2).

An essential dimension of any cultural field is the presence of narratives. By "narrative" I mean a set of ideas, debates, and understandings

---

[1] Searle likens his notion of background to Bourdieu's *habitus* (1995: 132): a set of capacities,
disposition, and know-how (127–47), a "certain sort of knowledge about how the world
works... a certain set of abilities for coping with the world" (131).

that present a coherent, overarching story (or stories) about some dimension or aspect of social reality. Narratives include judgments about which actors and identities are consequential and vary across time and space, but they provide meaning to even the mundane by organizing experience and structuring expectations. Yet every cultural field is characterized by the presence of multiple narratives that actors engage, contest, or ignore, and, through those processes, reconstruct. Even in authoritarian societies, where public discourse may be overwhelmed by a dominant, state-enforced narrative, alternative narratives always exist (Scott 1985, 1992), if only in carefully guarded private spaces or through sarcasm, irony, or feigned compliance and phony gestures (Wedeen 1999).[2]

Actors are an essential component of a cultural field, and through their practices they engage in, and reshape, these narratives. In this connection, actors also adopt practices that adhere to or reflect, with varying degrees of commitment, a range of worldviews. A worldview is a set of dispositions or understandings about the world, including but not limited to perspectives of what is wrong, what is possible, and what is just. An ideology, by comparison, is a particularly rigid, cohesive, and closed worldview. As a social science concept, the term *ideology* remains somewhat contested. It evolved from its original, neutral conception as "the science of ideas" used by Destutt de Tracy in 1796, to more pejorative (and inconsistent) usages by Marx and many branches of Marxian thought,[3] to a wide range of usages in contemporary social sciences. Williams argues that ideology is "a relatively formal and articulated system of meanings, values, and beliefs, of a kind that can be abstracted as 'worldview'" (1977: 109). Rather than use *worldview* and *ideology* interchangeably in this way, I treat ideology as a particularly rigid worldview, a set of relatively closed, comprehensive, and cohesive beliefs, dispositions, and values.[4]

---

[2] Wedeen (1999) explores the cult of Syria's President Hafez al-Asad and asks why the regime spends valuable resources on a cult whose rituals of obeisance are transparently phony. Her answer is, *because it works*. It does not matter that Syrian citizens do not believe in the cult; it only matters that they act as if they believe because the outcome remains an effective disciplinary device. Even under Asad's repressive regime, however, Syrians find outlets for alternative narratives, transgressions that contract the atomizing effects of the cult while simultaneously and unwittingly shoring up a politics of public dissimulation.

[3] Compare, for example, the summaries of the development of the idea of ideology in Marxist thought presented by Williams (1977: 55–71) and Thompson (1990: 28–73).

[4] Religious fundamentalists and Leftists are often identified as ideological in the negative sense of dogmatism and closed-mindedness, though "liberalism," for example, may be just as much an ideology when it precludes other options or understandings.

Is "political Islam" an ideology? No, because what political Islam is varies dramatically in terms of the objectives and strategies of Islamist actors not only from the political Islam(s) of the early twentieth century, but also across spatial, class, and gender divides (to name but a few). However, an Islamist political actor may be *ideological* to the extent that her worldview entails a relatively cohesive and closed set of meanings and practices that largely exclude alternative understandings or perspectives. Not all Islamist actors are ideological, therefore, nor should they be assumed to be ideological in similar ways. In exploring moderation, my approach conceptualizes a continuum of worldviews, from highly closed ideologies to ones more open, inclusive, and tolerant of other perspectives. If the question is why or how inclusion increases moderation, these notions of practice, public political space, narrative, and worldview provide analytic purchase for investigating why and how political actors may become less ideological over time. Moderation is therefore identified not as change in political behavior, which leaves open the possibility of feigned moderation, but change in worldview of the sort that may be described as *ideological moderation*.

How does this change take place? Callon notes that an actor's "objectives, interests, will, and thus identity are caught up in a process of continual reconfiguration, a process that is intimately related to the constant reconfiguration of the network of interactions in which he or she is involved" (1998b: 253). Lynch argues that through processes of deliberation, "accepted truths become open to question, shared convictions about the role and purpose of the state become contentious, and new ideas and interpretations compete for hegemonic status" (1999: 14). In this regard, engaging in any political practice necessarily requires engaging one's worldview, and this engagement can take the form of reinforcing existing beliefs, values, and goals or of reconstructing those core beliefs, values, and goals (in ways that may be more moderate, more radical, or different from what they were previously in ways not captured by the terms *moderate* or *radical*).

Because narratives include judgments about which actors and identities are consequential, engaging particular narratives connects actors to certain networks. By virtue of entering certain debates, actors may also become disconnected from other networks. My interest in this cultural dimension of political contestation is to explore how Islamists may strategically adopt practices that engage and restructure various narratives – particularly Islam and democracy – and whether the engagement of these narratives (combined with participation in political openings) may lead them to become less ideological in the sense of greater openness and tolerance toward alternative worldviews. How can we theorize this type of ideational change and its connection to change in modes of political contestation and broader political opportunity structures? That is, even if we establish that moderation of this sort has taken place, can we identify the causal factors producing this change? A first step is to investigate the cultural contours of public political space in each country, including dominant narratives and competing worldviews. Can we identify in the IAF and Islah a growing commitment to inclusive, democratic practices over tight adherence to an exclusive, confessional worldview?

CULTURAL DIMENSIONS OF PUBLIC POLITICAL SPACE

As illustrated in Chapters 2 and 3, regime-led political openings and the introduction of pluralist political practices significantly restructured the fields of political contestation in Jordan and Yemen in the early 1990s. Because practice is meaningful action, how can we identify what actors understood themselves and others to be doing? What sorts of ideational constraints did these political actors encounter, and how did the adoption of new practices reshape them?

All political actors face a range of choices among various strategies of political engagement. Of the strategies that they see as available to them, why do they choose the ones they do? To begin with, actors consider only the range of options that are imaginable: that is, they cannot consider options they do not perceive to exist. The "imaginable" is thus an historically contingent dimension of any cultural field, shaped by social institutions, recent and distant memory, perceived threats and opportunities, the practices of actors, and understandings of local, regional, and global political trends. What is imaginable for a political actor at any point in time and space is therefore structured by her own experiences as well as by the meanings and practices present at that time, and is not necessarily shared by other actors. Like narratives, the range of what can be politically imagined is reproduced and restructured through the practices of both state and nonstate political actors. When state leaders "change the rules of the game," for example, they redraw the boundaries of the imaginable in ways that affect both themselves and their challengers.

Why must we be concerned with what is imaginable for a given society and for specific actors to understand what choices political actors make? Because questions of political change rest in part on perceptions of possibilities. Simply put, opportunities are not available if actors cannot first

imagine them, let alone consider them as possible. But how can conceptualizing a sphere of the *unimaginable* help us explore the question of
political moderation? Thinking about the unimaginable reminds us that
perceptions of possibilities are specific to time and place and always subject to change, sometimes in an instant and sometimes gradually. This is
not to suggest that certain social actors are *incapable* of imagining any
particular possibilities, but rather that they simply *do not* imagine them.
Occasionally, events of great magnitude produce ruptures that make the
unimaginable imaginable. These historical developments may resonate
locally, regionally, or globally, but in each case they introduce new ideas
about what is possible. The end of the Cold War, the AIDS epidemic, and
the attacks of September 11, 2001: each has raised new political possibilities that were previously unimaginable. At a more local level, events such
as the death of a powerful leader, the spread of ethnic rivalries, the collapse
of a long-standing alliance of powerful interests, a natural disaster, or the
technology that has brought global text messaging through cheap cell
phones to poor refugee camps around Amman may create new scenarios
for the future, new ways of imagining and understanding political, social,
and economic possibilities. Ruptures caused by events of great magnitude
are among those most easily identified, but even slower, localized, or mundane processes may introduce shifts in practice that effectively redraw the
boundaries of the imaginable.

The driving question of this study is to explain why some ideological
actors become more moderate while others engaged in similar practices
do not. The answer entails identifying the mechanisms through which new
possibilities are introduced into a given field of political contestation, that
is, when the historically unimaginable becomes imaginable within a specific field of political contestation. The attacks of September 11, 2001,
for example, provided such a mechanism. Because they were carried out
on U.S. soil by a radical Islamist group, let me return to the question
of Islamist political activism. The historical emergence of a new way of
thinking about Islamist groups illustrates precisely how events can shift
the boundary between the imaginable and the unimaginable, creating new
ways of understanding preexisting phenomena in ways that produce tangible political consequences. Although the rise of radical Islamist movements is often dated to the 1970s and particularly the period following the
Iranian revolution, in fact militant Islamist movements have been central
political actors in the Middle East for more than a century. As Mitchell
argues, various Islamist groups in Saudi Arabia (before and after the creation of that state) were not only instrumental for the establishment of

a particular political order (the creation of a state around a single family), but were also indispensible for the emergence of the fragile economic pact between local and global oil interests, facilitated by fundamentalist Islamists known as *al-muwahhidun* (those who embrace the "oneness" of God) through a movement known as the *Ikhwan* (not to be confused with the Muslim Brotherhood founded in Egypt). He argues, "the political economy of oil did not happen, in some incidental way, to rely on a government in Saudi Arabia that owed its own power to the force of an Islamic political movement. Given the features of the political economy of oil – the enormous rents available, the difficulty in securing those rents due to the overabundance of supply, the pivotal role of Saudi Arabia in maintaining scarcity, and the collapse of the older colonial methods of imposing antimarket corporate control of the Saudi oil fields – oil profits depended on working with those forces that could guarantee the political control of Arabia, the House of Saud in alliance with the *muwahhidun*. The latter were not incidental, but became an internal element in the political economy of oil" (Mitchell 2002a: 11).

This historic relationship has been either hidden, misrecognized, or ignored for decades, so that despite these interconnections the emergence of Islamist movements who challenged Western interests came as a surprise to many. By the 1960s, a wide diversity of Islamist movements had begun to challenge the local political order in many Middle Eastern states (but not only there). Many of these groups had been active for decades in complicated relationships with existing elites as well as against them, while others emerged around anticolonial struggles. In states such as Turkey and Jordan, Islamist groups were active in organizing social and political activities and even in participating directly in state institutions as ministers, deputies, and government employees. Political elites relied on Islamists to shore up their support bases in a variety of ways, so these relationships were far from benign. In states where regimes espoused socialist or secular national narratives, the often newly established political elite used Islamists at certain periods but saw them as a threat at other junctures and subjected them to increasing state repression (Moaddel 2002; Hafez 2003). In Egypt, for example, members of the Muslim Brotherhood were allies of the Free Officers movement that overthrew King Faruq in 1952. Just two years later, Nasser's new republican government saw these same individuals as a threat and enacted a series of repressive measures. As many were imprisoned and tortured over the next decade, the radical writings of the imprisoned Islamist Sayyid Qutb spread among Islamists in Egypt and elsewhere who had become frustrated with the limits of cooperating with existing regimes. Like the Saudi-based *al-muwahhidun* before him, Qutb advocated direct attacks not only on "infidel" regimes, but on all who supported or defended them (Haddad 1983). He was executed in prison in 1966 for allegedly plotting to assassinate Nasser, a move which elevated his status in the eyes of his radical followers. Although Qutb is far from the only contemporary radical Islamist thinker or even the most influential, his writings continue to resonate with many Islamists, including various branches of the Islamic Jihad (including the Egyptian branch of which assassinated Sadat in 1980), Egypt's Gama'a Islamiyyah, Palestine's HAMAS, al-Qa'ida, and diverse Salafi groups.

But against the popular narrative of radical Islam common in the West, militant Islamists did not emerge only in the 1960s with the Qutb's articulation of a justification for violent jihad. As Mitchell argues, the relationship of these groups with local elites (and in some cases, directly supporting the economy of oil) was a disjunctive one, as political Islam was oriented toward a different set of goals (2002: 12). The radicalization of certain Islamist groups from the 1960s onward might therefore have been anticipated, but instead came as a surprise. Even as Islamist movements used violence to shore up support for regimes such as Saudi Arabia and constructed secret militant cells as in Egypt, Islamist political actors had been generally viewed as social conservatives, located on the far right of the political spectrum distinct from but alongside other conservative political actors, including loyalists and some state nationalists. Even prior to the Cold War and the emergence of militant nationalism and the secular Left in the Middle East, the United States shared the view of many nondemocratic Arab regimes that these conservative religious groups could be employed – often literally – to serve as allies in projects as diverse as protecting oil interests and preventing the spread of Soviet-backed socialism in the region. In Afghanistan, the long-term outcome of U.S. support of the Islamist *mujahidin* against Soviet troops is infamous; less well-known is that the United States and Saudi Arabia began backing the *mujahidin* at least six months prior to the Soviet invasion in December 1979. Mitchell notes, "As U.S. national security advisor Zbigniew Brzezinski later confirmed, the United States hoped to provoke a war that would embroil the Soviet Union in 'its own Vietnam'" (2002a: 14).

As these largely conservative Islamists began to assert political projects that directly clashed with those of the region's regimes, they came under increased repression, which seems to have only strengthened radicals who espoused more revolutionary ideologies and strategies (Kepel 1986, 2002; Esposito 1997, 2002; Hafez 2003), leading to increasing divisions between certain radicals and conservatives (Zubaida 1996; Ismail 1998). Even though militant Islamists had operated for decades, it was only with the 1979 Iranian revolution that a radical vision of Islamist change became highly visible on a global scale, one that actively sought to overthrow non-Islamist regimes through the use of violence, if necessary. No longer were Islamist groups considered alongside other political actors with conservative agendas. As they came to be called "Islamic fundamentalists," their agendas for social reform seemed to outsiders (both domestic and international) more threatening than they had been. Particularly with the Iranian revolution, the "Islamic threat" became imaginable to a wide range of political actors (and from diverse perspectives) on a global scale (Esposito 1992, 2002; Huntington 1993, 1996; Roy 1994; Barber 1995; Kepel 2002) long before the emergence of loose transnational networks such as al-Qa'ida. This new imagining of Islamist politics, then, drew a sharp distinction between "moderates" and "radicals," where advocacy of the use of violence marked the key divide. This new imagining stood in stark contradistinction to the willful blindness of Western elites to the long-standing reliance of nondemocratic regimes in the Middle East on militant Islamist groups.[5]

The emergence of a sharp moderate-radical distinction to characterize Islamist groups illustrates an historical shift in the boundary between the imaginable and unimaginable. This reframing of radical Islam became politically consequential as regimes pointed to the "Islamist threat" as justification for harshly constrained political rights, a practice that continues. More recently, George W. Bush's "war on terrorism," which seeks to "win the war of ideas" in defeating radical Islam in particular, illustrates how newly imaginable outcomes shape political practices in profound ways. The example of militant and radical political Islam is instructive not only because it is germane to the substantive cases of this study, but because it illustrates how the introduction of a new narrative into a field of political contestation – that of moderate versus radical Islamism – can structure perceptions about possibilities and choice among available strategies.

The sphere of the imaginable, however, is more than merely the range of thinkable ideas. It encompasses dominant and subordinate narratives, and the particular way(s) in which those ideas are structured. Within the whole range of imaginable strategies and outcomes, not all options are really

---

[5] Mitchell (2002a) outlines the complex relationship between the militant Islamists and the Saudi family, but for other examples of how militants allied with a variety of local and international powers, see Cooley (2000), Rashid (2000), and Vitalis (2002).

TABLE 4.1. *Ideational Dimensions of a Cultural Field*

Sphere	Subdimension	Characteristics
Unimaginable		Ideas that are not present at a particular historic moment, the literally inconceivable
Imaginable	Fantastical	Ideas that are thinkable, but which seem so outlandish as to play no role in shared understandings of social reality
	Unjustifiable	Strategies and practices rejected as incongruent with an actor's worldview
	Justifiable	Strategies and practices congruent with an actor's worldview
	Dominant narrative	The most widely accepted (but not necessarily hegemonic) ideas, practices, and beliefs shared among political actors

possible for all actors. Actors may not be able to adopt certain strategies for the simple reason that they cannot justify them in terms of their own beliefs or their commitments to certain practices or narratives. The use of political violence, for example, is imaginable in most societies. But few actors consider it morally justifiable except when the survival of oneself or one's community is at state (which is, of course, subject to interpretation). In this regard, political violence is an available strategy, but few actors will consider using it. For strongly ideological actors, such constraints are particularly acute: their choice among "available strategies" may be severely constrained by what they can justify in terms of their ideological commitments.

Thus the imaginable has three distinct dimensions: the fantastical, the unjustifiable, and the justifiable (Table 4.1). The fantastical are ideas present in individual or collective thought that seem so implausible as to play no meaningful role in one's understanding of social reality. For many Americans, the events of September 11, 2001 were simply unimaginable the previous day, or at worst they were imaginable but fantastical. For decades to come, however, Americans may view similar attacks as not only imaginable but perhaps even likely. Not only did those events redraw the boundary between the unimaginable and the imaginable, but they led many to view a strongly interventionist U.S. foreign policy – even at the expense of alienating longtime allies – as not only justifiable but essential.

This conceptualization of the cultural dimensions of public political space gives us a tool with which to theorize the impact of even limited political openings on ideological political actors (e.g., some Islamist groups) and the interactive ways in which political openings restructure the institutional and cultural dimensions of political contestation. The adoption of new practices, in turn, also restructures public political space. Does political inclusion lead ideological actors to redefine what strategies and practices are justifiable, and in ways that are more inclusive and tolerant (and thus less ideological)? How do shifts in the imaginable and the justifiable affect actors and their practices in politically consequential ways? Answering these questions may provide analytic purchase on the inclusion-moderation hypothesis by suggesting how, and under what circumstances, ideological groups may become less so.

THREE NARRATIVES: ISLAM, DEMOCRACY, AND NATIONAL UNITY

The dominant narratives in much of the Muslim world are those of Islam, democracy, and national unity.[6] Narratives about Islam are common in the public spaces of states with majority Muslim populations. Many regimes have even inscribed a prominent role for Islam in their constitutions, for example by stipulating that the leader must be Muslim and/or that law must be wholly or in part based on *shari'ah*. Leaders often claim Islamic credentials in defending their authenticity and their "right" to rule, emphasizing descent from the immediate family of the Prophet Muhammad, strong personal piety, or advanced knowledge of Islamic teachings (Piscatori 1983; Halliday and Alavi 1988; Munson 1993; Zubaida 1993). Regimes sometimes also allow religious courts considerable autonomy on certain social issues. Narratives about national unity have proven essential components of state projects of building national identity, particularly in states whose borders were drawn by colonial powers. In recent decades, however, democracy narratives have become increasingly widespread in the Muslim world (as they have globally). Regimes and Islamist groups alike negotiate a field of political contestation in which these narratives provide opportunities and constraints at least as powerful as those of formal state institutional arrangements.

---

[6] Of course, Islam, democracy, and national unity were not the only narratives in Jordan and Yemen during the period of study. Others included Arab nationalism, socialism (including Islamic socialism), national liberation, and republicanism.

As argued in Chapter 2, the political elite in Jordan and Yemen were not responsible for introducing the idea of democracy into their countries. Debates about democracy had already spread throughout the Middle East through transnational public spaces and the transactions and dialogues among different networks of Islamist groups, human rights organizations, trade associations, grassroots reform organizations, and women's associations, to name but a few. In South Yemen, a number of YSP leaders had begun vibrant debates about the need for democracy, largely in response to the tragedy of the 1986 internal YSP conflict that cost thousands of lives within a matter of weeks. In 1987 and 1988, for example, YSP leader Jar Allah 'Umar prepared and presented to the party a major paper calling for political pluralism in South Yemen and within the YSP ranks. But neither country saw widespread mobilization around democratic ideas, and the few protests that materialized were largely framed to challenge economic conditions and, in particular, the types of economic restructuring projects mandated or encouraged by international institutions such as the World Bank and IMF.

The ruling regimes of Jordan and Yemen did, however, push the language of democracy to the center of public political debates about governance at a time when neither country was witnessing widespread demands for democratic reform. They did this by framing their own agendas and reform projects in terms of political liberalization. State and nonstate actors began to speak of such democratic notions as civil society (*mujtama'a madani*, or *mujtama'a ahli*) and pluralism (*ta'addudiyyah*), terms that had entered Arabic political discourse only in the 1980s (Browers 2005, 2006). Of course, we should not assume that an appeal to a democratic narrative (or for that matter any narrative) necessarily produces legitimacy (Wedeen 2002: 723). But we can establish the prominence of a narrative about democracy at a particular time and space by gauging the extent to which political actors appeal to a democratic narrative and engage in practices inscribed with democratic meaning(s).

In this connection, we can make arguments about why a particular narrative becomes prominent when it does. In both Jordan and Yemen, as political elites began to speak of democracy as a desirable, even preferable, framework for political organization, a democracy narrative quickly became prominent within public political discourse. Jordan's King Hussein and united Yemen's President Salih and Vice President al-Bid all celebrated the arrival of democratic practices and promised to uphold the ideals associated with democratic freedoms, political pluralism, and elected representative governance. They made these claims in speeches, in the state-owned media, and when making new political appointments, but the democracy narrative gained its most significant boost with the introduction of new pluralist (if not quite democratic) practices and institutional arrangements that accompanied the controlled political openings. A wide range of political actors immediately responded to the openings, as illustrated in the following text and in Chapter 5, both by adopting new practices and by engaging in public debate about democratization: its prospects, appropriateness for the nation, its compatibility with Islam, its western origins, and so on. Even after each regime retreated from some of the openings of the early 1990s, state elites continued to appeal to a democracy narrative. Yemen's President Salih became so fond of the phrase "emerging democracy" – borrowed from a 1999 regional conference in San'a organized by the U.S.-based National Democratic Institute – that he has used it to characterize virtually every dynamic of Yemeni politics as well as to justify the slow pace of progress toward democracy. Similarly, Jordan's King 'Abd Allah follows his father in repeatedly declaring his commitment to democratization in Jordan.

Just as regimes seek to use controlled political openings to undermine the power of political challengers by steering them toward particular modes and channels of contestation, so do they seek to impose structure and a particular order on the semiotics of political contestation. As Sewell puts it, "The typical cultural strategy of dominant actors and institutions is not so much to establish uniformity as it is to organize difference. They are constantly engaged in efforts not only to normalize or homogenize but also to hierarchize, encapsulate, exclude, criminalize, hegemonize, or marginalize practices and populations that diverge from the sanctioned ideal" (1999: 56). Such efforts create constraints on even dominant actors, however, and likewise can create opportunities for challengers. In this regard, the articulation of reforms by the dominant actors in democratic language elevated and strengthened the democratic narrative. These developments had tangible impact on public political space in both Jordan and Yemen, ranging from strategies for political contestation to the content of public political debate.

But how do these new opportunities create the possibility for ideological moderation? If a key dimension of the inclusion-moderation hypothesis is discerning when groups are, for example, committed to pluralist political practices and when they are merely acting as if they are committed, then public declarations of commitment alone are insufficient evidence of commitment to democratic or pluralist practices and the willingness to abide by the rules of the game. State actors throughout the Middle

East clearly adopt democratic language instrumentally, with little real commitment to meaningful reforms. Serious analysts have little reason to take these declarations seriously. Nonstate actors might certainly do the same, especially if they believe that acting as if they embraced democracy would bring tangible benefits. Thus the real challenge for strongly ideological groups is not to recognize and exploit new political opportunities by appealing to popular narratives, but to reconcile their decision to adopt new practices with their relatively closed worldview.

The political practices and developments examined here are predominantly the product of public political discourse centered in urban areas, notably the metropolitan capital centers of Amman and San'a. I focus on these urban centers because each constitutes the realm of formal political engagement between key political actors and with regard to state institutions of power. I do not suggest that these debates are reproduced identically in rural areas, or even across class or gender lines in urban centers. They represent the terms in which state actors, political parties, and civil society organizations debate politics within certain public political spaces. The issues I explore are also not exhaustive, but I chose them because of their relevance to the question of inclusion and moderation.

Narratives of Democracy and National Unity in Jordan

With Jordan's long history of nationally elected assemblies, Leftist and nationalist groups there had fairly consistently called for a return to the electoral politics of the 1950s. Jordan had banned all political parties in 1957 following the emergence of al-Nabulsi's socialist government and its efforts to reform the political system. Meanwhile, the Muslim Brotherhood was permitted to continue functioning as a charitable organization even though in practice it engaged in political activities. Government representatives, particularly agents from various security services, frequently attended public meetings organized by the Muslim Brotherhood, which held such gatherings only with government approval. This frustrated Muslim Brotherhood leaders, who felt that such close state scrutiny was not ideal for advancing their agenda. But with their legal status as a religious, charitable society, the group could spread its ideas in mosques and other public places without having to receive prior permission. In fact, Muslim Brotherhood leaders openly courted the regime by "routinely seeking official approval of even ordinary activities, such as the renting of a building or the building of a new one" (Kazem 1997: 17–18). For its part, the regime relied on the Muslim Brotherhood to both counter revolutionarly Leftist and nationalist narratives and to absorb and deflate more radical Islamist trends. The group thus found a way to negotiate activities and practices that were acceptable to government officials without compromising its own objectives. In a newspaper column published in 1972 in the then government-owned *Al-Ra'i*, Farhan (a minister at the time) wrote, "The Muslim Brotherhood has never been a political organization and has consistently respected the authority of the rule of the Hashemite family, who descended from the Prophet Muhammad, peace be upon him. ... The [Muslim Brotherhood] is working for the same goals [as the government]: to promote an Islamic way of life through education and the improvement of social conditions for all Jordanians."[7]

Both the Muslim Brotherhood and the regime have benefited by framing the activities of the Muslim Brotherhood as primarily nonpolitical. The government allowed an ally to operate while maintaining its opposition to political parties; the Muslim Brotherhood could promote its social reforms in a state-sanctioned sphere devoid of other legal political actors. In large part, the group's leaders sought to promote their reforms through education and healthcare while avoiding talk of the relegalization of political parties. In fact, a return to multiparty politics would likely have undermined the Muslim Brotherhood's privileged position as the only nonstate organization with access to high levels of political power. The Muslim Brotherhood–regime relationship was not without tension, however. The Islamist group was stridently opposed to establishing ties with western states and Israel, and it promoted *shari'ah* as the only legitimate reference point for legal and legislative matters. The group also opposed reaching any compromise with Israel, advocating full liberation of all Palestinian lands west of the Jordan River. The regime, however, engaged in ongoing relations with Israel and the United States (Nevo and Pappé 1994; Susser 2000),[8] which the Muslim Brotherhood consistently condemned. On such occasions, the group usually took the opportunity to also call for reform according to *shari'ah* (Kazem 1997: 18).

With Jordan's loss of the West Bank in the 1967 war and the 1970 Black September uprising in East Bank Palestinian refugee camps, public political debate by the early 1970s no longer focused on a return to the multiparty politics of the 1950s. The most powerful political actors – the

---

[7] *Al-Ra'i*, August 16, 1972.
[8] As Shlaim documents, Jordanian relations with Zionists predated the establishment of the state of Israel in 1948 (Shlaim 1988, 1998).

royal family, the loyalist members of the nonpluralist assemblies, and the Muslim Brotherhood – had simply stopped framing their programs and activities in the terms of pluralist electoral politics that flourished in the 1950s. In a draft internal document of the Muslim Brotherhood dated February 18, 1971, just five months after Black September, the group articulated its agenda in a form very similar to that of its post-1989 program, but without reference to domestic political contestation of any type.[9] Primary objectives included, "Spreading the Islamic faith in society, and reviving the faith of Muslims to restore the original spirit of Islam . . . promoting education and literacy . . . working to improve standards of living and health care . . . promoting national unity and protecting the nation's resources. . . ."[10]

The program, which apparently was never published, noticeably lacked the reference to electoral practices and representative politics that appeared in Muslim Brotherhood documents and newspapers in the 1950s.[11] Instead, they focused on such strategies for achieving these goals as the publication of a diverse range of materials, the establishment of social, educational, vocational, economic, and scientific institutions, and the construction of mosques, schools, medical centers, and clubs.[12] Islamist groups throughout the Middle East increasingly characterize these strategies as the promotion of civil society – a discursive shift from the writings of Muslim Brotherhood founder al-Banna (e.g., see 1979), who opposed democracy as un-Islamic – to present their activities in a language that has in recent years gained currency in the region as well as globally. In Cairo, sociologist Saad Eddin Ibrahim founded an institute called the Ibn Khaldoun Center for Civil Society and the Study of Democratic Development in the early 1990s, which publishes a monthly newsletter along with periodical books. In Amman, the New Jordan Research Center has funded and published numerous studies on civil society in the Middle East, including translations of English-language materials into Arabic.

From the 1970s through the early 1980s, then, calls for a return to national democratic elections in Jordan were not only infrequent but they were clearly taboo. If the regime did not want to talk about a return to

---

[9] The 1971 document does, however, continue to prioritize the liberation of Palestine – a decidedly political issue – even though the group had not supported the Palestinian militants in 1970 during their standoff with the Jordanian government.

[10] "Ahdaf al-Jama'at al-Ikhwan al-Muslimun," February 18, 1971.

[11] For example, see the series on elections in *Al-Kifah al-Islami*, March 1957.

[12] Also see Norton (1995–6), Schwedler (1995), and Browers (2006).

electoral politics, any actor who did so risked provoking the regime. But by 1983, King Hussein began talking about the importance of a nationally elected representative assembly and then called for bielections to fill seats from the 1967 assembly that had been vacated due to resignations and deaths. Public space for political debate incrementally expanded, even though the country remained under martial law. By the time the regime held bielections in 1984, it recognized a need to revamp the assembly in light of Jordan's immanent renunciation of authority over the West Bank, a move formalized in 1988. The populist Islamist Shubaylat had garnered a strong following and displaced an incumbent from the prominent Hadid family in 1984. His popularity rests in part on the ability to appeal to a range of narratives, from criticism of corruption and the lack of open political participation in Jordan to populist and Islamist rhetoric. These tentative discussions concerning electoral participation slowly began to reshape public political debate, though they did not become prominent until late spring 1989, when King Hussein announced the November 1989 elections and began speaking of a full-blown democratic transition. In the fall, calls for increased political freedoms and expanded political participation dominated many of the campaigns (Lynch 1999: 106–7). For its part, the regime sought to demonstrate its commitment to democratization through the establishment of local branches of the Arab Organization for Human Rights and Amnesty International, and by lending royal patronage to the Center for Freedom, Democracy, and Human Rights Studies (Brynen 1998: 76). The National Charter codified political freedoms and the regime's democracy narrative, but always within the context of bolstering the regime's power.

Throughout this period – from the suspension of debate about electoral politics in the late 1950s, through the introduction of martial law in 1967 and the expansion of space for public political debate in the early 1980s – other narratives also waxed and waned within Jordan's public political spaces. In addition to Islam (examined in the following text), Arab nationalist and socialist narratives gained followings throughout the region, though far more so in states where political leaders embraced these narratives (e.g., Egypt, Syria, and Yemen) than in monarchies that saw them as threatening (e.g., Jordan, Morocco, Kuwait, Saudi Arabia, and the United Arab Emirates). As Barnett argues, Arab political leaders in the early twentieth century were largely forced to address the narrative of Arab nationalism, as many states in the region sought and won (sometimes only through violent struggle, as in Algeria) their independence from foreign control (1998). While monarchies tended to appeal to the more

general populist notion of Arab unity, they shunned the nationalist debate
and instead emphasized various dimensions of the monarch's right to rule.
In Jordan, this narrative played out in terms of emphasizing not only the
king's descent from the prophet Muhammad, but also his commitment
to the welfare of the Jordanian people. As part of a sustained effort to
construct a single Jordanian national identity, the narrative of the monarchy's authority and benevolence seeks to obscure both the monarchy's
debt to British colonial powers in establishing its rule and the fact that,
as a unified entity, Jordan has no historical memory before the twentieth
century. The mechanisms of the construction of this narrative of national
identity have been closely examined by Layne (1994), Brand (1995a),
Lynch (1999), Massad (2001), and Katz (2004). At the same time, this
regime-led narrative sought to minimize, even deny the implications of a
presence of a (since 1967) majority Palestinian population. Here the question is not whether the so-called Palestinian-Jordanian divide is or is not
politically significant, but the extent to which the ruling family has sought
to exclude debates about this divide from public political discourse while
effectively engaging in practices that continually reinforce this cleavage.
Putting the "ethnic divide" issue on the agenda has meant challenging the
political elites' efforts to exclude it. The government's efforts to stop this
debate have been largely unsuccessful, making the extent and vigor of the
efforts all the more noteworthy. As Lynch notes, the regime's framing of
the political opening as democratization, including elections and engaged
debate about public freedoms and popular participation, had the effect
of entrenching "the norm of democracy as central to regime legitimacy"
(1999: 107).

Narratives of Democracy and National Unity in Yemen

Unlike Jordan, Yemen has had very limited historical experience with
pluralist, electoral, or democratic processes and representative institutions. As described in Chapter 2, united Yemen's initial foray into political
liberalization was the outcome of secret negotiations between the presidents of North and South Yemen to facilitate the 1990 unification. With
the republican victory against the royal family and the rise of a military
regime in North Yemen in the 1960s, the urban-based republican narrative was rather less dominant nationwide than the one that characterized
the landscape of engagement with state institutions of power in Jordan.
This was due in large part to the relatively decentralized nature of political authority in North Yemen, despite the formal allegiance of a range

of powerful actors to the revolutionary regime. The GPC, the national assembly created in North Yemen in the mid-1980s, did not introduce meaningful debate about democratization. The National Charter adopted by the GPC in 1982 prioritized "building an enlightened, powerful, democratic, central state" over the secondary goal of "realizing the principle of participation at the local level."[13] Despite the reference to democracy, meaningful representation was clearly of far less of a concern than building a strong centralized state, one that could exert sovereignty over even powerful tribal regions.[14] Thus, although the assembly was built in part "as a promised means for local voices to be heard at a national level" (Dresch 2000: 159), in practice the GPC did little more than institutionalize President Salih's patronage network and extend prizes to local allies. President Salih called for 70 percent of the seats to be filled through elections, but he did not engage in a political narrative about democracy in a substantive or sustained manner.

In South Yemen, the dominant frame of socialist development was largely restricted to the port city of Aden, while the public spaces of significant lands to the east – notably the dozens of villages in and beyond the relatively isolated Hadramawt valley – were for all practical purposes entirely cut off from these political debates. Discussion of democratization was virtually absent through 1986, with the ruling YSP suffering from conflict among internal factions that left a huge portion of the Politbureau dead in January 1986. One YSP leader, Jar Allah 'Umar, repeatedly tried in the aftermath of the bloodbath to open debate about implementing political pluralism (*ta'addudiyyah siyasiyah*) through his conversations with surviving party officials and particularly in a paper he authored that was circulated within the party. Again in a lengthy memorandum to the party secretary in spring 1989, he argued that pluralism was desperately needed because "the working class here is quantitatively and qualitatively weak" (Dresch 2000: 172). His call for democratization went unrealized for more than a decade, but when President al-Bid agreed secretly with President Salih to push forward with Yemeni unification, YSP leaders endorsed the union only on the condition that the new state would be democratic. If only in this respect, the aftermath of the bloody events of 1986 changed the possibilities for political debate and brought the beginning of a narrative about the need for pluralism and democratization.

---

[13] "Al-Mithaq al-Watani," translated in Dresch (2000: 156).
[14] Even today, the Yemeni government does not effectively exercise full authority over all of Yemen.

Unlike Jordan, North and South Yemen each lacked a single dominant national political narrative before unification. First, the land and
distribution of the population created obstacles to the creation of such a
narrative: 79 percent of Jordan's 5.4 million citizens live in urban centers,
with more than half the population located in metropolitan Amman. By
comparison, only 26 percent of united Yemen's 19.7 million citizens live
in urban centers (United Nations Development Program 2005). Shared
experiences resulting from living in proximity tend to produce, minimally, an awareness of other narratives and often engagement with them,
if only through the articulation of a counternarrative. Even after unification, most Yemenis continued to live in small rural villages, remote
in terms both of physical distance and of isolation from the political
debates that play out in capital urban centers. Second, Yemeni society
in general, but rural villages in particular, continue to be dominated not
by the infrastructure of centralized state institutions, but by a mix of
tribal structures, extended kinship units, and patronage networks that
have historically formed the basic social and political blocks experi-
enced by most of the population. This situation is changing, but not
at a rapid pace, and President Salih's regime does not exercise effective authority over the whole of Yemen. As a result, Yemeni society has
been marked less by a discernable dominant national political narrative,
particularly prior to unification, than has been Jordanian society. As we
shall see in the following text, these structural differences have significant
implications for the positioning of political actors vis-à-vis state sites of
power.

By 1990 democratization had emerged as one of the main facets of
Yemeni unification, but other themes circulated within various publics. A
narrative about national unity, for example, dominated public political
debate. Democracy was seen to be necessary not on its own merit, but
as a mechanism to guarantee the success of unification. Only certain YSP
leaders sought to push issues of democracy and pluralism to the front
of the national political agenda. At the same time, questions arose about
other power structures and their compatibility with unification and democratic processes. In this regard, the role of various tribal elites proved a
point of contention between the leaders of the North and South. To be
sure, stretches of both North and South Yemen were, to varying degrees,
dominated politically, economically, and socially by tribal and extended
kinship structures. The presence of tribes (sing. *qabil*) in Yemen has contributed to the idea that the country is "traditional" and (by implication)
somehow less than modern. But only about 25 percent of Yemenis are

tribal in any meaningful sense, and tribal units now most often serve to protect real estate and resources (Dresch 2000: 159–60).

The use and abuse of tribes as well as narratives about tribal power (not to mention violent conflicts between well-armed groups) have come to be seen as an obstacle to further democratization. With unification, for example, President Salih promoted retribalization as a tool to weaken the support bases of the YSP and extend his own patronage network. As journalist 'Abd Bari Tahir wrote in the Leftist newspaper *Al-Thawri*, "In Yemen, the government, people, parties, and even the press all endeavor to develop tribal or pseudo tribal affiliation.... After unification, [the government] began a policy aimed at the restoration of tribalism. The state turned into a tribe and the shaykh's authority began to eclipse any other authority...crimes are increasingly being channeled through the tribal system...[which has] given more prestige and power to the shaykhs at the expense of the civilian authorities...."[15] The narrative of democracy in Yemen must therefore be situated at the center of complex power struggles between diverse actors rather than as a set of core values about political participation (as some YSP leaders hoped).

Particularly as the 1993 elections approached, prominent candidates and parties were forced to negotiate their strategies within publics characterized by complex, sensitive issues, and sometimes conflicting narratives, including democracy, tribalism, national unity, and Islam (Table 4.2). In the main urban centers and particularly at *qat chews* (sing. *takhzin*), Yemenis gathered to debate these issues.[16] Even many of the most optimistic political observers recognized that real lines were not drawn over whether or not one supported democracy and/or unification, but over the eventual distribution of power with regards to the new institutional arrangements. In this regard, the elevation of an Islamist narrative emerged as a crucial political resource for the northern political elite.

The Narrative of Islam in Jordan and Yemen

Talk of Islam is interwoven into political narratives in Jordan and Yemen in complicated ways. Both societies are predominantly Muslim, with

---

[15] November 3, 1993.
[16] A qat "chew" (*takhzin*, literally "storage" because the chewed qat is stored in the chewer's cheek) is a gathering at which people chew fresh qat leaves for their mild stimulant effect. Chews are highly social events with, frequently, political importance as diverse actors meet and discuss various issues of common concern from land rights to electoral candidates to marriage arrangements to the negative effects of chewing qat.

TABLE 4.2. *Themes in Elections Platforms in Yemen, 1993*

	Democracy	Tribalism	National Unity	Islam
GPC	"... adheres to ... democracy based on the multi-party system ... the constitution, constitutional legitimacy, and the peaceful transfer of power...." "... pledges to the Yemeni people that it will do its utmost to achieve more democratic accomplishments...."	"... focuses its concern on the extended family as an essential core of society...."	"... a primary objective is to assure national unity...."	"... affirms its full adherence to the principles that are loyal to Almighty God ... adheres to Islam as a faith and shari'ah as a source of law...."
YSP	"... declares its main objective to be the promotion of national unity and democracy and to realize social justice...."	"... to find a solution to the problem of tribal power and the resulting anarchy...."	"... declares its main objective to be the promotion of national unity...."	"... wishes to see the creation of an Islamic university...."
Islah	"... committed to promoting democracy as a means to realize the freedoms guaranteed by shari'ah...." "... peaceful alternation of power through free and fair elections...."	"... the preservation of the family...." *Note:* no mention of extended family units	"... committed to opposing all threats to national unity...."	"... Islam provides the basis for all aspects of life...." "... reform the constitution in light of shari'ah, which must be the source of all legislation...." "... close the Aden brewery," which constitutes a "challenge to God's law...." "... creation of additional schools for Islamic learning...."

approximately 95 percent of Jordanians and virtually all Yemenis identifying as Islamic.[17] The constitutions of both countries define their nations
as Islamic, with *shari'ah* described as one of the main sources (Jordan) and
the main source (Yemen) for guiding state governance.[18] Political leaders in each state make public shows of their piousness, praying during
holidays and tense political moments. These performances of worship
are displayed nationally on televised broadcasts and promoted in state-
owned print media. How are Islamic narratives politically consequential? In Jordan, the Hashemite monarchy also suggests that its authority
to rule derives in part because descends from the family of the prophet
Muhammad. The Hashemites are a member of the Qurayshi tribe and
descend from the male bloodline of Hassan, grandson of Muhammad, and
likewise ruled Mecca and Medina (and thus the holiest sites in Islam) for
more than seven centuries (1205 to 1925).[19] King Hussein also appealed to
an Islamic narrative in presenting an image as the keeper of the two Islamic
holy sites of Jerusalem, the Dome of the Rock and Al-Aqsa Mosque,
where Sharif Hussein ('Abd Allah II's great-great-grandfather) is buried
and where King 'Abd Allah I was assassinated in 1951. This imagery was
represented in national textbooks and on stamps and coins (Katz 2004),
in print and broadcast media (Lynch 1999), and at an elaborate perma-
nent exhibition at the King 'Abd Allah Islamic Center in Amman (Katz
2004) that emphasizes the monetary contributions of the regime to the
restoration of the Islamic holy sites in Jerusalem. As argued in Chapter 2, King Hussein also used a narrative of Islam politically in an attempt
to weaken opposition to the regime by framing Islam as an authentic
expression of Jordanian identity against the spread of Arab nationalist,
socialist, and communist movements during the 1950s and 1960s. The
Muslim Brotherhood thrived during those periods, providing support for
the regime as the government faced crises as diverse as the challenge by
Leftists and nationalists in the 1950s and within the Palestinian camps in
Black September in 1970. Yusef al-'Azm, a prominent Muslim Brotherhood figure during those periods, appealed to the Islamic legitimacy of the
regime in an interview with the government-owned *Al-Dustur* newspaper
on October 13, 1970, just weeks after the Black September standoff: "His

[17] Perhaps a few hundred Yemeni Christians and a thousand Jews remain (latter primarily
    in the northern city of Sa'da), but in a population of more than 19.7 million, they are
    statistically insignificant.
[18] The struggles over the wording of each constitution concerning the status of *shari'ah* are
    discussed in detail in the following text.
[19] The Hashimites lost control of Medina just prior to World War I.

majesty King Hussein, descendant of the Prophet Muhammad, peace be upon him, stands at the vanguard of the struggle against the illegitimate Zionist occupation of Palestinian and the Islamic holy places there." Al-'Azm portrayed the regime as both leader of a Muslim community and an advocate for Palestinians. This discursive feat required some creative maneuvering, as the regime had just taken up arms against a Palestinian movement whose primary objective was to liberate occupied Palestinian lands.

Nevertheless, King Hussein continued his periodic appeals to Islam. By appointing several prominent Muslim Brotherhood leaders to powerful positions within the Ministry of Education in the late 1960s and 1970s, he encouraged the spread of Islamic imagery through the national curriculum (Antoun 1993). Over the course of his career, he frequently referenced Islam in his public statements and sought to utilize Islamic symbols to bolster his rule, by appealing to mobilized political groups (e.g., the Muslim Brotherhood) as well as by invoking a language that the wider Jordanian citizenry will find comprehensible. In the early 1980s, for example, the regime spearheaded an effort to have new constructions in Amman, particularly mosques and government buildings, adhere to Islamic and Arab architectural lines. As Boulby argues, "by identifying itself with Islamic tradition, the monarchy sought to capture the Islamic revival so that it would not be channeled into political opposition" (1999: 98). At an awards ceremony in Amman for the Aga Khan Award for Architecture, King Hussein said, "We live in the historic centre of the Muslim world, and are keenly aware of the need to associate our sense of identity with the best that Islamic history and tradition have to offer" (cited in Boulby 1999: 98).

In 1993 comments about the status of Jerusalem, King Hussein said, "We Hashemites have borne a special historic honor through our distinctive connection with Jerusalem. For it is the site where Allah took his Prophet for a journey by night.[20] And the site is the resting place of Hussein I. The soil of Al Aqsa Mosque has been moistened by the blood of my martyred grandfather, founder of the Kingdom 'Abd Allah bin al-Hussein."[21] Hussein made this statement as he was negotiating the

---

[20] The Qur'an tells of the prophet Muhammad being transported to heaven during the famous "night journey"; the point of departure from Earth was the rock under the Dome of the Rock in Jerusalem, also by tradition the rock on which Abrahim (Ibrahim) was to sacrifice his son.

[21] Hussein (1994: 91). For additional background on the Hashemite dynasty's claims to legitimacy based on Islam, see Katz (2004).

provisions of the Israeli-Jordanian treaty that would be signed in October 1994.

At the same time, the regime has sought to control the framing of the Islamic narrative in the country's network of mosques. The imams who lead the prayers at each mosque are appointed and tightly controlled by the Ministry of Religious Affairs and Endowments. Muslim Brotherhood and other nonsanctioned speakers often give sermons (sing. *khutba*) in defiance of state control, and the regime closely monitors what is said. On occasion certain individuals have been banned from addressing assembled worshipers, particularly during the Friday noon prayer, and Muslim Brotherhood members have not been exempt from this targeting. When the regime was negotiating a peace treaty with Israel in 1994, for example, Muslim Brotherhood deputy Abu Zant was allegedly assaulted by police after forcefully condemning the treaty in a sermon. Wiktorowicz reports that subsequent to the altercation, Abu Zant "went on a tirade in parliament, charging that preachers appointed by the ministry were imploring God to be merciful to the Israelis..." (2001: 61–2), which (if true) illustrates how the regime utilizes Islamic spaces to promote its political agenda while seeking to prevent open political debate in those publics. The regime also appoints the preeminent Islamic scholar (*mufti*) of Jordan. This figure ostensibly issues religious opinions (sing. *fatwa*) independent of state influence, but in practice he consistently supports state policy. In response to the broad-based boycott of the 1997 elections, for example, Mufti Sa'ad al-Hijawi issued a *fatwa* invoking the principle of public interest (*maslaha mursalah*) to compel Jordanian citizens to vote.[22] Outside this sphere of officially sanctioned Islamic voices, the regime seeks to control the Islamic narrative by regulating independent Islamic social organizations and establishing a network of some two dozen Islamic cultural centers under the direct management of the Ministry of Religious Affairs and Endowments (Dabbas 1997: 193–259). One requirement of teachers at these Islamic centers, for example, is that they not be affiliated with any political party, a move that has sharply restricted Muslim Brotherhood and Salafi influence in lessons.

By comparison, Yemeni political elite are more cautious about appealing directly to Islam because it reminds of the Imamate that ruled Yemen in the name of Islam until the 1962 revolution. Northern leaders have strongly promoted Islamization since unification, however, and conservative dress has become commonplace in Aden, where as recently as

---

[22] *The Jordan Times*, October 26, 1997.

1995 women were routinely seen wearing western fashions. British colonial authority did not embrace Islam, though it put forth few if any real efforts to secularize southerners. The eastern regions of Hadramawt and Maharah remained religious and conservative throughout the colonial period, but both were well outside of the Aden-based British authority. With the departure of the British from South Yemen in the 1960s, the new socialist leaders sought to reshape social organizations in such a way as to displace tribal and Islamic authority with a secular socialism as the dominant political ideology. The initial strategy was not so much to criticize Islam as to minimize its role and turn it to the service of the socialist state. As Dresch argues, "The state in the South had treated Islam as a feeble, rather distant case of socialist reform and turned it solely to the ends of nationalism. A textbook on religious education for the fourth year of secondary schools, for instance, begins with 'general conscription and defense of the homeland,' for 'love of country,' according to a Tradition [of the Prophet Muhammad] quoted, 'is part of godliness.' Islam had aimed to free humanity from slavery, says the text, and the chapters jump directly from the conquest of Mecca to the nineteenth century…" (2000: 172). Despite these efforts, an Islamic narrative began to reemerge in public spaces by the 1980s. The governing board of Aden University, for example, tried in 1985 to ban Islamic dress, which had begun to reappear along with various Islamist groups and the discussion of Islamist ideologies (Dresch 2000: 173). These efforts to suppress an Islamic narrative appear to have been only superficially successful, given the rapid pace and extent to which both Islam and tribalism have resurfaced in the South since unification. Thus while Islamic narratives were diminished under socialist rule, they were never entirely absent.

In the North, by comparison, Islam had a much different history vis-à-vis the political elite. Prior to the 1962 revolution, North Yemen was governed by an Imamate, a hereditary dynasty that ruled in the name of Islam but paid little attention to the welfare of the Muslim community (*ummah*). Parts of the North's strong tribal structures were linked to Zaydi authority, though the two should not be conflated.[23] The revolution was made not so much in the name of secular authority over religious authority, but as a populist republic over an exclusionary and hereditary monarchy. Indeed, among the supporters of the revolution were members of diverse Islamist groups, including scattered followers of a conservative

---

[23] For a detailed examination of this dimension of tribalism in North Yemen, see Dresch 1989.

Wahhabi Islam (compliments of Saudi influence), the small and loosely organized Muslim Brotherhood, traditional Zaydi Islamic notables with tribal links (sing. *sayyid*), and a handful of prominent figures with small personal followings. But in significant contrast to Jordan, descent from the prophet's family became not a resource but a political liability in the postrevolutionary North because it echoed the claims made by the Yemeni Imamate.

Nevertheless, while the new northern republic did not claim the moral right to rule in the name of Islam, neither did it seek to suppress Islamic imagery as had the southern political elite. Indeed, the military regime of the postrevolutionary North was strongly supported by a number of prominent Islamists. Some of these took up arms to defend the regime from southern-based rebels in the 1970s and eventually formed the Islamic Front in 1979 that fought against the NDF. Steady and substantial Saudi funding further facilitated the growth of both conservative and radical Islamist groups as a means of challenging the Left. When al-Zindani was appointed Minister of Education in 1973, he set up a series of Islamist scientific institutes (sing. *ma'hid 'ilmi*) that taught a highly conservative and (particularly beginning in the 1990s) increasingly radical, Salafi-influenced version of Islam. Although he upset so many people that he was removed from his post after only a short time and subsequently left the country for Saudi Arabia, his institutes continued to flourish in part due to continued Saudi funding. Dresch reports that by 1987 there were some 1,126 of these religious schools, which claimed 118,000 students the following year (2000: 173).

President Salih further encouraged Islamist movements, portraying them as fully compatible with the National Charter of 1982. Presidential Decree No. 61 of 1986 reads, "The national slogan of the YAR shall be as follows: *God, The Nation, The Revolution.* The text and spirit of this slogan must be adhered to in the order and arrangement mentioned, to deepen faith in God and strengthen loyalty to the nation and revolution."[24] As noted in Chapter 3, the Yemeni Muslim Brotherhood began publishing *Al-Sahwah* in 1985, also with the blessing of the regime. Thus through official slogans, the establishment of Islamic institutes, the Islamicization of public school curricula, and the publication of Islamist periodicals (where few alternatives existed) combined with other factors to ensure a strong basis for an Islamist narrative in diverse public spaces since at least 1973.

[24] Translated and cited in Dresch (2000: 174).

Within this context (of regime-Islamist cooperation in the North and regime-Islamist tensions in the South), postunification politics entailed, in part, a struggle over an Islamic narrative that presented particular moral frameworks as more authentic (i.e., locally generated rather than imported through foreign intervention) and appropriate to Yemeni society. YSP leaders responded by weaving socialist ideas into conformity with the symbols and narratives of both Islam and national unity. The provisional constitution formally characterized the unified Republic of Yemen (ROY) as Islamic,[25] and Islah emerged from the 1993 elections as a powerful "third" party. Given the resonance of Islam in the vast majority of unified Yemen, the YSP and other Leftist groups sought to distance themselves from the atheism of Leftist movements elsewhere and increasingly portrayed themselves as *Muslim* socialists. Some even began to regularly attend the Friday prayer in their local mosque. In a statement issued following a meeting of the YSP's general congress in June 1991, YSP Secretary-General (and Yemeni Vice-Chair of the Presidential Council) al-Bid explained the efforts to establish a new ideological base for the party, "These documents are the fruits of our long struggle, and they are based on a series of reviews of the theoretical and practical underpinnings of our party. We intend to overcome any form of intellectual stagnation." This new orientation reframed the YSP's objectives for promoting social equality partially in Islamic terms. For example, the first of the new tenets of the party were these four items, in order (emphasis added):

- To struggle for the sovereignty of the nation, to protect national unity, oppose secessionism, sectarianism, localism, and parochialism and any other factors that might destroy the unity of the nation and the people.
- To work for the achievement of a comprehensive and balanced socio-economic development, and for the construction of a modern national economy.
- To draw from *the teachings, values, and morals of our Islamic Faith* all the constituents of our struggle to help the weak, to achieve justice and equality, to push towards knowledge and work, and to confront oppression and tyranny. All this is to be achieved by *our strict adherence to the Islamic faith* and its sublime foundations and objectives, as *Islam is a force for progress, brotherhood, and equality.*
- To solidly stand by democratic values in the organization of political life....[26]

---

[25] Article 1.
[26] Document translated in *The Yemen Times*, June 8, 1991.

The ordering of these agenda items – national unity, economic reform, Islamic faith, and finally democracy – marks a significant departure from earlier YSP platforms, which made minimal mention of Islam. In this regard, the party's reframing of its objectives following unity demonstrates its recognition that an Islamic narrative circulated powerfully within various public spaces and, consequently, could not be ignored or dismissed. The YSP sought to thwart criticism that the party was not committed to the Islamic faith.

The political significance of these Islamic narratives in Jordan and Yemen plays out in another way: political elites often engage an Islamic narrative, but they also seek to keep the power of potential political challengers – notably Islamists – in check. In this regard, the ruling regimes are careful in their portral of Islamist groups, even those that may be longtime allies. These political elites may want to draw on "Islam" as a powerful idea while not paving the way for Islamist groups to usurp their power base or fundamentally challenge the existing hierarchies of power on which one's rule rests. In an effort to discredit challengers, state leaders can portray Leftist and secularist groups as foreign agents, but directly criticizing Islamist groups can be much trickier, particularly when a regime claims authority to rule at least in part on historical Islamic "credentials" and/or appeals to a narrative of Islam in speeches and official documents. For example, regimes characterize Leftist groups as foreign imports or colonial relics, and thus less locally authentic. By defining certain groups as outside of "legitimate" debate, the ruling elite attempt to exclude certain political challengers. Regime leaders seek to exclude other groups by framing them as outside the realm of legitimate politics due to their ties to "foreign" or "pan-national" organizations – and thus less loyal to the nation. The political elite may draw yet another line by adopting a narrative of democracy in tandem with strategic liberalization processes.

Within a narrative of democratic political contestation, however, regime leaders must also allow for some "democratic" competition, typically pluralist competition in elections even when the elected assemblies play a minimal role in actual governance. As the electoral manipulation in Jordan and Yemen illustrates, the political elite go to great lengths to engineer electoral outcomes that produce proregime majorities while leaving opposition groups with modest (and manageable) levels of representation. At the same time, they may strongly support an Islamic narrative while characterizing particular individuals or trends within Islamist parties as extremist and thus outside the boundary of legitimate political contestation. Since its creation in 1990, for example, Islah has been often described as a fundamentalist Islamist party, one that threatens Yemen's pluralist social and political vision, the country's incipient transition to democracy, and, by connection, the very stability of the nation. As Dresch and Haykel note, these characterizations are typical not only of the foreign press, but of accounts in the Arab and Yemeni press as well (1995: 405–9). Prominent government officials have also criticized Islah as radical, despite the closeness of Islah and the GPC. One GPC minister told me (in English), "Islah's leaders want you to think they are moderate and progressive, that's why they arrange for you to meet [Muhammad] al-Yadumi and Nasr Taha [Mustafa] and ['Abd al-Wahhab] al-Anisi. These aren't the hard-liners, they wear suits and shake your hand and will speak with you as long as you like. But they aren't the ones who pull the strings. You met al-Akwa, right? He's not even really with the party. And did you ask to meet Daylami, what did they tell you? Or Zindani? He refused to meet you, right? This is the true side of Islah, don't be fooled by their clever tactics. If they gain power their whole story will change."[27] This portrayal of Islah, although directed at me as a western female researcher, is not atypical. At the same time, the GPC has worked consistently to incorporate former Islamists. Among the more prominent is Tariq al-Fadli, who spent time training in Afghanistan, but won a parliamentary seat in 1993 as a GPC candidate. By the late 1990s, even a few former Islah members, such as Nasr Taha Mustafa and Faris Saqqaf, had either joined the GPC ranks or become closely associated with the regime.

Similar portrayals of Islamists can be seen in Jordan. When members of the Muslim Brotherhood were given five cabinet positions in Badran's cabinet reshuffle in late 1990, these Islamists had their first chance since liberalization at implementing some of Muslim Brotherhood programs through their control of certain ministries. As the regime expected, the group also found itself under increased public scrutiny. Muslim Brotherhood ministers sought to implement many reforms, but certain of them were held up by the independent and government-owned media alike as illustrative of how radical and out of touch with society at large these Islamists "really" are. For example, the Muslim Brotherhood made a list of demands on the government in exchange for accepting the cabinet positions, including a ban on alcohol sales, a ban on alcohol served on all Royal Jordanian flights, and segregation of sexes in schools.[28] As

---

[27] Interview with author, April 26, 1997, San'a, name withheld by request.
[28] For a summary, see Gharaybah (1997a: 49–50).

noted in the preceding text, one of the new measures that raised the strongest objections was a ban on fathers and male family members watching young girls (and thus their daughters) compete in gymnastic competitions. The incident was remarkable not only for the level of public outrage against the ban, but for the extent to which it continues to be mentioned a decade later as an example of the kinds of radical measures Islamists secretly plan to implement as soon as the opportunity arises. Some leaders in the group, like Farhan, argue that the policies were not necessarily bad ideas, but were poorly thought out: "We tried to accomplish too much too quickly. Critics were looking for something to challenge us on, and the media participated in characterizing us as out of touch with modern society. In fact, we implemented lots of policies that are still in place, and no one credits us for them.... We have learned to move more slowly, and to make sure there is public education about the goals of our policies."[29]

As in Yemen, government officials participated in characterizing the Muslim Brotherhood ministers as radical. The former Prime Minister Tahir al-Masri is typical: "They [the Muslim Brotherhood] were given a chance and they showed their true colors. Jordanians do not want them in power. Some are attracted to their rhetoric about authenticity and an ideal Islamic society, but when [the Muslim Brotherhood ministers] put forth their policies, the public was outraged."[30]

SUMMARY

Powerful narratives create opportunities as well as constraints for a whole spectrum of political actors. These narratives are given greater or lesser force in part due to the decision of the ruling elite to engage in particular narratives, but also due to the response of other political actors. Within various publics, competing narratives emerge, circulate, are subject to challenge, become dominant, or fall into disuse. These narratives can structure political actions in ways that are equally if not more constraining than institutions, and thus may be critical factors in explaining how inclusion may produce moderation. In this regard, ideological change may result not from participation in pluralist processes per se, but from engaging with multiple narratives. Even so, the key puzzle remains: Why do two groups participating in similar pluralist processes and engaging in similar

---

[29] Interview with author, March 31, 1997, Amman.
[30] Interview with author, February 9, 1997, Amman.

narratives not become more moderate in the same way? To explain this final dimension of moderation, I combine the two structural dimensions – new political opportunities resulting from political openings and internal group dynamics (including structure and decision-making practices) – with an ideational dimension, linking public political narratives with the evolution of ideology through internal party debates.

5

Justification and Moderation

Central to the inclusion-moderation hypothesis is the idea that when given the opportunity to participate in pluralist, democratic processes, political actors will, through some combination of experience, constraint, and learning, come to see the logic of continued participation. As a result, they will also become more moderate as they embrace democratic norms and practices. As argued in Chapter 1, this basic idea has a long history in a wide range of scholarly literature. But the lack of empirical evidence and a clearly specified mechanism for change seems discouraging for the inclusion-moderation hypothesis. Groups facing similar institutional constraints and incentives, for example, may not all become more moderate. Even more, how can we resolve the paradox of democracy, that is, identify when a group is feigning moderation and when it has become truly committed to democratic and pluralist practices? In this chapter, I present a framework for explaining why similar actors participating in similar processes will not necessarily become moderate, or moderate in the same way. Contrary to much of the literature, the institutional constraints of political openings are not a sufficient mechanism to produce moderation. And contrary to the literature on political learning, the accumulation of experiences does not tell us why some actors become moderate and others, gaining the same experience, do not. While I do not dispute the importance of these mechanisms, I focus on identifying changing boundaries of justifiable action and their implications for moderation. I begin by conceptualizing the boundaries of justifiable action for particular political actors and the mechanisms that can lead to a redrawing of these boundaries that is far more complex than the mere "opening" of the political system. I then illustrate the interconnectedness of the dimensions of public political space and various narratives explored in the preceding text. Finally, I explore how these processes play out differently for the IAF in Jordan and the Islah party in Yemen.

BOUNDARIES OF JUSTIFIABLE ACTIONS

As argued in Chapter 4, a cultural field is characterized not only by multiple narratives, but by the boundaries of what can be imagined by various political actors. Within any given context, a political actor's perceptions of possibilities will shape her actions and agendas. As Callon argues, an actor's "objectives, interests, will, and thus identity are caught up in a process of continual reconfiguration, a process that is intimately related to the constant reconfiguration of the network of interactions in which he or she is involved" (1998b: 253). This means that through practice – as political actors set agendas, engage narratives, interact with others, and seek to take advantage of new political opportunities – they construct boundaries of acceptable practices, conceptual frames within which they act to realize their objectives. As Lynch argues, "the process of formulating justifications in the public sphere, and of articulating the relationship between identity and interests, establishes the meaning and range of legitimate action" (1999: 21). Within the realm of available political strategies, all actors will not be able to justify all courses of action in terms of their own worldview.

I have suggested a dynamic approach to exploring questions of moderation, one that seeks to identify interactive effects of changes in one dimension of public political space on other dimensions. In a continuously reconstructed political space, changes in one area act as mechanisms for change elsewhere. As argued, the introduction of new political opportunity structures (e.g., participatory political processes and a liberalized sphere of political debate) can compel groups to reorganize to take advantage of these openings. At the same time, these reorganizational efforts reconfigure the contours of the political space, particularly as multiple groups emerge. *These mechanisms are causal*, but they are interactive rather than unidirectional or path dependent. They take place within a social context, but the relevant structures are not separate from action and must be considered as more than mere constraints that channel or restrict social action, as much of the literature on transitions and political opportunity structures suggest. Rather, structures are also enabling, and they are both "the *medium* and the *outcome* of social action" (emphasis in original; Sewell 2001: 55). The challenge, then, is to explain how practices (conceived of as meaningful actions) and structures evolve interactively over time, in ways that can result in ideological moderation of specific political actors. Which sorts of mechanisms might produce not just new institutional forms but a moderation in the beliefs, agendas, and commitments of ideological political actors, such as Islamist parties? What sorts of evidence would demonstrate that such a change has actually taken place?

One means of conceptualizing such a transformation is to think in terms of political boundaries: distinctions made by political actors about what is possible, who are friends and adversaries, and which of the available options are justifiable in terms of one's worldview. For all political actors, boundaries create opportunities and constraints in the same ways as institutional changes. The idiom "sleeping with the enemy" illustrates the significance of such ideational boundaries. Actor A, one who has engaged in relations with actor B, is subject to criticism for the sole reason that she has previously identified herself with a specific project or position in which B is implicated as either the problem or an obstacle to its resolution. The content of A's project is of no relevance to the prohibition; what matters is that a process of defining who is excluded from A's group has taken place. Anyone can engage in relations with B, but A cannot justify such relations because of the way she has previously drawn or accepted that boundary.

This example illustrates an interesting effect of boundaries. Rather than creating distance between those political strategies that an actor can and cannot justify, boundaries have the effect of establishing and strengthening relations between those strategies, as well as between the actors and practices that fall on either side of the boundary. That is, there is no specific relationship between A and B until A draws a boundary excluding B. Once A has implicated B as holding some level of responsibility for certain problems within society, the boundary separating them creates a close relationship between the two where none had existed. If enlightened A now "sleeps with" enemy B, the former has crossed a boundary with an action that is seen as either betrayal or hypocrisy. In either case, A's action cannot be justified without rejecting or redrawing the original boundary, or reframing such interactions as necessary for the pursuit of a larger, common objective. This is not to suggest that all boundaries are self-consciously drawn by political actors; new boundaries may emerge as a consequence of taking other decisions and justifying particular courses of action or as a result of shifts in the boundaries of the imaginable. In the aforementioned case, a boundary is explicitly drawn by identifying "them" in juxtaposition to "us." Most significant for this study is the observation that where boundaries have not been explicitly drawn, tensions about what is inside and what is outside of a boundary – that is, what is and what is not justifiable – may emerge only when new developments bring the location of boundaries into question.

Moderation not of political practices but of worldview – from one ideological in its rigidity to one more open and tolerant of alternative views – can be identified through evidence that, for a particular actor, these and other boundaries have been gradually redrawn to include or at least tolerate a wider diversity of actors, practices, and narratives. For all political actors, but particularly for ideological actors, adopting new practices requires that one justify that move in terms of one's core beliefs, goals, and commitments. Choosing to participate in pluralist political practices may make sense strategically, but to be considered within the realm of the possible, one must be able to justify it in terms of one's ideology. This requires internal debates and considerations, the outcomes of which may have the effect of redrawing boundaries, even when those boundaries are not themselves at issue. As Lynch argues, attention to acts of justification identifies not only the claims of particular actors, but the details of the debates reveal the relative power of competing narratives. "[T]he proffered justification represents a potential redeemable validity claim which is judged, accepted, rejected, or contested by other communicatively competent members of the society. . . . Justification and argumentation appeal to the force of the better argument, but what counts as a powerful argument depends on the ability to frame a validity claim in terms of shared norms, identities, and goals" (1999: 41). Even more, Lynch argues, "actors must share a 'will to consensus' or a commitment to maintain the conditions of interaction" (42). When such a will to consensus exists and when justifications are put forth and accepted, the practice entails both an appeal to particular norms, identities, and goals, and an act of restructuring, reinforcing, or rejecting particular narratives. In this sense, accepting pluralist, democratic practices as acceptable on moral grounds may redraw the boundaries of what practices will be justifiable in the future. We, therefore, should be able to establish through empirical investigation precisely when moderation has taken place – that is, when boundaries have been meaningfully redrawn so that a rigid and closed worldview evolves into one more tolerant and open. Attending to this dimension allows us to differentiate between when political actors are merely "playing by the rules of the game" while harboring secret antidemocratic agendas, and when they have meaningfully evolved in ways that can be characterized as moderation.

In the remainder of this chapter, I first briefly explore the question of reconciling Islam and democracy as distinct worldviews. Although this question has received perhaps more attention in the study of Middle East politics than any other in recent years, it remains relevant because it colors much of the debate about the participation of Islamist groups in democratic processes. Then I focus on changing boundaries of justifiable action within each Islamist party as a means of exploring whether ideological moderation has occurred. In particular, I identify the mechanisms that bring about change in various dimensions as well as obstacles that keep change from happening. I focus on the interactive effects of new pluralist political practices, internal group reorganization, and engaging multiple narratives. Changes in any of these dimensions may produce effects in the others that lead to the production of new boundaries of justifiable action.

Reconciling Islam and Democracy

Are Islam and democracy reconcilable? This question has been explored in innumerable books, articles, and conferences for decades throughout the Muslim world as in non-Muslim and western contexts. But what precisely needs to be reconciled? Are they competing ideologies? Many of these debates explore the issue from a theological perspective, asking whether the basic norms and beliefs of Islam as a religion can be reconciled with those of democracy as a system of governance.[1] Other studies examine the diverse practices and experiences of Muslims and Islamists in pluralist political processes, arguing that theoretical and theological debates hold little relevance when Muslim groups have been participating in democratic processes for decades.[2] Many of these debates

---

[1] The literature is truly vast, but some examples of summaries, syntheses, and interpretations of these debates include Binder (1988), Enayat (1988), Jabiri (1990), Esposito and Piscatori (1991), Krämer (1993), Zubaida (1993), Azmeh (1994), 'Ali (1996), Esposito and Voll (1996), Kurzman (1998), Tibi (1998), Moussalli (1999, 2001), Hashmi (2002), Moaddel and Talattof (2002), and Hofman (2004).

[2] For example, see Esposito (1992, 1997), Burgat (1993, 1997), Tamimi (1993), Kilani (1994), Krämer (1994, 1995a), Ma'aytah (1994), Nasr (1994), Roy (1994), Salamé (1994), Brynen et al. (1995), Ali (1996), Beinin and Stork (1996), Eickelman and Piscatori (1996), Mustafa (1996), Ayadat (1997), Clark (1997, 2003), Schwedler (1997), Bayat (1998), Hamzeh (1998), Lawrence (1998), Boulby (1999), Hefner (2000), Wiktorowicz (2001), Kepel (2002), Moaddel (2002), and Hafez (2003).

take place *among* Islamists, particularly around the issue of whether participation in democratic processes is justifiable in terms of a larger Islamist agenda – one that locates (at least for Sunnis) *shari'ah* at the center of projects for social, economic, and political reform. These debates are critical because they illustrate that the strategies and practices of the IAF and the Islah party are neither taken in a vacuum nor bound to the territorial constraints of individual states. Rather, the practices and boundaries of justifiable action of each party also contribute to and are informed by large, vibrant, and ongoing transnational debates among Islamists.

As detailed in Chapter 1, the contours of these debates have led many scholars to employ the terms *moderate* and *radical* to characterize the two poles among Islamists: those who view participation in democratic practices as justifiable or even necessary, and those who view such participation as illegitimate. For Islamists who argue that the richness of Islam is precisely its applicability to a wide variety of historical circumstances, the process of reconciling Islam and democracy is easily accomplished through consideration of Islamic concepts such as *shura* (the idea that decisions affecting society should be taken through a process of consultation) and *ijma'* (that decisions should be reached through consensus). Many Islamist thinkers also reference *ijtihad*, a process of interpreting classic texts for application to contemporary circumstances. Islamists engaged in these debates have not only reconciled their own reading of Islamic ideas with democratic practices, but they have found a means of justifying and defending adherence to the pluralist "rules of the game." Among the implications of this reconciliation is that these Islamists must justify their participation in a field of political contestation in which non-Islamist (though often, necessarily, Muslim) actors are counted as equals. This is of considerable importance, as part of the "bargain" of gaining the right to participate is formally acknowledging that those who oppose Islamist agendas also have the right to participate. For Islamists who had long condemned Leftists as infidels and critiqued their secular social programs and state-centered economic reforms, tolerating Leftists may entail more than a strategic decision: it may require a justification for tolerating one's former enemy. Not all Islamists will find room for such accommodation as it may stray too far from what they view as core principles and objectives. Still others may choose to participate while never fully accommodating competing norms.

These debates are vital for this comparative study of the IAF and the Islah party because they help us locate the particular issues faced by each party in the context of ongoing debates among Islamists regionally and globally. While it is outside of the scope of this book to thoroughly examine Islamist arguments about democracy in the modern and contemporary periods, I will note aspects of these debates in the analysis of the IAF and the Islah party that follows. This will serve as a means of situating some particular instances of shifting boundaries of justifiable action within larger transnational debates about Islam and democracy.

JORDAN'S MAINSTREAM ISLAMISTS

For the Muslim Brotherhood in Jordan, the question of Islam and democracy did not suddenly appear in their sights in the late 1980s when the regime moved toward political liberalization. As detailed in earlier chapters, Jordan has electoral experience dating to the 1920s and its first experiment with a pluralist political space emerged in the 1950s. The Muslim Brotherhood was active in these processes almost from its founding in the mid-1940s, contrary to al-Banna's opposition to democracy as an un-Islamic Western import into the Muslim world. Al-Banna initially opposed political parties as derisive, but later came out in favor of participation in nationally elected assemblies as a means of advancing reforms. Jordan's Muslim Brotherhood fielded candidates as independents in the parliamentary elections in 1951 and 1954, and in 1956 it put forth candidates under its own banner. But that participation did not happen without considerable debate. Abu Qurah, who founded and led the group until 1952, seemed to have resigned as a direct result of the decision to participate in elections. 'Azmi Mansur reports that Abu Qurah's son told him, "One reason behind my father's withdrawal from Muslim Brotherhood ranks was his attitude towards the elections, for which preparations were underway in the early 1950s. In brief, he saw that the Brotherhood should not take part unless they could put up enough candidates to garner a parliamentary majority. A minority presence in parliament will not enable Brotherhood leadership to implement Islamic Law. A leadership majority, on the other hand, saw that it was impossible for the Brotherhood to form a majority in the coming parliament, and conceded that staying away from the house would not offer them the chance to voice their views, oppose policies they do not approve of, or introduce Islamic ideas better than if they were under the dome. The majority had its way" (cited in Gharaybah 1997a: 73, n. 1). Abu Qurah was consistent in his emphasis of supporting the struggle in Palestine, and so when members of the group sought to move toward domestic political contestation, he viewed the engagement in elections as a distraction particularly given that outcomes were uncertain.

The question for the movement at that time was whether participation would likely bring sufficient gains to justify the costs – symbolic as well as material – of working through formal political channels and within a pluralist context. If such a victory could not be assured, participation could not be justified because it would violate the larger mission of reforming all aspects of state and society in accordance with a modernist reading of Islamic scriptures. While there remains little documentary evidence of the details of the intragroup debate at that time, those who did not resign with Abu Qurah have been among the most vocal supporters of democracy in subsequent years.

At the same time, Muslim Brotherhood leaders showed sensitivity to the popular characterization of the group as highly conservative and to competing narratives put forth by the nationalists and Leftists. Through a careful reading of *Al-Kifah al-Islami*, the Muslim Brotherhood's weekly of the time, Boulby discovered a statement that seems to express a much more liberal position toward women than espoused by the group in the 1990s: "We do not want a return to the past, to an old era and lifestyle ... and it is inevitable that women associate closely with men and become acquainted with men to the greatest possible degree. A man who prevents his wife from just associating with another man must fear that she will love another man" (February 8, 1957, quoted in Boulby 1999: 71). Thus from an early stage the party was characterized by a diversity of positions, the most critical of which were internally debated while other, less serious issues (e.g., the role of women in the party) was left rather unspecified. As Boulby argues, "The most distinctive feature of the Brotherhood's ideology, apart from its moderation, was its imprecision. Concepts of the future Islamic order or state were ill-defined and the implications of the implementation of *shari'ah* were not stated" (Boulby 1999: 38). This practice has left the party considerable flexibility in adapting to changing circumstances.

During the years between the suspension of multiparty politics in 1957 and the liberalization begun in 1989, the Muslim Brotherhood maintained close relations with the ruling regime, which proved a willing ally against revolutionary Leftist and nationalist groups. When the question of direct political participation reemerged in the 1980s, the group debated many of the same issues, albeit within a changed political context. As Boulby argues, the Muslim Brotherhood had always been a fairly pragmatic movement and underwent little intellectual development from the 1950s to the 1980s. Indeed, the group boasted no significant thinkers (1999: 115, 118), certainly not the sort who attracted the notice of Islamists outside Jordan. Muslim Brotherhood members contested the bielections of 1984, resuming their routine participation in elections established in the years before the 1967 war, but with a new generation of candidates. Many of the leading voices felt that participation was necessary and even natural for the group and cited Tunisian Islamist thinker Rachid Ghannouchi, who has argued since the 1980s that the Prophet Muhammad had set a precedent for Muslims participating in secular governments (1993). Ghannouchi's words are frequently invoked and referenced by Muslim Brotherhood groups throughout the world, reflecting the extent to which the contemporary Muslim Brotherhood branches have for the most part moved away from al-Banna's rejection of democracy. Jordan's Muslim Brotherhood leaders also reference contemporary Muslim Brotherhood voices in Egypt, such as Mustafa Mashhour and Ma'moun al-Hudaybi, who have incorporated the language of democracy, pluralism, and human rights into their policy statements (Abed-Kotob 1995; Wickham 2004). They have also been strongly influenced by Rashid Rida, who advocated the use of a constitution as a contemporary framework for Islamic governance (*al-hukumah al-Islamiyyah*) within the context of a modern state (*dawlah*), and a role for civic law (*qanun*) as subordinate to *shari'ah* where the latter makes no clear provision.[3]

The IAF's 'Arabiyyat put it this way: "The concept of *shura* is a central idea in Islam. It is the notion that no one individual has the authority to make decisions for a community. *Shura* and democracy are not identical concepts, but we see democracy as a contemporary form of *shura*, a mechanism through which we can govern in accordance with God's laws."[4] He notes, however, that ultimate sovereignty lies in the hands of God, and not the people, as "Western" versions of democracy demand.[5] This idea of sovereignty belonging to God rather than to the people is common throughout much of the Islamist debates, including in the writings of radical thinkers, such as Egypt's Qutb (1964) or Yemen's Muqbil ibn Hadi al-Wada'i, as well as in the writings of those who find democratic practices acceptable and even desirable, albeit within limits, such as Ghannouchi, Pakistan's Mawlana Mawdudi (1982), Sudan's Hasan al-Turabi (Moussali 1994), and Iran's Abdolkarim Soroush (2000). 'Arabiyyat stresses that every government should be accountable to its people, and democratic institutions are simply one institutional means of achieving that end. He

---

[3] For an extended discussion of Rida's influence on the Muslim Brotherhood, see Boulby (1999: 126–9).

[4] Interview with author, November 15, 1996, Amman.

[5] For example, see "Fi Majal Muraqibah al-Sultah al-Tanfithiyyah wa al-Huriyat al-'Am wa Huquq al-Wataniyyin," Muslim Brotherhood, July 1, 1989.

also argues that because parliament is a consultative body that can affect change in the constitution as well as in legislation, it is therefore a highly relevant site for Islamist activism. Thus even before the 1990s, when a democracy narrative was significantly elevated in Jordan's public political discourse, many of the leaders of the country's mainstream Islamists had already reconciled the compatibility of Islam and democracy and justified (in Islamic terms) the group's participation in pluralist political processes.

Still, the decision to participate again in 1989 was not without its dissenters. Several prominent members of the group characterized democracy as "an invading non-Islamic concept and a secular approach to community management" (Kazem 1997: 30). Among this dissenting group were Overseer-General Khalifah and several members of the Muslim Brotherhood's executive council, including Abu Faris, Ibrahim Khraysat, and Hammam 'Abd al-Rahim Sa'id (al-Abed), all of who resigned their positions during the 1989 elections as a sign of protest. They argued that participation in these state institutions would weaken the focus of the Muslim Brotherhood from its broader objective of Islamic reform by distracting members with issues such as coalition building, campaigning, and the need to negotiate with government and opposition groups. They were "also concerned that transformation into a party would lead them to the same destiny as all other parties – subject to the whims and decisions of different governments" (Gharaybah 1997b: 53). As Shaykh Muhammad al-'Alawinah argued, "If freedom and multi-parties are meant to reveal the truth, then they are not objectionable and [are] an urgent need. However, if they are meant to be, as in most countries of the world, 'parties just for the sake of having parties' and for highlighting a certain character, then I think this is selfishness conflicting with the teachings of Islam. I have no doubt it will be a harmful experience but we are trying through it to reach a better state of affairs" (interview in Sawt al-Sha'b, November 21, 1989, cited in Boulby 1999: 129–30). Boulby argues that at the time of the 1989 elections, "it seems clear that the Muslim Brotherhood does not ultimately seek a pluralist parliamentary system based on popular sovereignty" (1999: 134).

Nevertheless, a vote by the 1989 consultative council showed a strong majority in favor of participation, but that did not silence the debate while the group struggled with how to draft a formal position concerning participation in this period before political parties were legalized. Even some traditional "radicals" in the group supported participation, including Abu Zant, who subsequently won a seat in the assembly. These internal party debates illustrate Clark and Schwedler's argument that party moderates and radicals do not constitute well-defined blocs, and that those blocs may shift from issue to issue. In this regard, the notions of moderate and radical are most useful in describing positions on issues, rather than whole blocs of members.

In the meantime, the Muslim Brotherhood felt a need to formally respond to the issue, given its history of opposition to Leftist and nationalist groups and their secular agendas.[6] While moderate voices such as Farhan, 'Arabiyyat, and 'Akaylah gave interviews to the (still restricted) domestic press and to such Arabic-language papers as *Al-Hayat*, the group also formulated several comprehensive statements that were debated and circulated internally, but never released publicly.[7]

In its 1989 Elections Program, the Muslim Brotherhood declared a commitment to democracy and pluralism, while calling for a fight "against sectarian, regional, and ethnic chauvinism, which threatens the nation's unity and undermines the country's integrity" (quoted in Gharaybah 1997b: 59). By framing the issue this way, the group was able to downplay its acceptance of Leftists as equal political actors and focus instead on representing the democratic institutions as an acceptable mechanism for promoting national unity and integrity. The statement reaffirms the Muslim Brotherhood's antisecular credentials while portraying participation in the pluralist system as faithful to its core Islamic objectives. As al-'Alawinah argued with reference to the equality of other voices in the assembly, "Regardless of religious differences, our task in the [lower house] is to deal with new developments, and all deputies are entitled to participate in discussing all the proposed issues or finding a suitable solution to them" (interview in *Sawt al-Sha'b*, quoted in Boulby 1999: 131). He stressed that Christian minorities would be accepted, an idea underlined by Muslim Brotherhood spokesman Ziyad Abu Ghanimah: "Islam is very clear on the relations between Muslims and non-Muslims. We believe in Jesus Christ and Moses. We believe that Christians and Jews are the people of the book (*ahl al-kitab*) and we are ordered by God to behave with them very kindly..." (quoted in Boulby 1999: 131). As Boubly argues, however, "the Brotherhood's calls for Jordanian national unity are framed within an Islamic perspective and the main focus of Muslim-Christian cooperation relates to 'exposing Zionist ambitions and

---

[6] Interview with Ishaq Farhan, March 31, 1997, Amman.
[7] For example, see "Fi Majal Muraqibah al-Sultah al-Tanfithiyyah wa al-Huriyat al-'Amm wa Huquq al-Wataniyyin," July 1, 1989.

supporting the Christian Arabs in exposing Zionist endeavours at influencing Christians in the West..."' (1999: 131).

Nevertheless, when the Muslim Brotherhood obtained a license in 1991 to publish *Al-Ribat*, its articles focused primarily on political issues in the Arab and Islamic world, notably "strong support for other Islamist movements in Algeria, Sudan, and Tunisia, and its opposition to the Arab-Israeli peace process" (Boulby 1999: 118). At Boulby notes, the pages included interviews with such Islamists as Sudan's al-Turabi, who, like Jordanian Muslim Brotherhood members, framed his critiques of various efforts to suppress Islamists in Algeria and Sudan in terms of a democratic narrative, noting that although "Islam was adopted by the majority," "minority forces" prevented Islamic reforms from being implemented. Articles in *Al-Ribat* further illustrate that Muslim Brotherhood leaders praised the likes of al-Turabi and the Alergian Islamic Front for their "peaceful" efforts even in the face of harsh state repression (Boulby 1999: 118–19). In effect, the discussion of Islamists in foreign contexts provided a proxy for the Muslim Brotherhood to indirectly critique the Jordanian regime. This proved a useful strategy, as government censors interfered with the paper's efforts to criticize the Jordanian regime. On September 10, 1991, for example, *Al-Ribat* published a report by a parliamentary committee that contained detailed accounts of torture of detainees by the secret police. All copies of the paper were confiscated. On occasion even articles critical of other Arab regimes were also censored, as on February 17, 1992, when an article criticized the Tunisian government's repression of the Islamist group Al-Nahdah (Boulby 1999: 118).

Immediately following the elections and the strong Muslim Brotherhood victory, the group issued a statement that stressed that its two primary goals remain the complete liberation of Palestine and the implementation of *shari'ah*. The statement declared that the group would work for these goals through the legislative process, but with the ultimate goal of amending "the Jordanian laws that are not in harmony with Islam" (Boulby 1999: 141). In an interview to *Sawt al-Sha'b*, Muslim Brotherhood deputy Ya'qub Qarrush also stressed the group's commitment to adhere to the constitution and respect public liberties: "Our first demand will be on activating the constitution articles, returning real power to the people, allowing them to participate in the running of the country, regaining the prestige of this power within the constitution, restoring daily popular participation through the release of general liberties, and then discussing the economic crisis" (quoted in Boulby 1999: 141).

Very quickly, however, issues surfaced that tested the depth of the Muslim Brotherhood's commitment to pluralist political competition. The first challenge emerged with the drafting of the National Charter. The document was to formalize the principles of democratic governance and thus mark the transition of Jordanian politics toward democracy, though at the same time it placed limits on political parties that negatively affected the Muslim Brotherhood in particular. For example, political parties were forbidden to have ties to foreign organizations or to accept funds from nondomestic sources. Through the introduction of multiparty competition, the document would also ensure that the Muslim Brotherhood was no longer the only game in town.

King Hussein appointed a committee of prominent political figures to draft the document. Whereas the large Islamist bloc in parliament had not necessitated Muslim Brotherhood cooperation with political rivals, the National Charter committee put Islamists side by side with nationalists and Leftists. To be sure, the Gulf War of 1990–1 did see groups across the political spectrum unified against the U.S.-led invasion, but it was a position that commanded broad popular support across the country. With the drafting of the National Charter, however, Muslim Brotherhood leaders were able to overlook historic rivalries, particularly with Leftists, to find common ground in the name of national unity. The debate extended into the public political sphere: "Charter deliberations were generously covered in the daily press, and involved much of Jordanian political society in a dialogue over the most basic principles of Jordanian political order. Since the Charter was to establish general norms of Jordanian behavior, actors took the identity and interests of the collective as the frame of reference. It provided the framework for 'national action' in all spheres of political life..." (Lynch 1999: 108). The document formalized the right of political expression and codified the rights of citizens to organize politically and was signed by all the committee members on June 9, 1991.[8]

A second and more troublesome situation strained the extent to which the Muslim Brotherhood leaders could justify their equal participation alongside Leftists. In 1991, the lower house of parliament began to debate an amendment to the constitution introduced by Muslim Brotherhood deputies. The proposal advocated a change in the wording

---

[8] Subsequently, the National Charter's strong democratic narrative – even more than that of the constitution – has become the principle point of reference for both the political elite and the opposition groups who wish to challenge specific state practices and policies.

of the constitution concerning the status of *shari'ah* and its role in governance, calling for the wording of the document to stipulate *shari'ah* as the
source (*al-masdar*) – and thus the only source – of legislation regarding
governance, rather than merely the *primary* source. The incident placed
the Muslim Brotherhood in an awkward position. If the group was to
demonstrate its commitment to working within a pluralist political system and supporting Jordan's incipient transition to a democracy, it would
have to acknowledge the right of the parliament to take such a decision
and then respect the outcome of the vote. But as prominent Muslim Brotherhood members such as Abu Faris and Hammam Sa'id argued, such a
move suggested that fundamental Islamist objectives were open to debate.
Even more troublesome was the fact that secular Leftists would be among
those casting votes. For many within the Muslim Brotherhood, the situation took the group too far from its core objective of implementing
shari'ah. Yet a victory would vindicate those who had advocated pluralist participation by illustrating that the group's core objectives could be
achieved through democratic practices, and success was not far-fetched.
In addition to the seats controlled by Islamists, many independents were
sympathetic to socially conservative programs that might be advanced by
implementing *shari'ah*. After King Hussein came out in opposition to the
amendment, however, many of those who the Islamists had hoped would
support the measure decided to vote against it. The loss was devastating for the Muslim Brotherhood and brought forth tremendous internal
debate. Should Muslim Brotherhood deputies resign from the assembly?

Instead of withdrawing from the assembly or rejecting pluralist practices, however, the Muslim Brotherhood leadership portrayed the decision to continue participating in the lower house as an illustration of how
truly dedicated they were to supporting the new democratic processes. As
Farhan put it, "The press tried to portray it as if there was a major conflict
within the Brotherhood over the outcome, but that was not the case. We
debated the issue, like we debate all issues, because internally we function
democratically and decisions are taken by vote. There was no problem
when the vote did not go our way, as we were fully prepared to accept the
outcome."[9] Statements issued at the time reflected similar justifications.
Although accepting such an outcome might have been unacceptable just
a few years earlier – and notably before Khalifah and others opposed
to pluralist participation had resigned from the movement – Muslim
Brotherhood leaders now were able to reconcile acceptance of the

---

[9] Interview with author, March 31, 1997, Amman.

outcome through reference to earlier decisions taken by the movement about participation in democratic institutions. To reject the outcome of the vote as illegitimate would mean not only withdrawing from parliament and running counter to the popular democratization process, but contradicting the group's repeatedly stated commitment to honoring democratic outcomes. Thus despite dissent from Abu Faris and others, the party leadership prevailed in defending continued participation in the lower house not because it was desirable strategically, but because it was defensible on Islamic terms.

This example illustrates one way in which changing the boundaries of justifiable action can act as mechanisms for political change. Had the group not previously reconciled democratic practices and acceptance of the constitution with its core agendas for political reform, and had it not won such a large bloc within the national assembly, its leaders might have never raised an amendment in parliament that sought to change the wording in the constitution with respect to *shari'ah*. As leaders debated and then justified on Islamic grounds the Muslim Brotherhood's decision to participate in democratic processes, they reconstructed the boundary of justifiable practices, affecting what strategies would be possible to justify in the future. In this way, their engagement with a democratic narrative created the opening for a previously unacceptable outcome to be justifiable ideologically as well as strategically.

Nevertheless, members of the group continued to strongly oppose pluralist participation (Abu Roman 1991; Robinson 1997), and in 1992 the group organized a forum during which members could express their views. At issue was not only continued participation, but whether to form a political party to best compete in the 1993 elections. Two of the speakers were 'Umar al-Ashqar, who supported participation, and Abu Faris, who opposed it. Both had circulated booklets laying out their arguments, and the debate was captured on videotape and circulated among members as well as to branch offices outside of Amman. Abu Faris strongly opposed participation both as a party contesting for seats in parliament and as ministers in the cabinet. He argued, "As *shari'ah* must govern the Muslim community, participating in government will only serve to support a non-Islamic organization of society."[10] Al-Ashqar, however, argued that participation was justifiable on Islamic terms as long as it served the larger purpose of furthering the moral objectives of the movement as a whole. In fact, if through participation the group could hope to achieve

---

[10] Videotape of the forum, circa September 1992.

some of its primary objectives, they would be irresponsible to not participate. Both men cited scripture[11] to support their arguments. Abu Faris also emphasized a political issue, the regime's apparent rapprochement with Israel as contrary to the Muslim Brotherhood's primary objectives. Al-Ashqar's argument reflected the propluralist positions of most Muslim Brotherhood branches in the early 1990s, and he cited positive experiences in the pluralist process by Muslim Brotherhood members in Jordan as well as elsewhere. As such, al-Ashqar's arguments and justifications for continued participation most closely reflected the group's center, while those of Abu Faris were becoming increasingly marginalized. Abu Faris did not exit from the group, however.

Movement into Party

As argued in Chapter 3, the IAF was originally conceived as an umbrella party that would include Muslim Brotherhood members as its core while attracting independent Islamists. The party was formed as a separate entity from the Muslim Brotherhood, but it quickly came to be seen as that group's political wing, particularly after twenty-two of the founding members resigned in protest following the party's first consultative council elections. The IAF formulated a political program and an electoral platform for the upcoming November 1993 elections. These documents largely reflected Muslim Brotherhood positions, but they clearly elevated the democratic and particularly pluralist narratives that Muslim Brotherhood leaders were using with increasing frequency.[12] Whereas the Muslim Brotherhood's election program in 1989 called for the general promotion of public freedoms, the IAF's 1993 program names and emphasizes specific freedoms. The shift was in part a response to the language and content of the programs being advanced by other political parties (Hourani et al. 1993a: 20–1). At the same time, the new IAF was considerably concerned that the legalization of parties would provide Leftist parties with the opportunity to expand their support bases and therefore threaten the Muslim Brotherhood's prominence throughout the kingdom (Hourani et al. 1993a: 8). The program therefore also stressed an advanced role for women: "legitimate women's rights have to be respected, as does the

---

[11] Islamic scripture includes three sources: the *Qur'an* (the literal word of God as dictated to the Prophet Muhammad through the angel Gabriel), the traditions (*sunna*), and the sayings (*hadith*) of the Prophet Muhammad.

[12] "Al-Barnamaj al-Siyasi," IAF, n.d., circa early 1993; and "Al-Barnamaj al-Intikhabi," IAF, July 1993.

role of women in the development of society, within the framework of Islamic virtues. Women must be given access to participate in public life, and must have the chance to occupy leading posts." Like the discussion of other freedoms and human rights, this program for women's advancement is periodically qualified with phrases noting that such practices must be in accord with what *shari'ah* dictates.

In late summer 1993, as IAF leaders were hard at work preparing for the elections, the government introduced its new elections law. Among the most significant changes was the introduction of a system of single nontransferable vote within multimember districts. IAF leaders recognized that the law was indented to reduce the number of Islamist seats in the new assembly, an assessment shared by many non-Islamists. As Farhan wrote repeatedly in his weekly newspaper columns in August and September,[13] the new law violated the democratic spirit of free and fair participation: "The government says that this is a one-person, one-vote system, but the weight of individual votes are not the same. . . . The government knows that we [the IAF] have considerable popular support, which is why they have corrupted the democratic process in order to prevent us from achieving a majority."[14]

Meanwhile, the government continued to speak in terms of Jordan's transition to democracy, insuring that democracy remained at the center of public political debate. This government rhetoric, combined with the drafting and passing of the National Charter in 1991, holding regular rounds of national and local elections, lifting martial law (which had been in place since 1967), increasing press freedoms, and legalizing political parties, created a climate of vigorous democratic debate and the appearance of real democratic activity. Although few failed to recognize that the royal family held tight to the reins of power, even many government officials believed that the country had moved irreversibly toward a more open and pluralist, if not quite democratic, political system. As former Minister of Information Ibrahim 'Izzidin put it, "We were sure that democracy had begun to take hold, everyone was talking about pluralism, and even the opposition parties had demonstrated their willingness to play by the rules of the game. Certain government officials were against further democratization, though we fought them on it."[15]

---

[13] His columns appeared regularly in the Islamist weekly *Al-Sabil* as well as in the partially government-owned daily *Al-Dustur*, and occasionally in other publications.
[14] *Al-Sabil*, August 2, 1993.
[15] Interview with author, April 22, 1997, Amman.

Within this climate of democratic debate and preparations for Jordan's first multiparty elections since 1956, the IAF found itself not only frustrated by the new elections law, but also struggling with the Ministry of the Interior for the requisite permits to hold campaign rallies. As detailed in Chapter 3, Muslim Brotherhood leader Thunaybat successfully sued the ministry on behalf of the IAF for failure to process the party's requests to organize campaign events. While the suit was pending, however, IAF and Muslim Brotherhood officials debated whether to boycott the elections entirely, a move that IAF leaders 'Arabiyyat and Farhan strongly opposed. The pages of the Islamist weekly *Al-Sabil* reflected proparticipation stances as well as the widespread concern about the co-optation of the movement and the government manipulation of the elections. Many argued that a boycott would not be tantamount to a rejection of democratic processes per se, because the elections law was undemocratic.[16] The IAF consultative council voted on whether to boycott, and the outcome indicated strong support for continued participation: 87 of 101 members (of the party's 120 total) opposed the boycott.[17]

A comparison between the intraparty debates around the 1989 elections and the 1993 elections suggests some interesting developments in terms of changing boundaries of justifiable action. Whereas the decision to participate in 1989 was one that Muslim Brotherhood leaders sought to reconcile in terms of the group's Islamist orientation, these debates were entirely absent in 1993. In their place, IAF leaders criticized the new elections law and the actions of the Ministry of the Interior for failing to support the democratic process in deed and spirit. Prominent party members continued to debate the pros and cons of participating in pluralist political processes, but the question was not whether participation was justifiable on Islamic terms but whether it remained practical given that regime's efforts to affect the results by rewriting the elections law.[18]

Indeed, the need to justify participation in pluralist processes had almost entirely disappeared. IAF documents emphasized that the party's decision to contest the elections demonstrated its strong commitment to

---

[16] *Al-Sabil*, September 14, 1993.
[17] "Bayan al-Mu'tamir al-Sahafi li al-Amin al-'Amm li Hizb al-Jabhah al-'Aml al-Islami Hawl I'lan al-Musharikah 'Amaliyah al-Intikhabat al-Niyabiyah li-l-Majlis al-Niyabi al-'Urdunni al-Thani 'Ashr," IAF, October 19, 1993.
[18] In addition to IAF, "Al-Barnamaj al-Siyasi," n.d., circa early 1993; and IAF, "Al-Barnamaj al-Intikhabi," July 1993; see IAF, "Muqadimah: al-Ahdaf wa al-Muntalaqat," n.d., circa 1993.

democratic processes as a legitimate means of political reform.[19] In August 1993, for example, Muslim Brotherhood Overseer-General Khalifah – who had briefly resigned in 1989 in opposition to Muslim Brotherhood participation in those elections – now issued a press release stating that the IAF had decided to participate in the elections in direct response to King Hussein's call for "the preservation of Jordan's stability and well-being, and to further the drive toward democracy and *shura* initiated by the king."[20] With the exception of the reference to *shari'ah*, Khalifah's statement made no argument for participating on Islamic grounds, a stark contrast from movement statements and publications circa 1989 and from his own earlier opposition to democratic processes. Farhan wrote in several newspaper columns and in an IAF press release that the group chose to participate despite the problems with the law because it felt that to boycott would "not contribute to the strengthening of democracy in Jordan, and we are very committed to seeing that process thrive."[21] The Muslim Brotherhood's Thunaybat gently criticized the government while expressing a long-view commitment toward democratic reform: "We understand that the democratic and consultative experiment in Jordan is still in the incubator, despite its relative advancement compared to other parts of the Arab world" (cited in Kazem 1997: 31). Three years later, with the new elections law still in effect, he was more blunt with his assessment of the government's undemocratic practices: "The government has not been fair. The new electoral law was designed – and government officials admit this to us – for the sole purpose of reducing our share of seats in the chamber of deputies. But we oppose the law because it is unfair, and there are others who agree with us even though our loss was their gain. We support Jordan's move toward democracy, but we want a real democracy, where the people choose the government they want."[22]

Following the IAF's loss of seats in the 1993 elections, it sought to increase its political power by gaining seats on university councils and municipal assemblies and by thorough gradual rapprochement with the secular opposition forces, notably nationalists and Leftists (Kazem

[19] See "Al-Barnamaj al-Siyasi," IAF, n.d., circa early 1993; "Al-Barnamaj al-Intikhabi," IAF, July 1993; "Muqadimah: al-Ahdaf wa al-Muntalaqat," IAF, n.d., circa 1993; and "Bayan al-Mu'tamir al-Sahafi li al-Amin al-'Am li Hizb al-Jabhah al-'Aml al-Islami Hawl I'lan al-Musharikah 'Amaliyah al-Intikhabat al-Niyabiyah li al-Majlis al-Niyabi al-Urdunni al-Thani 'Ashr," IAF, October 19, 1993.

[20] "Taqrir sahafi," Muslim Brotherhood, August 25, 1993.

[21] "Taqrir sahafi," IAF, September 11, 1993.

[22] 'Abd al-Majid Thunaybat, interview with author, November 15, 1996, Amman.

1997: 25). The Muslim Brotherhood and later the IAF had long characterized themselves as *loyal opposition* to the regime, a term that captured
their close ties with the political elite while distancing themselves from
certain policies and practices of the regime. As detailed in Chapter 3,
with the IAF's considerable loss of seats in the 1993 elections, party leaders began to explore more formal and routinized relations with a number
of smaller political parties, and together they formed an opposition bloc
that spanned the political spectrum. The IAF joined a number of independents and eight other parties, including Leftist and nationalist groups,
and the bloc began to meet regularly to coordinate activities and negotiate
cooperative parliamentary strategies. To be sure, there are considerable
tensions between some of these groups. Tujan Faisal, for example, the first
woman elected to a seat in Jordan's lower house,[23] became the target of
attacks by certain Muslim Brotherhood and IAF members (acting independently) for her progressive feminism and secular views. The substance
of their criticisms has been to label her an unbeliever (*kafir*), thus framing their opposition in terms of dissonance with Islam.[24] Yet this entire
group, including Faisal, met regularly at the IAF headquarters in Amman
from 1993–7, the locale chosen for its ability to accommodate the entire
group.[25]

Participation in the diverse opposition bloc was a significant development for the IAF. Just a few years earlier, the group had dedicated considerable energy to justifying its participation in pluralist institutions in
which Leftists would be equal players. Islamists justified that participation
on Islamic grounds while failing to debate the implications of pluralism
in terms of putting Leftists on equal political footing with Islamists. At
a time when an Islamist-Left alliance in the 1989 assembly would have
given opposition voices 60 percent of the seats, Muslim Brotherhood leaders rejected any such cooperation. With the parliamentary vote on the
status of *shari'ah* in the constitution, Islamist leaders defended the movement's commitment to democratic institutions to justify a process – Leftist

---

[23] Faisal was the only woman elected until the 2003 elections, when the government introduced a quota system to ensure that at least six women would hold seats. The seats would
be filled by the six women who won the largest percentage of votes in their districts. Faisal
won her seat outright in 1993, but she ran as a Circassian candidate (a minority quota
seat).

[24] The early attacks on Faisal prevented her from contesting the 1989 elections. She was
elected to a Circassian seat in Amman in 1993; she lost that seat in 1997.

[25] After its boycott of the 1997 elections, the IAF remained involved in the opposition bloc,
but its role was diminished until it contested the 2003 elections.

infidels (sing. *kafir*) having a say on the status of *shari'ah* – that was clearly unacceptable on ideological grounds. Muslim Brotherhood deputies continued to express their dissatisfaction with successive governments by denying them their vote of confidence while continuing participation in the lower house.[26] But with the loss of seats in parliament, the IAF now found little difficulty justifying its cooperation with Leftist and national groups – longtime ideological rivals of the Muslim Brotherhood – in a united opposition bloc. This does not necessarily mean that the group had evolved to such an extent that it could no longer be considered Islamist, or that Islam was no longer central to the group's diagnosis of the problems faced by contemporary Jordanian society and the group's prognosis for solutions. But gradually redrawing the boundaries of justifiable practices, the Muslim Brotherhood and the later the IAF came to explore and accept practices and actions that seemed unthinkable just a few years earlier. Strategies that once triggered considerable debate no longer required any justification at all.

The Muslim Brotherhood remained active in the social sphere while the IAF forged alliances in the political space. By one count, at least 66 nonpolitical Islamic institutes were functioning in Jordan in 1996, the vast majority of which were sponsored by the Muslim Brotherhood, the IAF, or prominent individuals from among their ranks (Dabbas 1997: 257–9). The opposition bloc met regularly and often coordinated their strategies in parliament, particularly concerning such issues as the 1994 Israel-Jordan Peace Treaty.

The Unjustifiable Peace with Israel

As the Jordanian regime moved steadily toward peace, the leadership of the IAF faced a serious internal crisis. In July 1994, a vocal group within the party insisted that IAF deputies resign from the lower house in protest, arguing that continued participation in any government body would signal acceptance of the treaty. The crisis was significant, as promoting the "liberation of Muslim Palestine" was one of the party's central objectives, second in priority only to the "resumption of Islamic life and the

---

[26] The Muslim Brotherhood deputies gave a vote of confidence to the Badran government formed in 1989, and to the one in which they participated following a cabinet shuffle in late 1990. Beginning with the Masri government that replaced Badran and for every subsequent government, the Muslim Brotherhood and later the IAF denied a vote of confidence.

application of *shari'ah* in all fields."[27] In fact, since the formation of the Jordanian Muslim Brotherhood in the 1940s, the group sought to spread Islamic ideas as a means of combating Zionism in Palestine (Kazem 1997: 15).[28] The group had consistently argued against any sort of compromise with Israel, advocating the liberation from Zionist/Israeli control of all Palestinian lands west of the Jordan River. They argued that Palestine belonged to all Muslims, not just to Palestinians, so no government or group – Muslim or otherwise – had the right to concede any parts of historic Palestine to Israel. Some four decades later, the IAF found itself participating in a political body that was on the verge of endorsing a Jordanian-Israeli treaty.[29]

The debate about how the party should respond was open to all members of the IAF and Muslim Brotherhood, hundreds of whom squeezed into a crowded hall in Amman to debate the issue. Key speakers included Abu Faris, who continued to criticize participation in democratic processes without resigning from the party, and Farhan, then Secretary-General of the IAF. The debate lasted several hours, with an even number of Palestinian members divided. As in 1992, the party circulated videotapes and audiotapes of the session to members not in attendance, and various trends published booklets that represented their position. The IAF consultative council met a few weeks later to vote on the issue. Some argued that working within the elected national assembly still offered promising means of achieving their Islamist goals. They defended democratic practices as congruent with Islamic principles and argued that the decision to participate had never been merely tactical. Others suggested that if they withdrew, the move might provide fuel to critics who argued that the IAF never truly had been committed to working within a

---

[27] See "Al-Barnamaj al-Siyasi," IAF, n.d., circa early 1993; and "Muqadimah: al-Ahdaf wa al-Muntalaqat," IAF, n.d., circa 1993. The latter document dedicates four pages (of thirty-six) to the Palestine issue: "Thawabitna 'ala sa'id al-qadiyah al-Filastinah" (31–4).

[28] Numerous Islamist groups, but particularly Muslim Brotherhood groups, have argued that God allowed the Zionists to gain control of Palestine because Muslims had deviated from their path while Jews remained pious. Muslims would reclaim Palestine, they argued, when they began to live according to their faith.

[29] The party has also issued regular statements at various stages of the Israeli-Palestinian peace process. For example, see "Khiyar 'Gaza-Iriha . . . Awalah' Mu'amirah Amrikiyah-Sahwiniyah . . . ," IAF, September 8, 1993; "Bayan Sadr 'an Hizb al-Jabhah al-'Aml al-Islami bi Munasibah Sadur Qarar al-Mahkamah al-'Aliya li-l-Kiyan al-Yahudi al-Ghasib," IAF, October 16, 1993; and "Bayan Sadr 'An Katalah Nuwab Jabhah al-'Aml al-Islami Hawal Ittifaqiyah Hizb al-Jabhah al-'Aml al-Islami Hawar Ittifaqiyah 'Arafat-Perez fi-l-Qahirah," IAF, February 22, 1994.

democratic system. Abu Faris led the opponents of continued participation, arguing that the party could not justify participation as it took the group too far from its primary goals. When the consultative council finally voted, a majority agreed to continue participating in both houses of parliament, but to refuse to join the government at the cabinet level. Anyone who violated this decision was required to leave the party, and indeed the executive has since revoked the membership of a few prominent members who accepted cabinet positions.[30]

The outcome preserved the group's ability to take advantage of certain institutional channels to power while expressing continued commitment to the Palestinian cause and opposition to Jordan's treaty with Israel. However, the decision also illustrated that the IAF was now willing to accept outcomes that fundamentally contradicted its primary objectives as long as they were processed through democratic channels. This was indeed a profound change from the group's position only four years earlier, when its members debated the decision to participate and concluded that participation could be justified as long as it moved the group toward realizing its primary objectives. IAF leaders stressed that the democratic process by which the decision was reached was integral to the party's internal organization, a claim supported by historical record. IAF deputies then headed a campaign in the lower house opposing the treaty. On the day of the parliamentary vote, many IAF deputies were notably absent, signaling not only a rejection of the treaty but also a desire not to antagonize the regime. In the end, a majority of Jordan's parliamentarians voted in favor and the treaty was enacted in October 1994.

The refusal to participate at the cabinet level was largely symbolic: no prime minister had offered the IAF any portfolios since 1991. But something else was at stake. Following the decision to participate in elections following the 1989 liberalization, the group was able to reconcile its worldview with certain democratic practices, even though it meant

---

[30] In 1998, the IAF revoked the membership of Bassam'Ali Salameh Amoush, a member of the founding committee and the executive committee, for accepting a post as Minister of Administrative Development in al-Majali's government following the party's boycott of the 1997 elections. Two other IAF members, 'Akaylah and Muhammad al-Azaydah had their membership frozen for not withdrawing their candidacies in accordance with the boycott. Both were reinstated in June 1998, unofficially giving the IAF two seats in the lower house. Amoush was not reinstated, though two IAF officials vociferously lobbied the party leadership to do so. Interviews with Farhan, plus several who wished to remain anonymous, March–June 1998, Amman.

accepting the right of longtime rival Leftist groups to participate. The peace treaty, however, was something else. If participation in pluralist political institutions was merely a means to realize other objectives, how could the group remain engaged when the process produced the antithesis of one of its primary goals?

To be sure, IAF members were strategic in their decision to continue their participation in the assembly. Withdrawing would not only mean that the group would lose access to certain political opportunities, but it might suggest that the IAF never had been committed to working within democratic processes. In the five years from the 1989 political opening to the peace treaty of 1994, the group had invested much effort in arguing that democratic institutions provided acceptable means of realizing its broader agenda for social reform. But given the group's long-held high prioritization of the liberation of Palestine on its political agenda, the continued participation of the party illustrated more than an accommodation of democratic practices for strategic reasons. Rather, the internal party debates and particularly its practices illustrate that the group had seriously incorporated elements of a democracy narrative that effectively redrew the boundaries of what practices and strategies the group could justify.

Indeed, the most persuasive evidence of this evolution lies not in the public statements of various party leaders and dissenters, but in the intraparty debates about this and other issues. In addition to the video-tapes mentioned in the preceding text, party leaders authored articles and columns in the Islamist weekly *Al-Sabil* that reflected a diversity of perspectives and serious contention among party leaders and consultative council members, far too much to dismiss the decision for IAF deputies to remain in the assembly despite the treaty. As the aforementioned pamphlets, newspaper columns, and videos of intraparty debates illustrate, many of the arguments in favor of continued participation – including those by party leaders Farhan and 'Arabiyyat – engaged a democratic narrative as integral to the movement's larger Islamist agenda. Democratic processes had become central to intraparty practices both institutionally and discursively. In this regard the decision to continue participating was certainly strategic, but participation under these conditions – within a government that could make peace with Israel – had become possible when it would not have been so just four years earlier.

Of course, both the Muslim Brotherhood and the IAF continued to oppose the treaty, the popular position as well as that of the other members of the opposition bloc. Even after the October 1994 signing, Islamists continued their active engagement in activities critical of Israel and in solidarity with Palestinians. But these activities no longer followed the earlier practice of maintaining separation between Islamist activities and those of Leftists and other political trends. As preparations for the 1997 elections began, several significant events brought the opposition groups to not only coordinate their strategies but to cooperate in planning activities. As argued in Chapter 3, the January 1997 protests against the Israeli trade fair was successful due to the sustained efforts of cooperation and coordination among Islamists, Leftists, independent opposition voices, business organizations, and a prominent former prime minister. The demonstrations illustrated how far the relationship between the Islamists and Leftists had developed in the eight years since liberalization, from guarded official tolerance to partner in executing a large-scale demonstration challenging a government policy. Whereas the Muslim Brotherhood had been careful to skirt the issue of coexistence with Leftists in 1989 and had portrayed its subsequent acceptance of Leftists as equal political actors only in terms of pluralist principles, by 1997 the IAF saw no need to justify cooperation between the ideologically distinct trends over issues of common interest. At the demonstration, 'Akaylah argued that the event demonstrated Jordan's national unity in opposing the peace with Israel: "Today we see all of the political trends in Jordan standing united in defense of our nation. We have embraced democracy, and through democracy we are expressing our opposition to these economic ties with Israel . . . and the devastating effects they will have on the Jordanian economy."[31] Such statements were made possible in part because earlier needs for justification of strategies had made Islamist-Leftist cooperation possible, particularly following the formation of a formal opposition bloc that brought diverse parties together for meetings at the IAF headquarters. Yet while the group had gradually stopped shunning cooperation with other parties when issues of common interest arose, it continued criticizing the policies advocated by these parties and certain individuals in terms of violating basic Islamic principles. As the party increasingly practiced internal democratic procedures, democratic and related activities became justifiable on their own terms. This near full acceptance is evidenced by the disappearance of the debates about Islam and democracy that had marked party statements and publications in the early

---

[31] Speech at the trade fair, January 8, 1997, Marj al-Hammam, Jordan.

1990s.[32] In this regard, the events surrounding the trade fair demonstration illustrate the extent to which cooperation with Leftists had become acceptable on democratic terms without having to justify it in Islamic terms. To be sure, IAF leaders have been more able to justify these cooperative strategies in some settings than in others. In 2003, IAF Secretary-General Mansur admitted that the support base of the party was less interested in the party's commitment to democratic participation than it was to its conservative social agenda and its long-term objective of implementing *shari'ah* in all spheres.[33] But within the party's inner circles, the leaders had reached the consensus that Islamist-Leftist cooperation was not problematic and was desirable in terms of presenting a united front on vital issues (e.g., the treaty with Israel, opposition to U.S. presence in the region, particularly the U.S.-led invasion of Afghanistan and Iraq).

Many of the democratic openings initiated in the early 1990s had been reversed by the summer of 1997, creating a dilemma for opposition parties. For the IAF, the question of a boycott was raised again as the November 1997 elections approached and the problematic elections law introduced before the last elections remained unchanged. In May, *Al-Sabil* published a list of likely IAF candidates for the upcoming elections taking many Muslim Brotherhood and IAF members by surprise. The party quickly stated that it had not yet reached a decision about fielding candidates. Farhan and 'Arabiyyat strongly favored participation, but a younger cohort within the party's consultative council were pushing to boycott. After several heated debates – including one for which an Egyptian Muslim Brotherhood leader was flown in to moderate the discussion – the consultative council voted in favor of a boycott.

Farhan argued that unlike in 1993, the IAF had demonstrated a sound commitment to working within democratic institutions, so boycotting proved less a problem on those grounds. Public opinion held that the regime had blatantly violated the democratic principles that had been formalized in the National Charter. As noted, the 1997 boycott document was signed not only by opposition bloc members, including the IAF and secular parties, but also by diverse individuals including two former prime ministers. The Muslim Brotherhood issued its own statement on July 13

---

[32] For example, compare "Al-Harakah al-Islamiyyah wa al-'Aml al-Niyabi: Nazrah Taqwimiyyah," Muslim Brotherhood, n.d., circa summer 1989; and even "Al-Barnamaj al-Siyasi," IAF, n.d., circa early 1993; and "Muqadimah: al-Ahdaf wa al-Muntalaqat," IAF, n.d., circa 1993; with statements issued around the question of press freedoms and the 1997 elections.

[33] Interview with author, June 29, 2003, Amman.

in defense of the boycott, which when compared to the group's rhetoric from 1989 is striking in the extent to which it appeals to a democratic narrative. The document begins:

> In 1989 the grand hope for democratic transformation that could foster develop-ment and prosperity in Jordan (the society and the state) was revived. The Mus-lim Brotherhood responded positively to the new political developments which formed a part of their comprehensive project of building the country and serving the society through a moderate methodology. Through this project, the Muslim Brotherhood has realized, over several decades, significant achievements for the society in the charitable, social, cultural, educational, public service, and health fields in addition to its ongoing ethical guidance. It had interacted positively with the requirements of these transformations and participated in the 11th parlia-mentary session, in laying down the National Convention [Charter] in cooper-ation with other intellectual trends and political powers, and in the formation of the 1991 cabinet amidst critical local and regional circumstances. The Mus-lim Brotherhood responded positively and honestly to political pluralism. The Muslim Brotherhood participated in the 1993 elections despite the dissolution of parliament before the end of its legal mandate and the issuance of the temporary law of "One Man One Vote" in 1993 which, according to many local, Arab, and international leaders of public opinion and public work, aimed to diminish and contain the Islamic movement . . . (cited in Moaddel and Talattof 2002: 301–3).

The statement continues to discuss a wide range of irregularities and devi-ations from democratic practices on the part of government officials, con-cluding with a set of seven recommendations to the government. The first six call for constitutional reforms formalizing separation of legislative and executive authority, revising the elections law, canceling the tempo-rary press law, ceasing arbitrary actions against political parties and civil society organizations, rejecting IMF influence over economic reforms, and expanding freedoms. The last calls for "ceasing the normalization of rela-tions with the Zionist state" (cited in Moaddel and Talattof 2002: 307). The document opens and closes with short Qur'anic verses, but the text is otherwise absent references to Islam. Thus the Muslim Brotherhood increasingly made claims engaging a democratic narrative, a practice that effectively reconstructed the boundaries of justifiable practices for the group.

Indeed, cooperation with Leftists and other non-Islamists no longer even required comment. As the 1997 elections approached, many of the boycotters formalized their alliance as a group called the Conference for National Reform (*Quwa al-Islah al-Watani*). The group's founding statement, "The Way to National Reform," is signed by the Muslim Brotherhood, the IAF, eight other political parties including Leftists and nationalists, the lawyers association, and eleven individuals without party affiliation. Like the boycott statement, the document is broadly secular (rather than religious) in its language of justification and fully invokes a democratic narrative, emphasizing that the boycott opposes not democratic processes but the fact rather that the regime was not honoring its commitment to uphold democratic processes.[34]

YEMEN'S MIXED BAG OF ISLAMISTS

Yemen's Islamists did not share Jordan's history of participation in pluralist and democratic processes. Whereas 1989 brought reliberalization to Jordan through the return to national elections that had been suspended in 1967, a democratic narrative did not have significant roots in either North or South Yemen prior to unification. As argued in Chapter 4, leaders in both Yemens held periodic elections of varying scope and occasionally even referenced democracy or democratic practices in their documents and public speeches. But given the lack of meaningful pluralist political engagement, Yemen's Islamists had neither dealt with the practical issues of, for example, electoral competition, nor had they had any reason to seriously engage a democratic narrative. Indeed, among the challenges faced by the Islah party, internal party politics proved far more significant than they had for the Muslim Brotherhood and IAF in Jordan.

As illustrated in Chapter 3, the Islah party brought together a range of political actors under the banner of an Islamist political party in large part to aid the leaders of the former North in defeating the South's YSP in national elections and thus diminishing southern power in postunification Yemen. The decision to participate was not only about taking advantage of new channels for promoting an Islamic social and political agenda but also about insuring that the northern elite dominated. The actors that came together under Islah were not without their disagreements. Yemen's loosely organized Muslim Brotherhood had been led by al-Zindani until the late 1970s, when he was pushed out in favor of Qubati. After unification, the Muslim Brotherhood trend remained more moderate than al-Zindani's radical rhetoric and more in line with the ideological positions of Muslim Brotherhood branches in other countries. Never a moderate, in 1973 al-Zindani had set up a series of Islamic institutes that taught a radical version of Islam, and he absorbed even

---

[34] Quwa al-Islah al-Watani, "Al-Tariq ila al-Islah al-Watani," October 1997.

more radical Wahhabi views during his stays in Saudi Arabia as a guest of that regime. He continued to resent the Muslim Brotherhood leadership who had ousted him a decade earlier, and he built a personal following with the assistance of Saudi funding. Thus when the Islah party brought these trends together with conservative tribal leaders, many of the disputes that emerged within the party fell along the lines of these long-standing animosities, which also reflected significant differences in worldview. Al-Zindani opposed the terms of unification altogether because they provided for a democratic system of governance and particularly for cooperation with and recognition of the South's avowedly secular, Leftist regime. The Muslim Brotherhood seemed to have less of a problem justifying participation in democratic processes. This was not only because of prior experience in Yemen, but because Muslim Brotherhood branches elsewhere had been grappling with the question of Islam and democracy for decades and Yemen's Muslim Brothers had followed and participated in these debates. These transnational debates play out in a variety of media, from regional conferences, reciprocal invitations between research institutes, and visits to other Muslim Brotherhood branches. Various arguments in these debates are put forth and exchanged through newspapers, interviews, videotaped sermons, lectures, books, pamphlets, articles, and, increasingly, using the Internet. And, of course, the party relied significantly on the support bases of various tribal personalities, above all that of Shaykh 'Abd Allah of the Hashid tribal confederation.

Nevertheless, Muslim Brotherhood members within Islah assumed leadership positions in the bureaus of the party headquarters. Each of these eight bureaus was tasked with formulating statements about party policies and objectives. In this regard, the political committee repeatedly sought to justify on Islamic terms the decision to participate in a democratic system.[35] Like Jordan's Muslim Brotherhood, these Islah officials framed policy statements and publications that drew on Islamic thinkers who argued that democratic practices provided an appropriate institutional form for Islamic governance. Islah's emerging positions on a variety of issues were reflected in the pages of *Al-Sahwah*, the Muslim Brotherhood–run paper established in North Yemen in 1985 that later became the official mouthpiece of the party.[36] Democracy was mentioned periodically,

---

[35] For example, see Al-Lajnah al-Siyasiyah, "Nashrah li Fa'aliyat al-Dawrah al-Siyasiyah al-Awala al-Munta'aqadah Tuhit Sha'ar: Nahwu'i Siyasi Rashid," September 11–13, 1991.

[36] For example, see "Fikrah al-Tajamma' al-Yamani" and "Ahdaf al-Tajamma'," both in *Al-Sahwah*, May 5, 1991.

but pluralism, freedom, justice, and the phrase "order and law" (*nizam wa qanun*) were favored instead.[37] Still, to the extent that the party did engage in a democratic narrative, such statements were generated almost exclusively from within the Muslim Brotherhood–dominated bureaucracy, and seldom reflected in the speeches and writings of al-Zindani, al-Daylami, or Shaykh 'Abd Allah.

While the party eventually put forth a relatively cohesive political agenda with references to pluralist practices framed within a conservative Islamist narrative, the emerging party leaders did not speak with one voice. In fact, from its earliest stages until today, the Muslim Brotherhood trend within Islah has been routinely frustrated by frequent statements from party leaders like Shaykh 'Abd Allah, al-Zindani, and al-Daylami that contradict official party positions. This distribution of standpoints resulted from the diverse personalities and trends that were brought together in the party. While each brought valuable resources, they also brought diverse and varying worldviews.

Many of these internal party differences stemmed from the sometimes divergent expectations and political objectives of those who founded the party. In practical terms, the tribal power within Islah took up the positions of authority necessary to tie the party as closely as possible to President Salih and his ruling GPC party while the younger, integrativist Muslim Brotherhood ideologues assumed responsibility for formulating official party policies across a wide range of issues. As a result, Islah publications, political and electoral programs, and official states overrepresented Muslim Brotherhood perspectives and downplayed the more radical visions of al-Zindani as well as the political outlook of Shaykh 'Abd Allah, who held conservative Islamist views but never prioritized Islamist objectives over maintenance of his bases of tribal power.

In this regard, the party saw a division of labor in which Shaykh 'Abd Allah represented ties to the highest levels of power, the Muslim Brotherhood leaders ran the party bureaucracy, and al-Zindani continued to control the Islamic institutes that taught a radical reading of Islam and provided local military training and recruits that joined the *mujahidun* in Afghanistan. Although undesirable to many of the more progressive Islamist voices within Islah, al-Zindani was seen as a key personality for the solidification of a strong Islamist bloc that could challenge the power and programs of the YSP. While Muslim Brotherhood members in the

---

[37] In addition to article in *Al-Sahwah*, see "Al-Barnamaj al-Siyasi li al-Tajamma' al-Yamani li al-Islah," 1993.

Islah leadership often expressed frustration and concern over al-Zindani's extremism, they appeared powerless to challenge him and instead sought to keep him at arm's length.

The Islah party's newness and its position as a close ally of President Salih and the GPC therefore presented a different relation to the political elite – and thus different opportunity structures – than did the Jordanian Muslim Brotherhood's symbiotic relationship with the monarchy. Whereas the Jordanian group went to great lengths to justify its decision to engage in democratic practices within a field of pluralist political contestation – leading to the resignation of some members over the decision – Islah members were more divided. Segments of the party seemed to adopt democratic practices for purely strategic purposes (e.g., Shaykh 'Abd Allah), others seemed willing to explore whether an Islamist worldview could accommodate democratic practices (e.g., the Muslim Brotherhood members), while yet others rejected democracy entirely but did not defect from the party (e.g., al-Zindani).

As argued in Chapter 4, Yemen's dominant postunification narrative was primarily one of national unity, with a democratic narrative prominent in some debates, but certainly not viewed as a priority by all political actors. Of the three most powerful political parties, only the YSP leadership seemed deeply concerned with advancing democratic processes, a commitment that stemmed in part from its internal crises in 1986 and its own debates about democratic reform from that period onward. For the GPC and many within Islah, the electoral dimension of democratic reforms was seen as a mechanism for tipping the North-South power balance so that conservative northern agendas would dominate under unification. Islah party platforms and statements reflected the efforts of Muslim Brotherhood members to formulate policies that served this larger purpose of the party, but they also reflected their own efforts to grapple with a democratic narrative in a manner similar to Muslim Brotherhood branches in other countries. In one early statement of party goals, for example, building a "democratic and just society" is listed as the fourth goal, after resolving internal disputes that divide the nation, building a strong national army to protect the state, and improving the level of economic, cultural, social, and political status of the people.[38]

The fact that Muslim Brotherhood members dominated the party bureaus but not the positions that tied the party to the highest levels of state power explains why official Islah policies often appear in discord

---

[38] "Ahdaf al-Tajamma'," *Al-Sahwah*, May 5, 1991.

with the individual statements of al-Zindani and Shaykh ʿAbd Allah. It also explains why the two are able to continue expressing their opinions, seemingly regardless of how far they diverge from official party positions. Despite official party endorsement of democratic processes, al-Zindani was highly critical of participating in democratic institutions from the beginning, characterizing democratic practices as secular tools of Western imperialism: "Political pluralism and secularism copied from the West are inappropriate for our Muslim society in Yemen. . . . Whoever joins a political party in the name of pluralism has betrayed his country by promoting sectarianism and secular governance."[39] His radical Islamist worldview is perhaps the most rigid of the party's main leaders, in accordance with other Salafi radicals, such as al-Daylami, as well as Salafis on the party's fringe, such as Muqbil ibn Hadi al-Wadaʿi.

In contrast, Shaykh ʿAbd Allah approaches politics from a perspective that emphasizes an Islamist worldview and locates *shariʿah* at the center of reform projects. He certainly endorses many official Islah positions, sharing more with Muslim Brotherhood perspectives than those of al-Zindani, and has authored a textbook on the oneness of God (*tawhid*). In practice, however, his reliance on patronage, loyalty, and kinship ties contributes to the reconstruction and maintenance of those social and political arrangements.

Shaykh ʿAbd Allah's commitment to promoting democratic practices appears to be shallow, as evidenced by the infrequency with which he invokes any aspect of a democratic narrative, even when directly asked. When questioned in 1992 by a reporter as to whether Yemen should organize a single national conference to establish a code of conduct on the details and procedures for democratic elections – which various tribes and groups had been debating at large conferences independently organized throughout the country – Shaykh ʿAbd Allah responded, "My personal position is that I see no need for the event. I am certain it creates more problems than it solves. If this trend continues [of holding conferences], we may have a national conference in this tribe, and another national conference in that governorate. I feel *we already have the institutions to agree on those things*, and there is no reason to introduce new or additional complications."[40] In essence, he argued that Yemenis did not need to create new forums for debating the structure, purpose, or import of democratic

[39] *Al-Thawri*, a weekly publication of the YSP, November 30, 1995, quoted from an interview published in *Al-Shoruq* magazine, published in the United Arab Emirates.
[40] Interview in *The Yemen Times*, June 10, 1992, emphasis added.

elections. Indeed, he portrayed new or additional means of facilitating public political debate as "complications" that should be avoided. Furthermore, he did not envision a weakening of tribal or kinship structures, and he seemed to imply that existing social and political institutions were sufficient to carry forth the political reforms associated with unification. Shaykh 'Abd Allah's apparent disregard for policies formally espoused by his party can be easily understood in light of the broader power relations that characterize Yemeni society. In fact, few seem to find Shaykh 'Abd Allah's behavior hypocritical or problematic, seeing him instead as fulfilling his primary role as tribal shaykh and only secondarily – and when strategically viable – accommodating his role as head of a party within the new field of pluralist political competition.[41] Thus while some Islah positions from the early 1990s did engage a democratic narrative to a limited extent,[42] the party did not have internal debates about whether participating in pluralist processes and democratic practices could be justified in Islamic terms, as did the Muslim Brotherhood in Jordan. Islah leaders made no systematic effort to deal with the issue of accommodating the Leftist YSP and many party members, notably al-Zindani, demonstrated extreme intolerance of Leftists, whom he routinely labeled "communists, infidels, and non-believers."

But the larger reason why the party did not debate questions of democracy was that the party was never a cohesive unit. A wide range of members expressed that they were well aware of fundamental ideological differences among the leadership, differences that few thought could be resolved through debate. Even Muslim Brotherhood leaders expressed doubt that al-Zindani could be persuaded that Islam and democracy were highly compatible. The Islah party never even debated the question of coexistence with Leftist groups, except within Muslim Brotherhood circles inside the party bureaucracy.

Indeed, many Islah leaders did not feel the need to accept Leftists as equal players, as had the Muslim Brotherhood and IAF in Jordan. In fact,

---

[41] This conclusion is based on my highly unscientific survey of several dozen politically conscious Yemenis in San'a between February 1995 and September 1998. In Jordan, I interviewed no one who found a problem with 'Arabiyyat's dual role in the 1997 elections: he boycotted the elections as a leader of the largest and most powerful political party, but he also played a leadership role choosing local candidates in Salt, where he is a prominent tribal figure.

[42] For example, see al-Lajnah al-Siyasiyah, "Nashrah li Fa'aliyat al-Dawrah al-Siyasiyah al-Awala al-Munta'aqadah Tuhit Sha'ar: Nahwu'i Siyasi Rashid," September 11–13, 1991; and "Fikrah al-Tajamma' al-Yamani" and "Ahdaf al-Tajamma'," both in *Al-Sahwah*, May 5, 1991.

al-Zindani and others so opposed Leftists that had there been debates within Islah, they might have resulted in either a rejection of pluralism or the collapse of the party. Even the frustrated Muslim Brotherhood members did not push for consensus. Competition with the YSP, meanwhile, was viewed not only in terms of contests over parliamentary seats, but perhaps even more in terms of an ideological struggle for moral soul of Yemen. The Islah party allied with the GPC in a contest over the political control of the country. In Jordan, by comparison, the Muslim Brotherhood and IAF shared a field of political competition in which the ruling regime – the monarchy – was not even a player.

Thus the nature of the competition between Jordan's Islamists and Leftists was much different than that in Yemen, where Islah shared the GPC's objective of total defeat of the YSP. This shared commitment toward total YSP defeat extended not only to electoral competition, but to political violence. From 1991–3, GPC operatives and Islamists associated with the Islah party together engaged in attacks against YSP members, including some 150 assassination attempts.[43] While not all Islah members were as hostile to the socialists as al-Zindani, even the more moderate Muslim Brotherhood leaders refrained from condemning the attacks in the pages of *Al-Sahwah*.

As a party, Islah leaders did not engage in the sort of substantive debates about what practices could be justified on Islamic terms, and therefore the party did not see an evolution in its boundaries of justifiable actions in the same way as did Jordan's Muslim Brotherhood and IAF. Islah held party conferences every two years and the consultative council met three to six times a year, but these sessions were more about formulating strategies and coordinating objectives than about reconciling internal party divisions.[44] Muslim Brotherhood leaders ran the bureaucracy, formulated official statements, and published *Al-Sahwah*, but the positions put forth in these venues did not reflect a unified or even consensus position of all party factions.

In 1991, Islah leaders faced a dilemma regarding the national referendum of united Yemen's constitution. Like the Muslim Brotherhood in Jordan, Islah leaders objected that the wording of the document did not stipulate *shari'ah* as *the* source of reference for legislation regarding

---

[43] This number is based on estimates of YSP officials and on media reports. See also Dresch (2000: 191), International Crisis Group (2003), and Wedeen (2003).

[44] For example, see "Al-Mu'tamir al-'Am al-Awal: al-Bayan al-Khitami," September 24, 1994.

governance, calling it instead merely the *primary* source. Yemenis were to accept or reject the new constitution (and its offending status of *shari'ah*) through national referendum. When Islah leaders raised the issue of changing the wording, they were criticized even by GPC figures as failing to support national unity. Shaykh 'Abd Allah defended Islah's position against the draft wording, arguing, "Those who support the constitution as it is [i.e., without stipulating *shari'ah* as the only source of legislation] are either members of the YSP, who see an anti-*shari'ah* constitution as a means of promoting their secular principles, or government officials who aim only to preserve the positions and privilege, or common people who believe that anything done by the state is an additional achievement of the revolution."[45] Going further in his criticism, Shaykh 'Abd Allah characterized the decision to put the new constitution to a national referendum as a ploy to frame the adoption of the document as a democratic process, when in fact, he argued, government officials had forced the referendum on citizens by suggesting that a "no" vote would be unpatriotic, a vote against national unity. President Salih remained silent on the issue.

As plans for the referendum moved forward, Islah organized a boycott of the poll, though it was not very successful. Indeed, the press criticized boycotters as opponents of national unity and reconciliation, charges that were widely debated in *qat chews*. At the same time, a coalition of parties organized several protest marches in opposition to the amendments, marking one of the few early instances in which diverse groups cooperated (though of course the YSP, Yemen's predominant Leftist group, opposed changing the wording to elevate the status of *shari'ah*). A march on May 12, for example, saw some 30,000 march on the presidential palace, where representatives of the Islah party and the League of the Sons of Yemen presented a joint letter addressed to President Salih asking that the wording be amended before the referendum was held. President Salih met the delegation but stated only that the cabinet and presidential council would look into the matter.[46]

Interestingly, the situation led to the Islah party's first serious engagement of a democracy narrative (and the only one for several years). Party leaders defended their efforts to amend the constitution as fully democratic, emphasizing that their objection was precisely because the referendum presented citizens only with a "yes" or "no" vote and did not allow open debate on substantive issues. As Islah's official spokesperson Faris

[45] Interview in *Al-Sahwah*, March 20, 1991.
[46] *The Yemen Times*, May 15, 1991.

Saqqaf stated, "Islah is committed to the creation of democracy in Yemen based on order, law, and justice, and to promoting national unity. We object that the wording of the constitution was not put forth for discussion and we call on the government to withdraw the constitution until such a debate is had."[47] In this regard, the utilization of a democratic vocabulary proved useful in making a political appeal. President Salih, however, used the consensus around national unity to mobilize people to support the constitution. He appealed primarily to national unity, but stressed that the referendum marked a critical stage in united Yemen's transition to democracy. On May 16 and 17, 1991, 98.3 percent of Yemenis who voted cast a "yes" ballot in a referendum for the new constitution.[48]

The issue marked a first "democratic" loss for Islah leaders, who then concentrated on weakening the YSP as a political force in the upcoming elections, but it harbored considerable resentment at the outcome.

1993 Parliamentary Elections

By 1992, the North-South coalition regime was dragging its feet in planning Yemen's first national elections. Several opposition and tribal groups organized large rallies that criticized the regime on a variety of issues, each issuing "written demands for the rule of law, pluralism, economic development, and local autonomy" (Carapico 1993b: 4).[49] On December 27–30, 1992, Islah leaders organized a party conference under the banner "Unity and Peace" that adopted the slogan, "The Qur'an and the Sunna supercede the constitution and [secular] law" (*Al-Qur'an wa al-sunna fowk al-dustur wa al-qanun*). The slogan represented an aggressive intervention into national debates about democracy and Islam, and seemed aimed at antagonizing YSP leaders, who were being targeted in hundreds of assassination attempts.

Meanwhile, public political space continued to evolve as more political parties emerged and various social and political groups organized large-scale gatherings to debate political issues. As Carapico argues, "These conferences, both tribal and urban-based, involving tens of thousands of people, were among the transition period's most critical political developments. In response, the regime felt compelled to adopt its own mold of political conduct, ... accept the principles of local elections, and adopt a

---

[47] *Al-Sahwah*, clipping n.d., circa early May 1991.
[48] *The Yemen Times*, May 22, 1991.
[49] These groups included 'Umar al-Jawi's progressive Unionist Party and 'Abd al-Rahman al-Jifri's League of the Sons of Yemen.

rhetoric of electoral rights" (1993b: 4). As Wedeen argues, the question of national unity at times seemed at odds with democracy in Yemen, even as the country executed national elections that were deemed free and fair and expectations about the prospects for real democratic transition grew (2003).

Thus by the time the elections were held in 1993, a range of organizations had begun to mobilize around and engage two primary narratives: democracy and national unity. Islah leaders, with the exception of al-Zindani, drew on the increasingly popular democratic narrative, albeit with frequent reference to an Islamic narrative. Islah's electoral platform even engaged a democratic narrative, emphasizing not only the primacy of national unity but also "peaceful alternation of power by way of the ballot box."[50] Overall, however, the Islah party focused its campaign on the promotion of national unity while also advocating the implementation of *shari'ah* in all aspects of Yemeni society. Given that the political elite of former North and South Yemen were competing within the same field and that unification was accomplished through a secret pact between President Salih and President al-Bid, a GPC-YSP coalition after the elections was a foregone conclusion. As expected, the formation of campaign materials was left primarily to the bureau of the party. Campaign materials spoke of promoting democracy based on *shura*, but always framed in terms of the superiority of Islam over secularism. Qur'anic passages were prominently displayed on elections posters and pamphlets, though campaign slogans seemed aimed for wider appeal. The Islah party's symbol, which appeared on their campaign materials, publications, and posters, shows an outline of a mosque and minaret with an open book – the Qur'an – above the mosque dome and with light radiating from it. But the symbol also includes symbols of modernity and development, including a large grain of wheat (cultivation), two smoke stacks attached to a factory (industry), and, in the center, a fired rocket (technology). The outer circle of the symbol bears a Qur'anic passage along the top and the name of the party along the bottom.

Still, Islah leaders recognized that certain ideas espoused by the YSP and other Leftist parties were somewhat appealing to Yemenis, so the party sought to engage a democratic narrative by employing Islamic terms. One of the YSP's key campaign positions, for example, advocated the promotion of equal rights for women in all spheres of life (Table 5.1). The official position of the Islah party was to not field (or even condone) female

---

[50] "Al-Barnamaj al-Siyasi li al-Tajamma' al-Yamani li al-Islah," 1993, sec. 1.

TABLE 5.1. *Theme of Women's Rights in Elections Platforms in Yemen, 1993*

General People's Congress	"...affirms its promise to exert its efforts to guarantee the rights of women from the Qur'an and the constitution...."
Yemeni Socialist Party	"...to guarantee the equal rights of women...."
Islah	"...the protection of women from exploitation...." From campaign posters: "Women are the siblings [*shaqa'iq*] of men; they have rights and responsibilities."

candidates, though party leaders encouraged women to vote and in some regions the party even provided transport to polling sites. Nevertheless, Islah leaders put forth a version of women's rights, stated in Islamic terms: "Women are the siblings of men, they have rights and responsibilities" [*al-nisa' shaqa'iq al-rijal; lahunna huquq wa mas'uliyat*]. This Islamic framing of women's rights emphasizes that women have prescribed roles and responsibilities, and within those boundaries they have rights to pursue courses to fulfill those roles and responsibilities. Al-Yadumi argued that the YSP did not have a monopoly on the promotion of women's rights, stating, "Our view of women's rights is one based on *shari'ah* and the teachings of the Prophet Muhammad rather than the secular socialism imported through British colonialism and Soviet influence. *Shari'ah* provides for women's rights."[51]

From Coalition to Opposition?

Islah did very well at the polls, gaining the second largest bloc of seats after the GPC. Unfortunately, Yemen's first national elections, which were remarkably free and fair for a first contest in a "transitioning" state, gave way less than a year later to armed conflict between the GPC and YSP. Although the dominant narrative during and after the conflict was one of preserving national unity, al-Zindani portrayed the war as a religious struggle (*jihad*) between pious Muslims and infidels, arguing, "We Yemenis are called upon by God to fight against the communists.... The YSP are communists, infidels, and non-believers... [who] have authorized liberal sexual policies and adultery... [and who] intend to convert

[51] Interview with author, March 13, 1995, San'a.

the *Ka'abah* [52] into a nightclub where alcohol is served. . . . The war we are fighting is jihad and I demand that all theologians declare it so. . . . All of us have to volunteer to fight. You do not need the permission of the rulers or your parents or spouse to volunteer. Just go ahead and do it." [53] Al-Daylami also issued a religious opinion in the summer of 1994 in which he justified the war as a confrontation between infidels (the YSP) and pious Muslims and rendered YSP members apostates.

Al-Zindani was named to head a committee to promote popular support for the North's war against the southern leadership. According to *The Yemen Times*, "The main task [of this committee] is to promote moral and financial support for the war efforts. The mosque preachers have been asked to galvanize the public, while financial and business leaders have been asked to contribute to pay for the war costs." [54] In the context of the conflict, and in contrast to the earlier "transition" period, al-Zindani's radical rhetoric was moved to the fore, though they did not really reflect a shift in the party toward a more radical agenda. Yet following the YSP's defeat and the exile of many of its leaders, al-Yadumi told *Al-Sahwah*, "Yemen has demonstrated to the world its commitment to democratic development. Ours is a democracy that is appropriate to Yemen and we reject efforts by foreign agents to force our political institutions to conform to secular, western democracy. The defeat of the socialists was not a failure for our democratic development, but a final victory against imperialism in Yemen and for national unity." [55]

With the YSP defeat the Islah party was awarded two seats on the presidential council and gained a number of ministries. With the YSP having lost its veto of constitutional amendments, the coalition of the GPC and Islah were able to press constitutional amendments through parliament, including the desired wording stipulating Islam as the source of all legislation. [56] A new article also made defending religion a sacred duty, [57] while women's rights were to be confined to those in accordance with Islam, giving men implicit predominance over women. [58] The GPC and

---

[52] Located in Mecca, the Ka'abah is Islah's holiest shrine and the site of the annual pilgrimage, or *hajj*.

[53] From a Friday sermon, quoted in *The Yemen Times*, June 20, 1994.

[54] *The Yemen Times*, May 30, 1994.

[55] Undated clipping, circa August 1994, given to author during an interview on February 24, 1995, San'a.

[56] 1994 Constitution, Art. 3.

[57] 1994 Constitution, Art. 59.

[58] 1994 Constitution, Art. 31. For a detailed discussion of the amendments, see Saif (2001: 75–76).

Islah concluded a series of agreements aimed at furthering earlier cooperation between the two parties. Record #1 of the coordinating committee meeting characterizes the gathering of seven GPC members and five Islah members as "a continuation and extension of past mutual efforts [between the two parties]," in which "the atmosphere of the meeting was filled with the spirit of understanding, seriousness, and care." The document further stresses "the safeguard of the Yemeni union, preventing secession [of the South], and implementing government programs for the lessening of citizen suffering."[59]

Yet despite significant victories in implementing conservative Islamist reforms following the 1994 civil war, the Islah party saw its political influence deteriorate over the next few years. Of course, prominent individuals such as Shaykh 'Abd Allah retained their privileged positions of power, and even al-Zidani remained influential despite President Salih's periodic efforts to wrest control of the Islamic institutes from his personal control. Ironically for the Islah party, the YSP's defeat meant that President Salih no longer needed Islah as a powerful ally for the GPC in offsetting the YSP's influence. As more and more Islah ministers resigned their posts over the next few years, certain party leaders began to question the party's formal relations with the GPC. Previously party leaders had stressed the strength of its coalition with the government, arguing that Islah would sometimes act as opposition on certain issues, but would remain part of the alliance with the GPC. As the alliance deteriorated, however, statements issued through the Muslim Brotherhood – dominated party bureaucracy as well as articles published in the Muslim Brotherhood – run *Al-Sahwah* appealed for adherence to democratic practices, particularly in framing critiques of the GPC. GPC membership ballooned, with a number of mid-level Islah leaders and administrators defecting to accept positions with the GPC or in government.[60]

Thus when the GPC announced during the summer prior to the April 1997 elections that it would seek to gain a majority of parliamentary seats, Islah leaders criticized the ruling party for acting undemocratically and undermining the basis of *shura*, namely, the presence of a multiplicity of voices in the national assembly. Gradually, Islah leaders began to

---

[59] "Muhadar Ijtima' Lajnah al-Tansiq, No. 1," April 30, 1994.
[60] These included Nasr Taha Mustafa, former head of the YCSS and Faris Saqqaf, former party spokesperson (who left the party to found an "independent" think tank, the Center for Future Studies, before formally rejoining the government).

identify the GPC's derailing of the democratic transition as central to Yemen's political problems. In private, Islah leaders worked hard to preserve the weakening GPC-Islah coalition and especially to come to some sort of agreement for the upcoming elections so that prominent Islah and GPC candidates would not run against each other. Continuing to stress the party's commitment to promoting national unity, party statements, communiqués, press releases, and sometimes newspaper articles made increasing reference to "enhancing the democratic *shura* approach to governance" and adhering to the provisions of the constitution. In one communiqué issued following the annual meeting of its consultative council in 1996, the party directly addressed its relations with the GPC, arguing that it wished to "... stress keeping them strong. These relations are not newly established but are based on strong historical and ideological grounds of shared struggle. The coalition between the two organizations is built on basic national foundations untainted by any narrow interests. Their basic and greatest aim is, first and foremost, to serve Yemen and alleviate the suffering of its people. They look forward to establishing the state of law and order, achieving justice and *shura*, erecting the correct social structure, guaranteeing freedom and human rights... and enhancing the democratic *shura* approach to governance." Among the specific issues the communiqué emphasized in this regard, was this item concerning mudslinging: "It is essential that the media belonging to the two parties should refrain from all harmful rhetoric and must offer a forum for objectivity and honest opinions."[61]

Perhaps more critically, representatives from the Muslim Brotherhood trend within Islah were holding talks almost simultaneously with the opposition bloc in consideration of future cooperation. Like the IAF in Jordan, the Muslim Brotherhood leadership within Islah had come to view such communications in terms of democratic practices and ideals, criticizing the government for violating democratic provisions now guaranteed in the constitution, particularly the manipulation of elections. Also like the IAF, the Islah party engaged a democratic narrative with greater regularity when it began to explore cooperation with groups that had differences with the party on ideological grounds. 'Abd al-Wahhab al-Anisi, the former Deputy Prime Minister who had served the highest cabinet post of any Islah member, responded to my question about possibly joining the

---

[61] "Bayan," no title, Consultative Council of the Yemeni Congress for Reform (Islah), October 26, 1996.

opposition bloc, stating, "I will never understand you foreign researchers and why you keep asking about our relations with other parties. Isn't that supposed to happen in democracies? From the first day Islah was founded we have consistently promoted *shura* and sought to work with all other political trends except those created and supported by foreign agencies."[62]

In an interview with *The Yemen Times*, a member of Islah's consultative council took a different approach, one that acknowledged a shift of strategy and expressed regret over Islah's history of isolation from other political parties: "Lack of dialogue with other parties was a gross error... Islah has a democratic aim especially after the Islamist movement in Yemen changed its attitudes and mechanisms."[63] Meanwhile, Islah leaders worked through Shaykh 'Abd Allah to try to reach an agreement with the GPC concerning candidate lists, but efforts crumbled by mid-winter. Yet while Islah portrayed its negotiations with both the GPC and opposition parties in the terms of a democratic narrative, the party adopted a new electoral symbol for the upcoming elections that emphasized an Islamic narrative: A rising sun was surrounded by the slogan, "Promoting *shari'ah*; fighting secularism." (The party's preferred symbol was a crescent moon, but the Nasserite party had beat Islah by one day in registering the symbol. Islah took the case to court, but the judgment found in favor of the Nasserite party.)

Thus while the Islah party emerged from the 1994 civil war as a full coalition partner of the GPC, that very success facilitated the decline of its importance as a political party. Party leaders have never enjoyed internal consensus on a range of issues, with various factions holding divergent expectations about where the party should be headed. It is not surprising that the Muslim Brotherhood members who staff the party offices and produce party literature present arguments quite similar to Muslim Brotherhood branches in other countries, including Jordan. In this connection, the party's gradual rapprochement with the reemerging YSP, particularly following the overwhelming GPC victory in the 1997 elections, has proven as interesting as it is controversial. At the same time, the Islah party has failed to reflect increasing acceptance of democratic practices and rhetoric demonstrated through significantly changed boundaries of justifiable action, as happened with the IAF in Jordan. Furthermore, Islah leaders did not practice the sort of internal democratic

---

[62] Interview with author, April 24, 1997, San'a.
[63] Interview with Muhammad Alawi, *The Yemen Times*, October 7, 1997.

procedures that characterized the Jordanian Muslim Brotherhood, from open forums to express and reconcile diverse opinions, to a democratic rotation of leadership (evidenced in Jordan by the 1998 upset that saw Farhan and 'Arabiyyat fail to be reelected to the consultative council). While the IAF had moved significantly in the direction of accommodating and even embracing democratic practices, the Islah party, as a whole, had not.

6

Conclusion: Does Inclusion Lead to Moderation?

In this study, I have examined the inclusion-moderation hypothesis – the idea that political actors included in pluralist processes become more moderate as a result of that inclusion – through a structured comparative study of two Islamist groups and find that the IAF in Jordan has become more moderate over time, while the Islah party in Yemen has not. The evidence from party documents, internal party debates, interviews, and evolving party practices suggests that the ideology of the IAF has indeed evolved from a relatively closed worldview to one that is more pluralist and tolerant of alternative perspectives. I do not claim that the IAF or Muslim Brotherhood are fully committed to liberal democratic norms and practices, but I do argue that the party has become ideologically more moderate – in the sense of being relatively more open and tolerant of alternative perspectives – than it had been prior to the 1989 political opening. In Yemen, the Islah party has not changed in a similar manner. In this chapter, I highlight several insights on democratization and moderation that emerged from this comparative study and then briefly review the three factors that explain the variation between the IAF and the Islah party. Finally, I situate these two political parties within a larger context of Islamist politics in both countries.

One observation is that much of the literature on democratization in the Middle East adopts the teleological language of the transitions literature, so we tend to emphasize progress toward democracy and use the language of stalled or failed transitions. Even the emerging "gray-zone" literature, to which Middle East scholars have begun to contribute, critiques the transitions paradigm primarily by suggesting new typologies of nondemocratic regimes. This continued spotlight on regime type, however, overlooks the often dramatic evolution in public political space that results from even limited political openings. For example, political parties organize, publish agendas, and seek to build a constituency. Public political debates expand, and the language of democracy is invoked by both state and nonstate actors. Actors that were formerly rivals may even begin to cooperate. These developments are often dismissed because the broader process is not "moving forward" and meaningful democracy is nowhere on the horizon. At a very minimum, scholars might fruitfully examine these ongoing changes within public political space when democratization or liberalization processes do not advance. As the cases of Jordan and Yemen illustrate, even small openings can profoundly impact how political actors organize and interact.

A second observation is that the inclusion-moderation hypothesis appears in a wide range of literature, but the specific mechanisms are often poorly specified. Most of the literature emphasizes the role of institutional constraints in shaping political behavior. In this view, liberalizing states create channels for legal participation that, in turn, structure opportunities for opposition groups to engage. But the cost of entry is "playing by the rules of the game," and so political actors that take advantage of these openings become constrained. Groups also face the practical distractions of routine operation: maintaining an office and staff, producing programs and press releases, campaigning for elections, forming strategic alliances with other political actors, forging relations with government officials, and so on. Thus, political openings provide both the opportunities and constraints that support the inclusion-moderation hypothesis. But these formulations assert rather than explain ideational change, that is, how a political actor may come to hold more moderate positions as a result of inclusion. Even more crucial is explaining the counterfactual: Why don't similar groups with similar experiences participating in similar processes under similar constraints all become more moderate, or moderate in the same way? Explanations that focus on institutional constraints alone cannot explain this variation.

A third observation is that arguments about inclusion often suggest a single continuum whereby more inclusion is assumed to lead not only to more moderation, but also to less radicalism. Conflating inclusion and exclusion in this manner has a tendency to obscure complex processes and practices. Even more, it offers little in terms of precise hypotheses about the effects of either inclusion or exclusion. I argue that entangled in the inclusion-moderation hypothesis are many propositions that need to be unpacked. For example, inclusion may "increase moderation" by:

- Turning radicals into moderates,
- Turning fence-sitters into moderates,
- Encouraging moderates to become even more moderate, and/or
- Providing moderates with opportunities to increase their visibility and efficacy.

Thus, the appearance of moderation may have little to do with whether political actors have actually become more moderate, and it may have everything to do with elevating certain political trends or disadvantaging others. That is, inclusion may not turn radicals into moderates, or revolutionaries into reformers, but rather deny radicals a large support base. The IAF and Islah, for example, are cited as evidence supporting the inclusion-moderation hypothesis: both participate in pluralist processes and elections, and both seek political change through reform rather than revolution. But both have been allied with the ruling elite since their earliest days, so labeling them moderate because they do not seek to immanently overthrow the existing regime fundamentally misses the point: not only were they never really radical, they were never really excluded. The question should be whether each party has become *more* moderate over time, as defined by movement toward a more open and tolerant worldview (and regardless of the starting point). Though the IAF and Islah participate in similar processes, the IAF has become more moderate in the fifteen years since Jordan's political opening, while over approximately the same period of time, the Islah party has not.

What explains this variation? I argue that three factors are at work, two of them structural and one ideational. The first factor is that the relation of the regime to public political space structures pluralist practices, even in so-called stalled transitions. In monarchies, the king and ruling family do not compete in elections, and thus they have different stakes in the outcome than do the ruling elite in a republic where the right to rule is at least theoretically and officially based on electoral outcomes (Herb 1999; Lust-Okar and Jamal 2002). Jordan has no "ruling" party in this sense, though the monarchy certainly encourages and supports "loyalist" candidates, particularly among local elite and tribal leaders. In Yemen, by comparison, President Salih's party must at least pretend to win elections, even if Yemenis all recognize, as Wedeen (2002) argues, that the contest is more of a performance of power than a substantive process to popularly elect leadership. Even when elected assemblies do not play a real role in governance – indeed, perhaps especially when that is the case – the direct participation of the regime in elections renders certain alliances among other parties more or less costly. For example since the early 1990s, in Jordan, the IAF has begun to explore a wide range of cooperative alliances with various Leftist, liberal, and nationalist parties, even though they remain political rivals in other areas. In Yemen, by comparison, even after the Islah party cautiously entered such alliances with opposition groups by joining the SCCO in 1997, it sought to maintain close relations with the regime rather than embracing an oppositional role because it did not wish to find itself completely outside of power.

The second factor is the internal organization and decision-making practices of each party. Yemen's Islah party is a coalition of tribal, mercantile, and religious interests, and the party is fairly fragmented. Quite frequently, its central bureaucracy announces formal policies and positions that are directly contradicted by the statements of prominent leaders in the party, notably al-Zindani and Shaykh 'Abd Allah. In the IAF, all major decisions are taken by vote and after sometimes considerable debate, with major party leaders adhering to those decisions. Following the contentious debates around the question of whether to boycott the parliamentary elections in 1997, for example, Farhan supported the boycott even though he had led the internal group that voted in favor of participation. Furthermore, Islah sees virtually the same party leaders elected year after year: al-Zindani, al-Yadumi, and Shaykh 'Abd Allah have each held the same executive office since the party's formation more than fifteen years ago. Within the IAF, leadership rotates every two years with even the most prominent eventually voted out of office. In this regard, the IAF's internal democratic practices and the cohesion of its central leadership distinguish the party from Islah, where decision making is fragmented in practice and party leadership is highly hierarchical and unchanging. Within the IAF the policy debates and mechanisms for decision making would be recognizable anywhere as democratic practices.

These two factors – the relation of the regime to public political space and the internal structure and decision-making practices of each party – explain only part of the variation between the cases. The third and most pivotal factor that explains moderation is that the IAF leadership as a whole has sought to justify new practices in terms of the party's central ideological commitments while Islah has not. The dimensions of change that appear as moderation within the IAF include not only the formation of new alliances, working within pluralist channels, and internal group organization and decision-making practices, but also changes in the boundaries of what the party can justify on ideological grounds and still recognize as Islamic practices. This process can be established empirically, for example, through the content of internal party debates, documents, interviews, and practices that evolve over time. Internal debates justifying new practices may have different impact on future practices, however, depending on how they were reached. That is, decisions reached through deliberation and debate are likely to redraw boundaries of justifiable action in a meaningful way recognized by the whole party, whereas decisions on contentious issues that are put forth by small factions whose opinions do not represent the views of the group overall are unlikely to constrain what is justifiable to the group in the future. For example, the IAF held heated debates about its decision to participate in elections in 1989. Those and subsequent efforts to justify electoral participation on Islamic terms created new possibilities to explore alliances with other political actors, and at each step, redrawn boundaries of justifiable action created new possibilities to adopt practices that were previously not justifiable. The IAF found alliances with Leftist and liberal parties unthinkable following the 1989 election, even though doing so would have given the opposition bloc 60 percent control of the assembly. Only after a series of justifications redrew the boundaries of acceptable practices did the now-commonplace Islamist-Leftist cooperation emerge.

For the Islah party, these boundaries have not been redrawn in a similar way. The Muslim Brotherhood trend within Islah may indeed have become more moderate and tolerant as the Islah party saw its share of power decline following the 1994 defeat of the YSP. But the party as a whole has not brought together its diverse trends to engage in meaningful debates in which all agree to adhere to the outcome. Al-Zindani continuously contradicts the policy positions put forth by the party bureaus, and Shaykh 'Abd Allah's actions appear more aimed at preserving his personal power than advancing the social and political agendas of Islah (although the two often coincide). Under Muslim Brotherhood control of the party bureaus, Islah has explored possible alliances with the YSP, but Shaykh 'Abd Allah has not encouraged this rapprochement and al-Zindani has not backed away from his inflammatory condemnations of the YSP dating to the early days of unification. These Muslim Brotherhood initiatives, forged in large part by Islah's political bureau leader, Muhammad Qahtan, enabled the party to realize a formal, if on-again, off-again, alliance with the YSP through the 2001 Joint Council for the Opposition. Islah formally invited YSP Deputy Secretary-General Jar Allah 'Umar to address the Islah general congress on December 28, 2002, on the subject of forging an electoral coalition in the upcoming April 2003 parliamentary elections. But unlike the IAF, the Islah party as a whole had not really redrawn the boundaries of justifiable action in ways that rendered cooperation with Leftists acceptable on Islamic terms in a way recognized across the party leadership and thus presenting a unified position. As 'Umar left the stage at the Islah meeting, he was fatally shot in the heart at point blank range by a radical member of the Islah party, one who (like al-Zindani and al-Daylami) did not share the Muslim Brotherhood members' view that an electoral coalition with the YSP was both justifiable and practical.[1] This incident is examined in greater detail in the following text.

Thus despite appeal to a democratic narrative, reconciling a broader Islamist agenda with democratic practices was less crucial to the Islah party than it had been for Jordan's IAF. Islah's leaders failed to present united positions on a number of issues, from the legitimacy of joining a coalition in which a socialist group participated, to the role of women within the party. The Muslim Brotherhood leaders who run the party bureau have been extremely frustrated by the failure of all party leaders to support party lines, but little has been done to alter the statements and actions of al-Zindani and Shaykh 'Abd Allah, whose power and resources buy them latitude. In Jordan, the Muslim Brotherhood faced considerably more public scrutiny of the details of its policies, a factor evidenced by the extent to which the group sought to sort out its differences internally and present a unified vision. Both parties publicly portray internal divisions and dissent as illustrative of their internal democratic workings, but the Islah party shows little evidence of internally justifying these new practices on Islamic grounds. These three factors explain not only why the IAF has become more moderate, but more crucially, why the Islah party as a whole has not. Shifting boundaries of justifiable action are one mechanism the can explain moderation, but certainly not the only one. Additional ethnographic study of other cases and practices will further expand our understanding of this critical process.

LOCATING ISLAMIST PARTIES IN A LARGER CONTEXT

While this study has unpacked the inclusion-moderation hypothesis and suggested one mechanism that may produce ideological change, the broader field of Islamist political activism begs comment. Just as Islamist parties practice and contest politics within a context of multiple and

---

[1] The assassin, 'Ali Jar Allah, was executed in Yemen on November 27, 2005, for the crime.

overlapping public spaces, competing narratives, and institutional constraints, so do they encounter, overlap, and come into conflict with other dimensions of Islamist activism: local and transnational networks, competing groups, discursive spaces inhabited by competing Islamists, alternative political claims, and so on. The IAF and Islah party are the most influential Islamist parties in their countries, but where do these parties fit within a broader spectrum of Islamist activism, domestically as well as regionally? The next stage of comparative study on Islamist politics will need to examine not only internal group dynamics, but also the complex and changing relations and practices between a diverse range of political actors. In the following text I outline some of these relations among competing Islamist groups within each country but with a view toward regional and transnational dimensions.

Islamists in Jordan

Jordan's Muslim Brotherhood and IAF overwhelmingly dominate other Islamist voices within many of the country's public political spaces. But other Islamist groups and networks exist throughout the kingdom and in the broader Middle East, and the Muslim Brotherhood has complex relations with many of these groups. Most obviously, for a long time the Jordanian Muslim Brotherhood has had close links to HAMAS, a militant group that emerged in Gaza from a Palestinian branch of the Muslim Brotherhood during the first weeks of the first Palestinian *intifada* in 1987. During the period from 1948 to 1967, when Jordan controlled the West Bank, the Palestinian branch of the Muslim Brotherhood was organizationally connected to the Jordanian Muslim Brotherhood. By most counts, the two groups functioned as one, sharing office space and members, although the Palestinian branch maintained a separate overseer-general. During this period, a separate Gaza branch of the Muslim Brotherhood existed under the patronage of the Egyptian Muslim Brotherhood, and the history of that group is more intertwined with the history of Islamist politics in Egypt than in Jordan.

When Jordan lost control of the West Bank in 1967, the West Bank branch of the Muslim Brotherhood began to cooperate more closely with the Gaza branch, though it continued to have ties to the Jordanian group, which provided limited support and continued to champion the Palestinian cause (and to confront many Arab states as well). In the 1970s and 1980s, Palestinian Muslim Brotherhood members did not directly challenge the Israeli government, however, and sought instead to provide social programs and build a wide base of support to spread Islamic values and education. At that time, the Israeli government (as well as the United States) viewed the group as a conservative force far preferable to the revolutionary Leftist guerillas who used political violence in their efforts to liberate Palestine. As a result, the Muslim Brotherhood was able to function relatively freely in the Palestinian territories throughout the 1970s and much of the 1980s. Indeed, some scholars have argued that the Israeli government even provided support to the Muslim Brotherhood as a counter to the Leftist militant groups such as the PFLP.

That was until the formation of HAMAS in 1987. HAMAS emerged as a political wing of the Palestinian Muslim Brotherhood, and its specific objective of armed resistance marked a departure from the Muslim Brotherhood's longtime strategy of reform-based engagement. As HAMAS gained in influence and popularity, however, the Palestinian Muslim Brotherhood and its predominantly social programs gradually became subsumed under HAMAS (Abu Amr 1994: 63–4). Organizationally, however, the Palestinian Muslim Brotherhood (now referred to almost exclusively as HAMAS) remains attached to the Jordanian Muslim Brotherhood, and a HAMAS office is still located within the Muslim Brotherhood directorate in Amman.

The close relations between the Jordanian Muslim Brotherhood and HAMAS have periodically caused conflict in the kingdom. In 1996, for example, Palestinian Chairman Yasser Arafat accused King Hussein of allowing HAMAS to use the kingdom as a base from which to organize acts of political violence in the territories. These militant activities, Arafat argued, were undermining the authority and stability of the Palestinian National Authority (Lynch 1999: 128). It also illustrates the complexities of Muslim Brotherhood relations between Jordan and the Palestinian territories. The Jordanian government periodically pressures the Muslim Brotherhood to contain HAMAS activities in Jordan, but at the same time the kingdom seems to support Palestinian Islamists, as when it negotiated the release from Israeli prison of Shaykh Ahmad Yassin, the spiritual leader of HAMAS. In Amman, Mossad agents had attempted to assassinate the prominent HAMAS leader Khalid Misha'al, who was responsible for planning and carrying out acts of political violence against Israeli targets. King Hussein was furious that Israel had launched the attack on Jordanian soil and was able to negotiate Yassin's release in the aftermath.

Within the Jordanian Muslim Brotherhood and IAF, the prominent members of Palestinian origin have not presented a cohesive or consistent bloc. Farhan, for example, is among the movements' more moderate voices, but was born in a Palestinian village in the West Bank prior to the creation of the state of Israel. Many of the more extremist voices among the groups' Palestinian members were refugees from the 1967 war, suggesting that to the extent that a cleavage over Palestine does exist within the Muslim Brotherhood and IAF, it is between 1948 and 1967 Palestinian refugees, rather than between Palestinians and Jordanians. Abu Zant, for example, was born in Nablus and became a refugee in Jordan after the 1967 war (he was studying in Saudi Arabia at the time). Considered one of the IAF's more radical voices, he has close ties to HAMAS leaders and frequently supports their activities in his sermons. When in the summer of 1999 the regime again sought to reign in HAMAS activities in the kingdom, "the Amman governor, Qaftan Majali, placed Abu Zant under administrative arrest detention [sic] for refusing to sign a pledge not to deliver pro-HAMAS sermons" and arrested him three times in a single week for not complying (Wiktorowicz 2001: 62). However, as a general rule the Jordanian Muslim Brotherhood has consistently put its own survival and relations with the monarchy over Palestinian liberation, most notably in supporting the regime during the 1970 events of Black September.

Several other Islamist groups within the kingdom were established by former Muslim Brotherhood or IAF members who disagreed with those groups' political tactics, strategies, or central ideological commitments. The Liberation Party (*Hizb al-Tahrir*) was founded in (Jordanian-controlled) Jerusalem in 1952 by Muslim Brother Shaykh Taqii al-Din al-Nabahani, a *shari'ah* court judge. He submitted an application on November 17, 1952 (Boulby 1999: 53) to the Ministry of the Interior in Amman to form a political party, but was denied because the party program failed to recognize the Jordanian constitution as the basis for pluralist political competition (Hourani et al. 1993a: 15) and sought to replace the monarchy with an Islamic state. Al-Nabahani and others had left the Muslim Brotherhood because of disagreements with the group concerning its strategy of working with the Hashemite monarchy to achieve its goals. According to Cohen, the group's platform rejected the monarchy and called for an elected ruler (1982: 210). Al-Nabatani had been an associate of Khalifah, but the two parted ways with the creation of Liberation Party as an illegal organization that sought to overthrow the monarchy and reestablish the caliphate. Muslim Brotherhood leaders speak of how the Liberation Party launched several assassination attempts against King Hussein and sought to seize power in 1962. Boulby argues, however, that the party has advocated only peaceful overthrow of the monarchy, and no records of violent activities exist. Party leaders tried again to register as a legal party in 1992, but were denied. Ihsan Samara, a senior official of the group, met Boulby in Amman at that time and told her, "We do not believe in using force to change society. We believe in building up the mentality in a practical way." While the Muslim Brotherhood and the Liberation Party maintain a competitive relationship, Boulby argues that there is very little ideological difference between them today (1999: 53). The party remains illegal, however, and a number of its members have been subject to periodic arrest, notably when spokesman Ata Abu al-Rishta and other members were arrested in May 1993 by the GID, which at the time confiscated party documents from the organization's office and the homes of arrested members.[2]

The liberal Islamic Center Party (*Hizb al-Wasat al-Islami*) emerged in 2003 with clear commitments to pluralism, social equality, and human rights. The founders include several of the independent Islamists who had been original members of the IAF in 1992, but who had resigned when the extent of Muslim Brotherhood domination of the party became clear. Nawal al-Faouri, who in the late 1990s became the first woman to win a seat on the IAF's consultative council, was also a pivotal figure in the formation of the new party. Another was Bassam Amoush, a former IAF member who left the party after the 1997 elections when he failed to honor the boycott and won a seat. The Islamic Center Party remains very small and unproven on the political scene, however, and is unlikely to seriously challenge the IAF for influence or members.

Outside the space of competitive parties, various Islamist networks and groups function throughout the kingdom, but have seldom played pivotal roles on the political scene. A mainstream Salafi movement emerged in the 1970s as Jordanians exposed to Salafi ideas while studying in Lebanon, Syria, and Egypt returned to the kingdom and began to spread their new-found ideas.[3] The leading Salafi figure in Jordan at that time was Syrian scholar Nasr al-Din al-Albani, who visited the kingdom frequently until he relocated there after Syria's crackdown on Islamists in 1979 (International Crisis Group 2005a: 5). Prominent Salafi leaders are located in Zarqa and

---

[2] *The Jordan Times*, May 24, 1993.
[3] Scholarship on the Salafi movements in Jordan is extremely thin. Wiktorowicz (2001) offered the first book-length study (actually a study of two groups, the Muslim Brotherhood and the Salafi), but ethnographic research by Arabic-speaking scholars is needed to expand on this pioneering but limited study. A report by the International Crisis Group (2005a) offers an excellent but brief overview, and Brisard (2005) presents a full study of al-Zarqawi, including his connections with a wide range of Islamists.

Irbid, and their circles gain members through the defection of Islamists from the Muslim Brotherhood and the Islamic Missionary Society (discussed in the following text), though primary recruitment continues to occur as followers invite friends and family to informal gatherings held largely in private homes (International Crisis Group 2005a: 5).

Jordan's Salafi movement gained strength in 1989 with the return of fighters – often called "Afghan Arabs" – from the Afghan war who brought highly critical views of the Hashemite regime (not to mention sustained military training and experience) and advocated the use of violence to achieve their objective of realizing a fully Islamic society. Since the 1990s, the movement has become somewhat fractured and decentralized, with competing reformist and *jihadi* trends. 'Abd Allah Azzam, a Jordanian of Palestinian origin and member of the Muslim Brotherhood, left a teaching position in Saudi Arabia to run a service bureau in Pakistan to assist Arab fighters on their way to Afghanistan. A strong advocate of *jihadi* activities, he split with the Muslim Brotherhood when the latter refused to urge Jordanians to join the *mujahidin*. Only a few hundred Jordanians eventually fought in Afghanistan, and the International Crisis Group argues that most did so out of economic opportunism rather than religious conviction (2005a: 3). Among the returnees was Ahmad Fadil Nazzal al-Khalaylah, who has gained notariety under the name Abu Mus'ab al-Zarqawi, and Isam Muhammad Tahir al-Barqawi, better known as Abu Muhammad al-Maqdisi. The two met and recruited followers in the poor Amman suburb of Zarqa, but would later become rivals of competing Salafi trends in the kingdom (Brisard 2005: 128–9).

This divide emerged in the 1990s as al-Maqdisi began to oppose the traditionalist view (advocated by al-Albani) against Islamist political activism. He insisted on the need to overthrow impious regimes, through violence if necessary, in contradistinction to the traditionalist view that Muslims must obey a Muslim ruler even if the latter rules unjustly. Al-Maqdisi led this new *jihadi* trend, which he named *Al-Tawhid* (Monotheism, or the oneness of God) in 1992, and the movement gained strength under al-Maqdisi and especially after al-Zarqawi joined in 1993 after returning from Afghanistan. Reformist Salafi followers, however, continued to advocate peaceful opposition to the monarchy. Jordan's peace treaty with Israel won the *jihadi* trend more followers, who launched some small-scale attacks in the mid-1990s, fire-bombing cinemas and liquor stores in Jordan (International Crisis Group 2005a: 5–6).

Al-Maqdisi and al-Zarqawi were both imprisoned in the mid-1990s: al-Zarqawi in 1994 for possessing illegal weapons and membership in a banned organization; al-Maqdisi in 1996 on similar charges. While in prison, both seem to have advanced the *jihadi* trend in Jordan but began to clash as al-Zarqawi increasingly acted as that movement's leader. When al-Zarqawi was released in 1999, he joined some 500 Jordanians who had gone to Afghanistan to support the Taliban against the Northern Alliance and left al-Maqdisi in the kingdom to became more vociferous in his criticisms of al-Zarqawi. During this period, the reformist trend appeared to dominate Salafi activities in the kingdom. The September 11, 2001 attacks and the subsequent U.S. wars in Afghanistan and Iraq served to energize the *jihadi* movement, however, as even one prominent reformist leader, Abu Anas al-Shami, joined the resistance in Iraq and was killed (International Crisis Group 2005a: 8–11).

Information about support for Osama bin Laden in the kingdom is very thin, and by all counts he had little following at all prior to the September 11, 2001 attacks, even among Salafi *jihadi* circles.[4] Al-Zarqawi joined forces with bin Laden in Afghanistan, but the two were reportedly at such odds that the Taliban leader Mullah Omar asked al-Zarqawi to lead a camp to train Arabs near the Afghan town of Herat (Brisard 2005: 210). Al-Zarqawi later formed *al-Tawhid wa al-Jihad* (Monotheism and Holy War) and in early 2001 took the first of several oaths of allegience to bin Laden. He was convicted in Jordan in absentia of participating in the failed millenium plot to bomb numerous sites in Amman, but he and other *jihadi* followers continued to plan attacks against targets inside the kingdom, including the fatal shooting of a senior U.S. Agency for International Development (USAID) administrator Laurence Foley on October 28, 2002 (for which al-Zarqawi was convicted and sentenced to death in absentia), a failed attack in Amman in April 2004 against several targets (GID headquarters, the prime ministry, and the U.S. embassy), and a failed rocket attack in the port of Aqaba that targeted two U.S. Navy vessels on August 19, 2005. On November 9, 2005, now the self-proclaimed leader of al-Qa'ida in Iraq, al-Zarqawi was successful in orchestrating a major attack inside the kingdom with the suicide bombings of three international hotels[5] in Amman that killed at least fifty-six people, including many members of a wedding party. The GID had in recent years arrested or detained hundreds of Jordanians with possible connections to various

---

[4] The International Crisis Group reports that the GID arrested 16 Islamists on suspicion of belonging to al-Qa'ida in 2000, 50 in 2001, and several hundred in April 2003 following U.S.-led war on Iraq (2005a: 12).

[5] The hotels were the Grand Hyatt, the Days Inn, and the Radisson SAS.

jihadi groups, including al-Qa'ida, and King 'Abd Allah told *The New York Times* that the security services had stopped at least 150 planned attacks inside the kingdom (November 16, 2005). Al-Zarqawi sent four Iraqis to carry out the attacks, however, exploiting a weakness in the GID's ability to monitor nonnationals and externally orchestrated *jihadi* activities (International Crisis Group 2005a: 1).

One final Islamic group of note is the Group for Preaching and Propogation (*Jama'at Tabligh wa al-Da'wa*), a *da'wa* ("call" to Islamic faith) movement that rejects direct involvement in political activities, but seeks to promote close adherence to Islamic practices. Based primarily in Zarqa, where the Salafi trends have significant support, this group spreads its peaceful vision through education, notably free literacy classes and discussion groups organized in poorer neighborhoods throughout the country.

In addition to these Islamist groups, Jordan has a number of independent Islamists of note. The most well-known is Laith Shubaylat, whom some Jordanian politicians refer to as *Hizb Laith Shubaylat* (the Party of Laith Shubaylat), a criticism of his perceived political opportunism. With moderate views toward political participation, vacillating views toward social issues, and a rigid opposition to peace with Israel,[6] he is a charismatic figure who draws large crowds to hear him speak and has a knack for grandstanding. He has also been imprisoned on several highly publicized occasions, which has only added to his credibility as an opposition figure though he has never significantly threatened the regime. Shubaylat has been elected president of the Engineers Association (the largest professional association in the kingdom) on several occasions, once receiving 90 percent of the vote even while in prison. At times he has criticized the Muslim Brotherhood as having been co-opted by the regime, while at other times he works as an ally of the movement. He often gives interviews to the Islamist weekly *Al-Sabil*, and he coordinates with Muslim Brotherhood and IAF leaders and professional association leaders (including Leftists and liberals) in organizing anti-American and antinormalization (with Israel) events.

Overall, the field of Islamist politics in Jordan is diverse, but clearly dominated by the Muslim Brotherhood and the IAF, who play an essential role for the regime in attracting Islamist activists into their ranks and thus tempering the expansion of various extremist trends. In this connection

---

[6] Shubaylat consistently calls for the liberation of all of Palestine from the Jordan River to the Mediterranean Sea (*min al-bahar ila al-nahar*).

the gradual moderation of the IAF's ideological commitments bodes well for the long-term prospects for democratization in the kingdom should the regime decide to implement more meaningful and deeper political reforms. Unfortunately, the reign of King'Abd Allah II has brought greater restrictions on political freedoms, further narrowing the opening initiated by his father a decade earlier.

Islamists in Yemen

The broader field of Islamist activism in Yemen is far more complex than that of Jordan, for two main reasons. First, the sheer size of the population (some 19.7 million compared to Jordan's 5.4 million) and terrain of the country (ill-defined borders, vast shoreline, rugged and inaccessible mountainous regions, etc.) facilitate a wider diversity of groups as well as increased flows in and out of the country. Second, President Salih's regime does not effectively exercise authority over portions of the country, nor did the YSP in the South prior to unification. Especially, but not only in the North, regions such as al-Jawf, Shabwa, Ma'rib, and Sa'dah are controlled by well-armed tribes, many of which have for years received considerable cash subsidies from Saudi Arabia. The government officials frequently note that Yemen has 60 million weapons for a population of approximately 19.7 million, and these arms are mostly outside of government control. Furthermore, Yemen remains predominantly rural and largely illiterate,[7] so the public political spaces of the urban centers are completely cut off from parts of the hinterlands.

These dimensions have created challenges not only for President Salih's regime, but also for a party like Islah that seeks a constituency throughout the country. Despite its sizeable network of regional offices, the Islah party, with its mix of tribal, mercantile, and ideological trends detailed in Chapter 3, does not dominate Islamist politics in Yemen the way the Muslim Brotherhood and IAF do in Jordan. Nor is the Islah party an ideologically or organizationally cohesive unit. In many ways, Islah is a microcosm of the broader field of Islamist politics in Yemen, with tribal, radical Islamist, and conservative Islamist dimensions intertwined.

The most obvious complicating factor, however, has nothing to do with Islamist politics per se: the extraordinary and often direct intervention of Saudi Arabia into Yemeni politics. The Saudi regime has for decades made sizeable cash payments to a wide range of actors for various

---

[7] In 2005, male illiteracy was 30% and female illiteracy was 71%. See UNDP (2005:20).

reasons: for example, convincing tribes along the border to adopt Saudi citizenship;[8] supporting various actors in both the North and South to keep power decentralized and to try to prevent unification; and supporting the YSP during the 1994 civil war (because a divided Yemen would pose less of a threat to Saudi Arabia), to name just a few. Perhaps even more divisive to Yemeni unity, Saudi influence has included ideational dimensions, such as the spread of Wahhabi thought in parts of Yemen and support for schools and other mechanisms for disseminating conservative and sometimes radical Islamist thought. Shaykh 'Abd Allah, the Islah leader mostly closely associated with Yemen's inner circles of state power, has reportedly received sizeable subsidies from Saudi Arabia for decades. Critics also note that his religiosity seems to have increased over time, as he has become more influenced by Wahhabi doctrine. Indeed, although he is closely associated with President Salih's regime, he has not been on good terms with the president at all times (Dresch and Haykel 1995: 420).

The other Islah leader often linked to Saudi Arabia[9] is al-Zindani, who is frequently at odds with Shaykh 'Abd Allah but who has strong affinities to a Wahhabi-influenced Salafi ideology. The terms *Wahhabi* and *Salafi* are often used interchangeably in talking about Yemen and elsewhere, in ways that obscure crucial complexities.[10] The term *Wahhabi* is best used to describe a Saudi-born school of conservative Islamist thought founded by Ibn 'Abd al-Wahhab. Wahhabis are certainly Salafi, and many so-called Salafi groups undoubtedly have ties to Saudi Arabia. But the term *Salafi* is best used to describe a general will toward a return to the teachings and practices of Sunni Islam's forefathers, especially the Prophet Muhammad. Salafis are highly conservative and insist on close and literal readings of Islamic doctrinal sources, though as the examples from Jordan illustrate, Salafi Islamists do not form a united movement. In terms of realizing their goals, they may advocate practices ranging from peaceful, gradual

---

[8] Tribes are widely said to have then burned their new Saudi passports in bonfires. Whether true (or whether the practice is widespread), these stories capture a popular notion of Yemenis as unwilling to be dominated by anyone (including the central government), but savvy enough to play various sides off each other and profit in the process.

[9] Shaykh 'Abd Allah and al-Zindani are not the only Islah leaders with links to Saudi Arabia, but Saudi support of two such different personalities illustrates both the complexities of Saudi intervention into Yemen and Saudi efforts to keep Yemen's various elite from becoming unified. Al-Yadumi, for example, is also said to receive subsidies from Saudi Arabia, though likely in sums far more modest than al-Zindani and Shaykh 'Abd Allah.

[10] For a discussion of the historical evolution of Wahhabism, see al-Fahad (2004).

reforms to radical and revolutionary methods. In Yemen, the term *Salafi* and especially *Wahhabi* have been used not only to refer to a particular worldview or ideology, but to imply connections with Saudi Arabia. But in fact not all followers of Wahhabi teachings (in Yemen or Saudi Arabia) accept the official state-sanctioned Saudi version, just as not all Salafi are Wahhabi.

In this connection, al-Zindani engaged official Saudi Wahhabi thought in a sustained manner during his stay in Saudi Arabia beginning in 1979. He is said to have become radicalized after fighting in Afghanistan in the mid-1980s, and by some reports was close to both bin Laden and his apparent deputy, 'Ayman al-Zawahiri.[11] As discussed in Chapter 4, al-Zindani has been able to spread extremist ideas through his influence over the thousands of Islamic scientific institutes (sing. *ma'hid 'ilmiya*) throughout Yemen. Control of these institutes has been a particular problem for the regime, which since 2000 has attempted to take them out of al-Zindani's control, but has run up against considerable opposition. In the 1970s, the institutes replaced the system of Islamic scientific schools (sing. *madrasa 'ilmiya*) established in the North as early as 1948 (International Crisis Group 2003: 10) and teach a version of Wahhabi thought officially endorsed by the Saudi state. These schools also seem to have served as recruiting stations to send fighters to Afghanistan in the 1980s and for the Islamic Front in the North. While some of them offered rudimentary military training, they do not seem to have operated large or sophisticated camps.

President Salih has sought to control these institutes, though with little success for fear of alienating al-Zindani and his militant followers. For example, in 1994 he established the Higher Council on Preaching to advocate a "moderate Islam" in mosques and in school curriculum (International Crisis Group 2003: 11), but the agency proved ineffective in reigning in extremist teachings. As recently as April 2005, Prime Minister 'Abd al-Kader BaJammal warned that some 4,000 scientific institutes continued to teach Wahhabi thought to 330,000 students. The result, he said, would be "a disaster to Yemen and this generation."[12] After the September 11, 2001 attacks, the regime stepped up its efforts to control the institutes and even deported hundreds of foreign students from one of

---

[11] I have been unable to confirm these rumors. Some critics have suggested that al-Zindani had little direct contact with bin Laden or al-Zawahiri and that these connections have been greatly exaggerated by al-Zindani and those around him.
[12] *Associated Press*, "Yemen Warns of Secret Extremist Schools," April 16, 2005.

them in the Abida district east of San'a, toward Ma'rib, because it was
alleged to have close ties to al-Qa'ida.[13] In November 2001, the regime
briefly closed the Islamic al-Iman University in San'a, which al-Zindani
had cofounded in 1994. Nevertheless, al-Zindani still controls many of
the institutes as well as the university, which continue to teach Wahhabi
orthodoxy. The institutes give him significant influence over education in
a largely illiterate country with a poor national school system.

In recent years, the tensions among the various trends (*tayarat*) within
Islah have threatened to split the party apart, particularly as the Muslim
Brotherhood trend running the central party bureaucracy have pushed
to envigorate the party's role as an oppositional actor. Extremists such
as al-Zindani and his followers strongly oppose any alliance, even tactical, with Leftists and liberals. Tensions between more progressive Muslim
Brotherhood party leaders and al-Zindani have escalated into personal-
ized attacks covered in local newspapers, perhaps marking the inability for
the party to continue presenting a united image to the public when deep
ideological and philosophical divisions have existed since Islah's founding
in 1990.

Much has been made in recent years of the radical Salafi Islamist groups
in Yemen, some of which are affiliated with al-Qa'ida and others of which
may be loosely connected or entirely independent. Like much of the Middle East, Yemen has been home to militant Islamist groups for decades,
however, and not only since the return of Afghan Arabs in the late 1980s
and 1990s, or the emergence of al-Qa'ida. A former Minister of the Interior, Hussayn al-'Arab, estimated that by 1993 the number of Afghan
Arabs in Yemen may have been as high as 29,000.[14] Soon after unification, these militants took a variety of career paths, from joining legal
parties, such as Islah and the GPC, to reengaging with local tribal politics, to forming underground militant groups. Of the latter, two primary
groups emerged that have been responsible for attacking Islamic shrines
and mosques in the South associated with Twelver Shi'a, bombing a brew-
ery in Aden, launching attacks on YSP leaders that claimed more than 150
lives, and bombing foreign targets in Yemen.

The first of these groups is the Aden-Abyan Islamic Army (AAIA).
Located in the South, the AAIA is said to have been created in the 1990s

---

[13] As with many conflicts in Yemen, the regime's measures against this institute in Abida
were also tied up in regime-tribal conflicts, as discussed in the following text. For more
on these and other regime-Islamist-tribal conflicts, see International Crisis Group (2003).

[14] *The Yemen Times*, April 2, 2001. Abu al-Miqdad, who leads the Islamic Jihad movement
in Ma'rib, a small town east of San'a and on the frontier with Saudi Arabia, put their
numbers as high as 50,000. See *The Yemen Times*, August 27, 2001.

by former Afghan Arabs with ongoing connections to al-Qaʻida. In December 1998, the group kidnapped sixteen tourists from the United States, Canada, and Great Britain. The AAIA is apparently linked to Egyptian radical Islamist Abu Hamza al-Masri, who heads the Finsbury Park mosque in London, and kidnapped the tourists in hope of exchanging them for the release of several British Muslims (including al-Masri's son) arrested in Yemen a few days earlier. Because this was not a typical tribal kidnapping,[15] President Salih sent forces to rescue the hostages, four of whom were killed in the ensuing battle. Several AAIA members were arrested, convicted, and executed, including Zayn al-Abidin Abu Bakr al-Mihdar, the group's Yemeni founder and leader. The regime declared that it had eliminated the group, but in 2000 the AAIA claimed responsibility for bombing the USS Cole on October 12[16] and the British Council in San'a that same month, and attempting to bomb the USS Sullivans soon thereafter. When the regime arrested several AAIA members accused of planning to bomb the U.S. embassy in 2001, President Salih again claimed to have eliminated the group (International Crisis Group 2003: 17). On October 6, 2002, the AAIA claimed responsibility for an explosion on the Limburg, a French oil tanker docked in Mukalla (a mid-sized port east of Aden), though it remains unclear whether the group was actually responsible.

While the bombings of U.S. and French vessels have commanded high international media attention, the AAIA also has been responsible for numerous violent attacks against Yemenis, particularly targeting southern regions seen to be morally lax. Although ties to Afghan Arabs and al-Qaʻida have colored the group as Salafi, Carapico notes that the name of the AAIA "connotes an appeal to the right wing composed of deposed aristocrats, mujahideen and religious ultra-conservatives, but also to some extent echoes the frustrations of Yemenis from Aden, Abyan and elsewhere in the former South, including liberals and socialists as well as social conservatives" (2000). In this connection characterizing the AAIA as merely a group of Afghan Arabs obscures connections to local conflicts and dissatisfaction with other dimensions of Yemeni politics.

The second of the extremist groups connected to the return of Afghan Arabs is the Islamic Jihad Movement (IJM, *Harakat al-Jihad al-Islami*),

---

[15] Tribes frequently kidnap foreigners and other prominent individuals in an effort (often successful) to exact economic concessions ranging from government and oil jobs to cell phone towers constructed in isolated regions.

[16] Carapico notes that two previously unknown offshoots of the Aden-Abyan Islamic Army – Muhammad's Army, and the Islamic Deterrence Forces – both claimed responsibility for the Cole attack (2000).

which has followers in both the North and South. The IJM has ties to conservative tribal leaders and seems to have been in existence well prior to 1990, but was able to significantly expand its numbers by recruiting among the Afghan Arabs (International Crisis Group 2003: 9). Tariq al-Fadli, a prominent Afghan Arab from the South and the heir to former Abyan nobility, led the IJM in Abyan in the late 1980s and early 1990s. He left the group to join the GPC and since 1993 has held a seat in parliament. The IJM also has a strong following in Ma'rib, where it is led by Abu al-Miqdad. Al-Fadli says both the AAIA and IJM appear to have at least loose links to al-Qa'ida, including personal ties to bin Laden.[17]

The relationship between President Salih's regime and Yemen's many and diverse militant Islamists is complicated. Even though these groups are seen as threats to the regime and destabilizing to Yemeni politics, many of them were instrumental in bolstering the power of the GPC in the early 1990s, first by launching attacks against YSP officials and then by directly fighting with the GPC to defeat the YSP in the 1994 civil war. It is difficult to make sense of these connections, and easy to exaggerate the strength and extent of militant Islamists and their networks in Yemen. Indeed, untangling political violence connected to radical Islamists is complicated because diverse tribal leaders and government officials of various countries have interests in either exaggerating or downplaying such links as serves their purpose (International Crisis Group 2003: 18).

Following the September 11, 2001 attacks, President Salih brought together all the major political elites, including Islamists and Leftists alike, and made very clear in no uncertain terms that there were not to be major demonstrations against the United State's response to the attacks, whatever it was. The efforts were largely successful, though with the launch of the U.S. invasion of Afghanistan, Shaykh 'Abd Allah's son Ahmad organized a large demonstration north of San'a. Cassette tapes of bin Laden's interviews, both old and recent, were widely available on every street corner in Yemen immediately after the September 11, 2001 attacks and were widely debated in various publics (Burgat 2002: 17). President Salih has become invested in Yemen's relationship with the United States, despite his initial reluctance and ongoing efforts to demonstrate otherwise to a domestic and regional audience. He perhaps remains fearful that the United States might invade because of the presence of (and lack of state control over) various al-Qa'ida–connected radical Islamists, and

[17] Interview in *al-Quds al-'Arabi*, cited in International Crisis Group (2003: 11).

has struggled to position himself as committed to the "war on terrorism" while maintaining a delicate balance at home. Burgat calls this "a pact of moderation against those who may have been tempted to act against the United States and its allies" (2002: 17). However, Burgat reports that President Salih is fond of telling foreign visitors that this fragile equilibrium "burns the hand of the state leader" (17), particularly as the United States places increasing demands on President Salih to both apprehend al-Qa'ida radicals and to allow U.S. agents free access throughout the country, or at least the parts of Yemen that the regime effectively controls. Nevertheless, since 2000 the regime has arrested hundreds of Islamist extremists and exported thousands more who were not Yemeni nationals.

Without a doubt, al-Qa'ida operates in Yemen, though the extent of its members remains unclear due to the complexities of Islamist-tribal-regime connections suggested in the preceding text. The group's supposed chief agent in Yemen was Qa'id Salim Sinan "Abu 'Ali" al-Harithi, who was assassinated by a CIA-operated drone missile on November 3, 2002. Al-Harithi was from the Abida region east of San'a and reportedly had offered to surrender during the late 2001 conflict between Abida tribes and the regime if he was guaranteed a fair trial in Yemen rather than being extradited to the United States (International Crisis Group 2003: 20). The regime initially denied knowledge of the drone attack, though admitted a week later that President Salih had given his okay for the attack to move forward. Al-Harithi was believed to be largely responsible for the attacks on the USS Cole and the French Limburg, and was killed in the attack along with four members of the AAIA and an American citizen said to have been the head of a Yemeni al-Qa'ida cell discovered in upstate New York. The regime has continued its periodic arrests of suspected al-Qa'ida members, including 'Abd al-Raouf Nasib, arrested in Abyan on March 3, 2004. Nasib apparently escaped from the CIA drone attack and in April 2003 helped ten militants detained in connection with the October 2000 attack on the USS Cole escape from an Aden prison.

Within this larger context, the Islah party has played in many ways a mediating role between militant and radical Islamists and the regime. However, party leaders have not always been able to negotiate this balance even within its own ranks. As noted, the more moderate, Muslim Brotherhood leaders who head the party bureaucracy began to explore the possibility of forming an alliance with the YSP and other opposition parties. One of these initiatives was to explore the possibility of an electoral alliance between Islah and the YSP in advance of the April 2003 parliamentary elections. On December 28, 2002, YSP Deputy Secretary-General Jar Allah 'Umar addressed a gathering of Islah leaders and its general membership, and spoke about the possibility of such an alliance. As he exited the stage, he was shot and killed by 'Ali Ahmad Muhammad Jar Allah, who was sitting in a front row. 'Umar's assassination was followed two days later with the shooting deaths of three American health professionals working for a Southern Baptist missionary hospital in Jibla, south of San'a. Some regime officials claimed that the shooter, 'Abed 'Abd al-Razzaq Kamal, coordinated the murders with 'Umar's killer (Carapico, Wedeen, and Wuerth 2002). The affiliation of either with al-Qa'ida remains uncertain, though the Minister of the Interior told Saba, the state news agency, that 'Umar's killer was an Islahi activist. 'Ali Ahmad Jar Allah was taken immediately after the killing to the home of Islah leader and parliament speaker Shaykh 'Abd Allah, where he was interrogated before being transferred to the Criminal Investigation Department. Carapico, Wedeen, and Wuerth note that circumstantial evidence does link the killer with Islah's radical trend and that he was reportedly registered in the mid-1990s at al-Zindani's ultraconservative al-Iman University. Though he denied any partisan affiliation, the regime accused him of links to al-Qa'ida (2002). Islah leaders denied that 'Ali Ahmad Jar Allah had any affiliation with Islah, or that someone in the party had provided support by seating him in a row usually reserved for dignitaries. Islah quickly issued a statement "threatening to sue the government for slander. The party also issued a statement calling Jarallah Omar 'a martyr for democracy'" (Carapico, Wedeen, and Wuerth 2002). "Kata'ib Abu 'Ali al-Harithi – The Military Wing," a radical Islamist group known to be associated with bin Laden, issued a statement the day after 'Umar's assassination to commemorate the killing of al-Harithi a month earlier. The statement was particularly harsh in its criticisms of the regime for "selling out" to the United States. It warned the regime and its allies, "We can, as you know, get at you any time, and as we have children and relatives, so you do too" (Carapico, Wedeen, and Wuerth 2002).

Yemen is home to a number of additional extremist Islamist actors of Yemeni and non-Yemeni origin. One prominent individual is the Salafi *jihadi* Muqbil ibn Hadi al-Wada'i, who is based in Sa'adah, a town north of San'a that has endured considerable armed conflict among various tribal and Islamists groups. Al-Wada'i appears to have ties to Islah's more extremist trends, though his is not a member of the party. Another is Sayyid Imam al-Sharif, founder of Egypt's Islamic Jihad, who was reportedly arrested in Yemen in the spring of 2004. Al-Sharif moved to Yemen in 1996 and is said to have turned over control of the group to al-Zawahri at that time.[18]

Outside of Islah and these various loosely connected Salafi, Wahhabi, and *jihadi* actors, Yemen's Zaydi community is represented in formal politics by *Hizb al-Haqq* (The Right Party, as in "rights," not the opposite of Left). As argued in the preceding text, President Salih is Zaydi but does not claim authority to rule on either Zaydi or Islamic terms. The Islah party does count a number of Zaydis among its members and administrators, notably Shaykh 'Abd Allah, but the Wahhabi influence on him and other prominent party leaders and the fragmented nature of the party have created the "glass ceiling" preventing "ordinary" Zaydi party members from advancing in party ranks unless they adopt Wahhabi views. When the republican war defeated the Zaydi Immamate in North Yemen in the 1960s, the new political elite – though many belonged to Zaydi communities – strove to diminish the authority of the Zaydi elite by virtually banishing them from influential government posts. These traditional Zaydi elite maintained some authority through practice throughout much of the North, though Sunni teachers were given control of most local schools (albeit of a poor and fragmented education system). Zaydi Shi'i communities have been increasingly targeted by Wahhabi Sunnis who have gained ground in Yemen over the past two decades through Saudi sponsorship and the influence of the scientific institutes. Weir, for example, has written about the "clash of fundamentalisms" in the northern town of Razih, where a growing Wahhabi community has given rise to a sectarian conflict since the mid-1980s. Much of the tension, which manifests in part around Wahhabi opposition to the Zaydi religious leaders who claim authority due to their descent from the Prophet Muhammad, appears to be more related to ongoing rivalries between Zaydi elites and tribal leaders than about religion per se. Wahhabis presented a challenge to the Zaydi elites' "claims to religious nobility," accusing them of "divinely sanctioned social superiority" (Weir 1997: 22). The Zaydi elite accuse the Wahhabi activists of importing from Saudi Arabia a school of Islamic thought inappropriate for Yemen. Following the 1997 elections and the political fallout for Islah, which lost all of its cabinet positions, a prominent leader of Hizb al-Haqq was appointed as the Minister of Religious Affairs and Endowments (Weir 1997: 26).

Beginning in the summer of 2004, clashes between Yemeni security forces and the Zaydi *sayyid* cleric Hussayn Badr al-Din al-Huthi also

---

[18] "Yemen Says al-Qaida Member Is Arrested," *Associated Press*, March 4, 2004.

left hundreds dead and thousands injured in northern Yemen. The long-standing tensions escalated when police arrested some 640 followers of al-Huthi who were demonstrating outside of the Grand Mosque in San'a on June 18. Two days later, al-Huthi followers prevented the governor of the northern province of Sa'da from reaching a district to the west (Glosemeyer 2004: 44–5). The conflict between various government security forces and al-Huthi's followers continued for months until al-Huthi – a former member of parliament for Hizb al-Haqq – was killed in fighting in September 2004. The fighting has continued periodically since, though President Salih has declared the conflict over (Phillips 2005).

Like in Jordan, the diverse field of Islamist politics in Yemen has unfolded in a largely nondemocratic context, save the limited political opening of the early 1990s. Continuing to characterize particular actors as either wholly moderate or wholly radical obscures complex relations not only between Islamist groups, but between various social elites, diverse opposition movements, and state and nonstate actors.

SUMMARY

The inclusion-moderation hypothesis raises vital questions not only about Islamist parties, but about processes of democratization and the political inclusion of diverse and ideological political actors in general. These brief overviews of the broader field of Islamist politics in Jordan and Yemen, combined with the detailed comparative study of the IAF and the Islah party, suggest that systematic scholarly attention should be directed not at the behavior of particular groups or the expansiveness of transnational terrorist networks, but at the practices and narratives of various Islamic and non-Islamic publics and the wide range of actors who inhabit, animate, and indeed produce those spaces. This study calls also for detailed attention to the internal dynamics of particular groups, not to identify moderates from radicals but to reveal the range of activities, alliances, and debates that characterize entities often treated as unitary actors. It also underlines the need to study political practices outside of formal state institutions. Even within so-called stalled democracies such as Jordan, Yemen, and many other states in the Middle East, significant changes in public political spaces have resulted from limited political openings. In advancing our understanding of these evolving political spaces and practices, a next step would be to move beyond the "career model" of groups and parties, which focuses attention on when groups emerge, who joins, what they advocate, and how they evolve over time. Instead, new sets of questions might explore the dynamics of various publics and the actors who produce them, how narrative spaces shape political practices, and how sites of brokerage facilitate changes in practice as well as ideological commitments. In short, unpacking the inclusion-moderation hypothesis suggests numerous avenues for future research that move well beyond the substantial literature on Islamist politics, that is, beyond studies of individual movements or the compatibility of competing worldviews treated as if they exist apart from the practice of politics (e.g., the many studies on Islam and democracy, which treat each as an actually existing entity whose central components are fixed and beyond interrogation or debate). In a post-September 11 world, the stakes of the production of knowledge are extraordinarily high. The study of Islamist participation in pluralist processes provides a valuable opportunity for unpacking complicated processes of inclusion within even nondemocratic contexts and assessing their connection to ideological moderation, a process that carries perhaps the highest stakes of all.

References

Interviews

In accordance with Human Subjects Review standards and practices, interviewees who request anonymity are not publicly identified in any way. The following interviews were wholly or in part on the record.

Abu Bakr, Jamil, November 9 and 11, 1997, Amman
Abu Ghanimah, Ziyad, May 5, 1997, Amman
Abu Odeh, Adnan, October 21, 2003, Amman
Abu Risha, Zulaykha, May 5, 1997, Amman
Afandi, Muhammad al-, October 25, 1997, San'a
Amoush, Bassam, December 1, 1997, Amman
Anisi, 'Abd al-Wahab al-, March 26, 1995 and April 24, 1997, San'a
'Arabiyyat, 'Abd al-Latif, November 15, 1996 and November 3, 2003, Amman
Akwa, 'Abd Allah al-, September 14 and October 5, 1997, San'a
'Awran, Muhammad Salih al-, October 23, 2003, Amman
'Azm, Yusef al-, July 12, 1995, Amman
BaFadl, 'Abd al-Rahman, October 9–10, 1997, San'a
Fadli, Tariq al-, July 31, 1997, San'a
Faouri, Nawal, March 1, 1997, Amman.
Farhan, Ishaq Ahmad, March 31, 1997 and June 12, 19, and 22, 1997, Amman
'Izzidin, Ibrahim, October 2, 1996 and April 22 and June 11, 1997, Amman
Judih, Nasir, March 31, 1997, Amman
Madanat, Isa, June 22, 1997, Amman
Mansur, Hamzeh, June 29, July 3, and October 30, 2003, Amman
Maraqa, Ishaq, April 8, 1997, Amman
Masri, Tahir al-, February 9 and March 13, 1997 and June 27, 2002, Amman
Muasher, Marwan, March 31, 1997, Amman
Mustafa, Nasr Taha, numerous meetings in 1997, San'a
Nadish, 'Ali 'Abd Allah, November 24, 1997, San'a

Obaydat, Tamir, March 31, 1997, Amman
Qahtan, Muhammad, numerous meetings in 1995 and 1997, San'a
Rubaydi, Ahmad, October 18, 1997, San'a
Sa'adi, Muhammad, August 16, 1998, San'a
Sanabani, Faris 'Abd Allah al-, August 1, 1998, San'a
Saqqaf, Faris al-, October 12, 1997, San'a
Shami, Zayd al-, October 8 and 14, 1997, San'a
Shubaylat, Laith, April 6, 1997 and October 20, 2003, Amman
Tahbub, Tariq, January 24, 1997, Amman
Tayyib, Muhammad, October 20, 1997, San'a
Thunaybat, 'Abd al-Majid, November 15, 1996 and May 8, 1997, Amman
'Umrani, Fath Allah al-, October 24, 2003, Amman
Yadumi, Muhammad al-, March 13 and April 6, 1995 and October 13 1997,
    Amman
Zindani, Mansur al-, August 18, 1998, San'a

Newspapers and Magazines

26 September (Yemen)
Al-'Arab al-Yawm (Jordan)
Al-Ayyam (Yemen)
Al-Balagh (Yemen)
Al-Dustur (Jordan)
Al-Hayat (London)
Al-Islah (Yemen)
Al-Jamahir (Yemen)
Al-Kifah al-Islami (Jordan)
Al-Liwa (Jordan)
Al-Ra'i (Jordan)
Al-Ribat (Jordan)
Al-Sabil (Jordan)
Al-Sahwah (Yemen)
Al-Sharq al-Awsat (London)
Al-Shura (Yemen)
Al-Thawra (Yemen)
Al-Thawri (Yemen)
Al-Ummah (Jordan)
Al-Wahdah (Yemen)
Al-Wahdawi (Yemen)
The Jordan Times
The Los Angeles Times
The New York Times
Sawt al-Sha'b (Jordan)
Shihan (Jordan)
The Washington Post
The Yemen Times

Books, Articles, and Chapters

Abdalat, Marwan Ahmad Sulayman al-. 1992. *Kharitah al-ahzab al-siyasiyyah al-Urdunniyyah*. Amman: Dar al-Ubra.

Abd Allah, Umar. 1983. *The Islamic Struggle in Syria*. Berkeley, CA: Mizan Press.

Abed-Kotob, Sana. 1995. The Accommodationists Speak: Goal and Strategies of the Muslim Brotherhood in Egypt. *International Journal of Middle East Studies* 27(3) (August): 321–39.

Abu-Amr, Ziad. 1994. *Islamic Fundamentalism in the West Bank and Gaza: Muslim Brotherhood and Islamic Jihad*. Bloomington: Indiana University Press.

Abu Jaber, Kamel, and Schirin H. Fathi. 1990. The 1989 Jordanian Parliamentary Elections. *Orient* 31: 62–83.

Abu Khusa, Ahmad. 1991. *Al-Dimuqratiyyah wa al-ahzab al-siyasiyyah al-Urdunniyyah*. Amman: Shurakah al-Sharq al-Awsat li al-Tiba'a.

Abu Roman. 1991. *Al Harakat al-Islamiyyah wa al-Barliman*. Amman.

Adams, Linda Schull. 1996. Political Liberalization in Jordan: An Analysis of the State's Relationship with the Muslim Brotherhood. *Journal of State and Society* 38(3) (Summer): 1–32.

Adler, Glenn, and Eddie Webster. 1995. Challenging Transition Theory: The Labor Movement, Radical Reform, and Transition to Democracy in South Africa. *Politics and Society* 34(1) (March): 75–106.

Ahmed, Akbar S., and Hastings Donnan, eds. 1994. *Islam, Globalization, and Postmodernity*. London: Routledge.

Akailah, Abdullah al-. 1993. Jordan. In Azzam Tamimi, ed., pp. 93–101. *Power-Sharing Islam?* London: Liberty for Muslim World Publications.

Alavi, Hamza. 1972. The State in Post-Colonial Societies: Pakistan and Bangladesh. *New Left Review* 74: 59–81.

'Ali, Haydir Ibrahim. 1996. *Al-Tayarat al-islamiyyah wa qadayyah al-dimuqratiyyah*. Beirut: Markaz Dirasat al-Wahdah al-Arabi.

Allport, Gordon. 1954. *The Nature of Group Prejudice*. Reading, MA: Addison-Wesley.

Almond, Gabriel, and Sidney Verba, eds. 1989. *The Civil Culture Revisited*. London: Sage Publications.

———. 1963. *The Civic Culture: Political Attitudes and Democracy in Five Nations*. London: Sage Publications.

Alyushin, Alexey L. 1992. The Paternalist Tradition and Russia's Transition to Liberal Democracy. *Democratic Institutions*, vol. 1, pp. 1–19. New York: Carnegie Council on Ethics and International Affairs.

Amir, Y. 1969. Contact Hypothesis in Ethnic Relations. *Psychological Bulletin* 71(5): 319–42.

Anderson, Lisa. 1997. Fulfilling Prophecies: State Policy and Islamist Radicalism. In John Esposito, ed., pp. 17–31. *Political Islam: Revolution, Radicalism, or Reform?* Boulder, CO: Lynne Rienner Publishers.

———. 1995. Democracy in the Arab World: A Critique of the Political Culture Approach. In Rex Brynen, et al., eds., pp. 77–92. *Political Liberalization and Democratization in the Arab World, Volume I: Theoretical Perspectives.* Boulder, CO: Lynne Rienner Publishers.

———. 1994. Liberalism, Islam, and the State. *Dissent* (Fall): 439–44.

———. 1991. Absolutism and the Resilience of Monarchy in the Middle East. *Political Studies Quarterly* 106(1): 1–15.

———. 1987. The State in the Middle East and North Africa. *Comparative Politics* 20(1) (October): 1–18.

Anderson, Perry. 1977. Antinomies of Antonio Gramsci. *New Left Review* 100: 5–78.

———. 1974. *Lineages of the Absolutist State.* London: Verso.

Andoni, Lamis, and Jillian Schwedler. 1996. Bread Riots in Jordan. *Middle East Report* 201 (Fall): 40–2.

Angell, Alan. 2001. The International Dimensions of Democratization in Latin America: The Case of Brazil. In Laurence Whitehead, ed., pp. 175–200. *The International Dimensions of Democratization: Europe and the Americas,* exp. ed. New York: Oxford University Press.

Antoun, Richard T. 1993. Themes and Symbols in the Religious Lesson: A Jordanian Case Study. *International Journal of Middle East Studies* 20(4) (November): 607–24.

Aristotle. 1988. *The Politics.* New York: Cambridge University Press.

Aruri, Naseer. 1972. *Jordan: A Study in Political Development 1921–1965.* The Hague: Martinus Nijhoff.

Awad, Taleb. 1997. The Organizational Structure of the Muslim Brotherhood. In Jillian Schwedler, ed., pp. 79–92. *Islamist Movements in Jordan.* Amman: Markaz al-Urdunn al-Jadid.

Ayadat, Zaid. 1997. The Islamic Movement: Political Engagement Trends. In Jillian Schwedler, ed., pp. 143–65. *Islamist Movements in Jordan.* Amman: Markaz al-Urdunn al-Jadid.

Azm, Ahmad Jamil. 1997. The Islamic Action Front Party. In Jillian Schwedler, ed., pp. 93–141. *Islamist Movements in Jordan.* Amman: Markaz al-Urdunn al-Jadid.

Azmeh, Aziz al-. 1994. Populism Contra Democracy: Recent Democratist Discourse in the Arab World. In Ghassan Salamé, ed., pp. 112–29. *Democracy without Democrats? The Renewal of Politics in the Muslim World.* London: I. B. Taurus.

Baaklini, Abdo, Guilain Denoeux, and Robert Springborg. 1999. *Legislative Politics in the Arab World: The Resurgence of Democratic Institutions.* Boulder, CO: Lynne Rienner Publishers.

Banna, Hassan al-. 1979. *Risalat Imam Hassan al-Banna.* Beirut: Al-Mu'assassah al-Islami.

Barber, Benjamin R. 1995. *Jihad vs. McWorld: How Globalism and Tribalism Are Reshaping the World.* New York: Ballantine Books.

Barnett, Michael. 1998. *Dialogues in Arab Politics.* New York: Columbia University Press.

Bates, Robert H., Rui J. P. de Figueiredo, Jr., and Barry R. Weingast. 1998. The Politics of Interpretation: Rationality, Culture, and Transition. *Politics and Society* 26(4) (December): 603–42.

Bayat, Asef. 1998. Revolution without Movement, Movement without Revolution: Comparing Islamic Activism in Iran and Egypt. *Journal of Comparative Study of Society and History* 40(1) (January): 136–69.

Beinin, Joel, and Joe Stork, eds. 1996. *Political Islam*. Berkeley: University of California Press.

Bellin, Eva. 2004. The Robustness of Authoritarianism in the Middle East: Exceptionalism in Comparative Perspective. *Comparative Politics* 36(2) (January): 139–57.

———. 2003. *Stalled Democracy: Capital, Labor, and the Paradox of State-Sponsored Development*. Ithaca, NY: Cornell University Press.

Benford, Robert D., and David A. Snow. 2000. Framing Processes and Social Movements: An Overview and Assessment. *Annual Review of Sociology* 26: 611–39.

Benhabib, Seyla, ed. 1996. *Democracy and Difference: Contesting the Boundaries of the Political*. Princeton: Princeton University Press.

Berman, Sheri E. 2001. Modernization in Historical Perspective: The Case of Imperial Germany. *World Politics* 53(3) (April): 431–62.

Bermeo, Nancy. 1997. Myths of Moderation: Confrontation and Conflict during Democratic Transitions. *Comparative Politics* 29(3) (April): 301–22.

———. 1992. Democracy and the Lessons of Dictatorship. *Comparative Politics* (April): 273–5.

Bevir, Mark. 1999. Foucault and Critique: Deploying Agency against Autonomy. *Political Theory* 27(1) (February): 65–84.

Bhabha, Homi K. 1994. *The Location of Culture*. London: Routledge.

Binder, Leonard. 1988. *Islamic Liberalism: A Critique of Development Ideologies*. Chicago: University of Chicago Press.

Bohman, James. 1996. *Public Deliberation*. Cambridge: MIT Press.

Boulby, Marion. 1999. *The Muslim Brotherhood and the Kings of Jordan, 1945–1993*. Atlanta: Scholars Press.

Bourdieu, Pierre. 1991. *Language and Symbolic Power*. Cambridge: Harvard University Press.

———. 1987. What Makes a Social Class? On the Theoretical and Practical Existence of Groups. *Berkeley Journal of Sociology: A Critical Review* 32: 1–17.

———. 1977. *Outline of a Theory of Practice*. Cambridge: Cambridge University Press.

Brand, Laurie. 1995a. Palestinians and Jordanians: A Crisis of Identity. *Journal of Palestine Studies* 96(4) (Summer): 46–61.

———. 1995b. *Jordan's Inter-Arab Relations: The Political Economy of Alliance Making*. New York: Columbia University Press.

———. 1994a. 'In the Beginning was the State…' Civil Society in Jordan. In Augustus Richard Norton, ed., pp. 148–85. *Civil Society in the Middle East*, vol. 1. Leiden: E. J. Brill Publishers.

———. 1994b. Economics and Shifting Alliances: Jordan's Relations with Syria and Iraq, 1975–1981. *International Journal of Middle East Studies* 26(3) (August): 393–413.

————. 1991. Liberalization and Changing Political Coalitions: The Bases of Jordan's 1990–91 Gulf Crisis Policy. *Jerusalem Journal of International Relations* 13(4) (Fall): 1–46.

Bratton, Michael, and Nicholas van de Walle. 1997. *Democratic Experiments in Africa: Regime Transitions in Comparative Perspective.* New York: Cambridge University Press.

Brisard, Jean-Charles. 2005. With Damien Martinez. *Zarqawi: The New Face of al-Qaeda.* New York: Other Press.

Browers, Michelle. 2006. *Democracy and Civil Society in Arab Political Thought.* Syracuse, NY: Syracuse University Press.

————. 2005. Arab Liberalisms: Translating Civil Society, Prioritizing Democracy. *Critical Review of Society and Political Philosophy* 7(1) (Spring): 51–75.

Brown, Michael E., Sean M. Lynne-Jones, and Steven E. Miller, eds. 1996. *Debating the Democratic Peace.* Cambridge: MIT Press.

Brown, Wendy. 1995. *States of Injury: Power and Freedom in Late Modernity.* Princeton: Princeton University Press.

Brownlee, Jason. 2002.... And Yet They Persist: Explaining Survival and Transition in Neopatrimonial Regimes. *Studies in Comparative International Development* 37(3): 35–63.

Brumberg, Daniel. 2002. The Trap of Liberalized Autocracy. *Journal of Democracy* 13(4) (October): 56–68.

————. 1995. Authoritarian Legacies and Reform Strategies in the Arab World. In Rex Brynen, Bahgat Korany, and Paul Noble, eds. *Political Liberalization and Democratization in the Arab World, Volume 1: Theoretical Perspectives.* Boulder, CO: Lynne Rienner Publishers.

Brynen, Rex. 1998. The Politics of Monarchical Liberalism: Jordan. In Bahgat Korany, Rex Brynen, and Paul Noble, eds., pp. 71–100. *Political Liberalization and Democratization in the Arab World, Volume 2: Comparative Experiences.* Boulder, CO: Lynne Rienner Publishers.

————. 1992. Economic Crisis and Post-Rentier Democratization in the Arab World: The Case of Jordan. *Canadian Journal of Political Science* 25(1) (March): 69–97.

Brynen, Rex, Bahgat Korany, and Paul Noble, eds. 1995. *Political Liberalization and Democratization in the Arab World, Volume I: Theoretical Perspectives.* Boulder, CO: Lynne Rienner Publishers.

Bunce, Valerie. 2003. Rethinking Recent Democratization: Lessons from the Postcommunist Experience. *World Politics* 55: 167–92.

————. 1995. Should Transitologists Be Grounded? *Slavic Review* 54(1) (Spring): 111–27.

Burgat, François. 2002. The Sanaa Chronicle. *ISIM Newsletter* 9: 17.

————. 1997. *L'islamism en face.* Paris: La Découverte.

————. 1993. Bilateral Radicalism. In Azzam Tamimi, ed., pp. 43–8. *Power-Sharing Islam?* London: Liberty for Muslim World Publications.

Burgat, François, with William Dowell. 1997. *The Islamic Movement in North Africa,* 2nd ed. Austin: University of Texas Press.

Callon, Michel. 1998a. Introduction: The Embeddedness of Economic Markets in Economics. In M. Callon, ed., pp. 1–57. *The Laws of the Markets.* Oxford: Blackwell.

————. 1998b. An Essay on Framing and Overflowing: Economic Externalities Revisited by Sociology. In M. Callon, ed., pp. 244–69. *The Laws of the Markets.* Oxford: Blackwell.

Cammack, Paul. 1997. *Capitalism and Democracy in the Third World: The Doctrine for Political Development.* Dorset, UK: Cassell Academic.

Campagne, Joel. 1997. Press Freedom in Jordan. *Middle East Report* 206 (Spring): 44–8.

Carapico, Sheila. 2000. Yemen and the Aden-Abyan Islamic Army. *Middle East Report Online* PIN 35 (October 18).

————. 1998. *Civil Society in Yemen: The Political Economy of Activism in Modern Arabia.* New York: Cambridge University Press.

————. 1996. Yemen between Civility and Civil War. In Augustus Richard Norton, ed., pp. 287–316. *Civil Society in the Middle East,* vol. 2. Leiden: E. J. Brill Publishers.

————. 1993a. Campaign Politics and Coalition Building: The 1993 Parliamentary Elections. *Yemen Update* 33 (Summer and Fall): 38–40.

————. 1993b. Elections and Mass Politics in Yemen. *Middle East Report* 185 (November–December): 2–7.

————. 1993c. The Economic Dimension of Yemeni Unity. *Middle East Report* 184 (September–October): 9–14.

————. 1991. Yemen: Unification and the Gulf War. *Middle East Report* 170 (May–June): 26, 47.

Carapico, Sheila and Cynthia Myntti. 1991. Change in North Yemen: A Tale of Two Families. *Middle East Report* 170 (May–June): 24–9.

Carapico, Sheila, Lisa Wedeen, and Anna Wuerth. 2002. The Death and Life of Jarallah Omar. *Middle East Report Online* (December 31).

Çarkoglu, Ali. 1998. The Turkish Party System in Transition: Party Performance and Agenda Change. *Political Studies* 46(3) (special issue): 544–71.

Carothers, Thomas. 2002. The End of the Transition Paradigm. *Journal of Democracy* 13(2) (January): 5–21.

Caton, Steven C. 1990. Anthropological Theories of Tribe and State Formation in the Middle East: Ideology and the Semiotics of Power. In Philip S. Khoury and Joseph Kostiner, eds., pp. 74–108. *Tribes and State Formation in the Middle East.* Berkeley: University of California Press.

Center for Strategic Studies of Jordan University. 1998. *Public Opinion Poll on Democratization in Jordan, 1997.* Amman: Jordan University.

————. 1997. *Public Opinion Poll on Democratization in Jordan, 1996.* Amman: Jordan University.

————. 1995. *Public Opinion Poll on Democratization in Jordan, 1994.* Amman: Jordan University.

————. 1994. *Public Opinion Poll on Democratization in Jordan, 1993.* Amman: Jordan University.

Charillon, Frederic, and Alain Mouftard. 1994. Jourdanie: les elections du 8 novembre 1993 et le processus de paix. *Maghreb-Machrek* 144 (April–June): 40–54.

Chaudhry, Kiren. 1997. *The Price of Wealth: Economies and Institutions in the Middle East.* Ithaca, NY: Cornell University Press.

————. 1993. Myths of the Market and the Common History of Late Developers. *Politics and Society* 21(3) (September): 245–74.

Cigar, Norman. 1990. Islam and the State in South Yemen: The Uneasy Coexistence. *Middle Eastern Studies* 26 (April): 185–203.

———. 1985. State and Society in South Yemen. *Problems of Communism* 34 (May–June): 41–58.

Clark, Janine Astrid. 2005a. Cooperation across Ideological Divides: Islamist-Leftist Cooperation in Jordan. Unpublished manuscript.

———. 2005b. Islamist-Leftist Cooperation in Lebanon. Unpublished manuscript.

———. 2003. *Faith Networks, Charity, and the Middle Class: Islamist Services in Egypt, Jordan, and Yemen.* Bloomington: Indiana University Press.

———. 1997. Women and Islamic Activism in Yemen. *Yemen Update* 39: 13–15.

———. 1995. Democratization and Social Islam: A Case Study of the Islamic Health Clinics in Cairo. In Rex Brynen, et al., eds., pp. 167–86. *Political Liberalization and Democratization in the Arab World, Volume I: Theoretical Perspectives.* Boulder, CO: Lynne Rienner Publishers.

Clark, Janine Astrid, and Jillian Schwedler. 2003. Who Opened the Window? Women's Activism in Islamist Parties. *Comparative Politics* 35 (April): 293–313.

Cohen, Amnon. 1982. *Political Parties in the West Bank under the Jordanian Regime, 1949–1967.* Ithaca, NY: Cornell University Press.

Cohen, Youssef. 1994. *Radicals, Reformers, and Reactionaries: The Prisoner's Dilemma and the Collapse of Democracy in Latin America.* Chicago: University of Chicago Press.

Colas, Dominique. 1997. *Civil Society and Fanaticism: Cojoined Histories,* Amy Jacobs, trans. Stanford, CA: Stanford University Press.

Collier, David, and Steven Levitsky. 1997. Democracy with Adjectives: Conceptual Innovation in Comparative Research. *World Politics* 49(3) (April): 430–51.

Collier, Ruth Berins. 1999. *Paths toward Democracy: The Working Class and Elites in Western Europe and South America.* New York: Cambridge University Press.

Collier, Ruth Berins, and David Collier. 1991. *Shaping the Political Arena: Critical Junctures, the Labor Movement, and Regime Dynamics in Latin America.* Princeton: Princeton University Press.

Colomer, Josep. 2000. *Strategic Transitions: Game Theory and Democratization.* Baltimore: Johns Hopkins University Press.

Comaroff, Jean and John Comaroff. 1991. *Of Revelation and Revolution: Christianity, Colonialism, and Consciousness in Africa,* vol. 1. Chicago: University of Chicago Press.

Cooley, John K. 2000. *Unholy Wars: Afghanistan, America, and International Terrorism,* 2nd ed. London: Pluto.

Crystal, Jill. 1994. Authoritarianism and Its Adversaries in the Arab World. *World Politics* 46(2) (January): 262–89.

Dabbas, Aida. 1998. Protesting Sanctions against Iraq: A View from Jordan. Interview by Jillian Schwedler. *Middle East Report* 208 (Fall): 37–9.

Dabbas, Hamed. 1997. Islamic Centers, Association, Societies, Organizations, and Committees in Jordan. In Jillian Schwedler, ed., pp. 193–259. *Islamist Movements in Jordan.* Amman: Markaz al-Urdunn al-Jadid.

————. 1995. *Al-Harakah al-islamiyyah al-siyasiyyah fi al-Urdunn*. Amman: Al-Urdunn al-Jadid.

Dahl, Robert. 1971. *Polyarchy: Participation and Opposition*. New Haven, CT: Yale University Press.

Dann, Uriel. 1989. *King Hussein and the Challenge of Arab Radicalism*. Oxford: Oxford University Press.

Davenport, Christian. 2005. Introduction: Repression and Mobilization. In Christian Davenport, Hank Johnston, and Carol Mueller, eds. pp. vii–xli. *Repression and Mobilization*. Minneapolis: University of Minnesota Press.

————, ed. 2000. *Paths to State Repression: Human Rights Violations and Contentious Politics*. Lanham, MD: Rowman and Littlefield.

Detalle, Renaud. 1994. Pacte d'Amman: l'espoir déçu des Yéménites. *Monde Arabe: Maghreb-Machrek* 145 (July–September): 113–22.

————. 1993. The Yemeni Elections up Close. *Middle East Report* 185 (November–December): 8–12.

Diamond, Larry. 2000. Is Pakistan the (Reverse) Wave of the Future? *Journal of Democracy* 11(3): 91–106.

————. 1999. *Developing Democracy: Toward Consolidation*. Baltimore: Johns Hopkins University Press.

Diamond, Larry, Juan J. Linz, and Seymour Martin Lipset, eds. 1988–90. *Democracy in Developing Countries*, 4 vols. Boulder, CO: Lynne Rienner Publishers.

————. 1987. Building and Sustaining Democratic Government in Developing Countries: Some Tentative Findings. *World Affairs* 150(1) (Summer): 5–19.

Dietl, Wilhelm. 1983. *Holy War*. New York: Macmillan.

Dietz, Mary G. 1998. Merely Combating the Phrases of This World: Recent Democratic Theory. *Political Theory* 26(1) (February): 112–39.

Di Palma, Giuseppe. 1990. *To Craft Democracies: An Essay on Democratic Transition*. Berkeley: University of California Press.

Douglas, J. Leigh. 1987. *The Free Yemeni Movement, 1935–1962*. Beirut: American University of Beirut.

Dresch, Paul. 2000. *A History of Modern Yemen*. New York: Cambridge University Press.

————. 1989. *Tribes, Government, and History in Yemen*. Oxford: Oxford University Press.

Dresch, Paul, and Bernard Haykel. 1995. Stereotypes and Political Styles: Islamists and Tribesfolk in Yemen. *International Journal of Middle East Studies* 27(4) (November): 405–31.

Duclos, Louis-Jean. 1990. Les elections legislatives en Jordanie. *Maghreb-Machrek* 129 (July–September): 47–75.

Dunbar, Charles. 1992. The Unification of Yemen: Process, Politics, and Prospects. *Middle East Journal* 46(3) (Summer): 456–76.

Dunn, Michael Collins. 1993. Islamist Parties in Jordan and Yemen. *Middle East Policy* 44: 16–27.

Earl, Jennifer. 2003. Tanks, Tear Gas, and Taxes: Toward a Theory of Movement Repression. *Sociological Theory* 21: 44–68.

Eckstein, Harry. 1990. Political Culture and Political Change. *American Political Science Review* 84(1) (March): 253–7.

———. 1988. A Culturalist Theory of Political Change. *American Political Science Review* 82: 789–804.

Eickelman, Dale. 1989. *The Middle East: An Anthropological Approach.* 2nd ed. Englewood Cliffs, NJ: Prentice Hall.

Eickelman, Dale, and James Piscatori. 1996. *Muslim Politics.* Princeton: Princeton University Press.

Eikert, Grzegorz, and Jan Kubik. 1999. *Rebellious Civil Society: Popular Protest and Democratic Consolidation in Poland, 1989–1993.* Ann Arbor: University of Michigan Press.

Ellis, Richard J. 1993. In Defense of Cultural Theory. *Critical Review* 7(1): 81–128.

Enayat, Hamid. 1988. *Modern Islamic Political Thought.* Austin: University of Texas Press.

Esposito, John L. 2002. *Unholy War: Terror in the Name of Islam.* New York: Oxford University Press.

———, ed. 1997. *Political Islam: Revolution, Radicalism, or Reform?* Boulder, CO: Lynne Rienner Publishers.

———. 1992. *The Islamic Threat: Myth or Reality?* New York: Oxford University Press.

Esposito, John L., and James Piscatori. 2001. *Makers of Contemporary Islam.* New York: Oxford University Press.

———. 1991. Democratization and Islam. *Middle East Journal* 45(3) (Summer): 427–40.

Esposito, John L., and John O. Voll. 1996. *Islam and Democracy.* New York: Oxford University Press.

Euben, Roxanna L. 1999. *Enemy in the Mirror: Islamic Fundamentalism and the Limits of Modern Rationalism.* Princeton: Princeton University Press.

Fahad, Abdulaziz H. Al-. 2004. From Exclusion to Accommodation: Doctrinal and Legal Evolution of Wahhabism. *New York University Law Review* 79 (2): 485–519.

Fatton, Robert, Jr. 1999. The Impairments of Democratization: Haiti in Comparative Perspective. *Comparative Politics* 31(2) (January): 209–29.

Fearon, James, and David Laitin. 2003. Ethnicity, Insurgency, and Civil War. *American Political Science Review* 97(1) (February): 75–90.

Ford, W. S. 1986. Favorable Intergroup Contact May Not Reduce Prejudice: Inconclusive Journal Evidence, 1960–1984. *Sociology and Social Research* 70: 256–8.

Foucault, Michel. 1991. Governmentality. In Graham Burchell, Colin Gordon, and Peter Miller, eds., pp. 87–104. *The Foucault Effect: Studies in Governmentality.* Chicago: University of Chicago Press.

———. 1977. *Discipline and Punish: The Birth of the Prison.* New York: Pantheon.

———. 1967. *Madness and Civilization: A History of Insanity in the Age of Reason.* London: Tavistock.

Fraser, Nancy. 1992. Rethinking the Public Sphere: A Contribution to the Critique of Actually Existing Democracy. In Craig Calhoun, ed., *Habermas and the Public Sphere.* Cambridge: MIT Press.

Freij, Hanna Y., and Leonard C. Robinson. 1996. Liberalization, the Islamists, and the Stability of the Arab State: Jordan as a Case Study. *The Muslim World* 86(1) (January): 1–32.

Fukuyama, Frances. 1992. *The End of History and the Last Man*. New York: Free Press.

Gallie, W. B. 1956. Essentially Contested Concepts. *Proceedings of the Aristotelian Society 56*.

Gamson, William A. 1992. *Talking Politics*. New York: Cambridge University Press.

———. 1990. *The Strategy of Social Protest*. 2nd ed. Belmont, CA: Wadsworth.

———. 1988. Political Discourse and Collective Action. In Bert Klandermans, et al., eds., pp. 219–44. *From Structure to Action: Comparing Social Movement Research across Cultures*. Greenwich, CT: Jai Press.

Gamson, William A., and David S. Meyer. 1996. Framing Political Opportunity. In Doug McAdam, John McCarthy, and Meyer Zald, eds., pp. 275–90. *Comparative Perspectives on Social Movements: Political Opportunities, Mobilizing Structures, and Cultural Framings*. New York: Cambridge University Press.

Gause, F. Gregory. 1994. *Oil Monarchies: Domestic and Security Challenges in the Arab Gulf States*. New York: Council on Foreign Relations.

Geddes, Barbara. 1999. What Do We Know about Democratization after Twenty Years? *Annual Review of Political Science* 2: 115–44.

Geertz, Clifford. 1973. *The Interpretation of Cultures*. New York: Basic Books.

Gellner, Ernest. 1994. *Conditions of Liberty: Civil Society and Its Rivals*. New York: Penguin Press.

———. 1993. Marxism and Islam: Failure and Success. In Azzam Tamimi, ed., pp. 33–42. *Power-Sharing Islam?* London: Liberty for Muslim World Publications.

Gendzier, Irene L. 1985. *Managing Political Change: Social Scientists and the Third World*. Boulder, CO: Westview Press.

Ghabra, Shafeeq N. 1997. The Islamist Movement in Kuwait. *Middle East Policy* 5(2) (May): 58–72.

Ghadbian, Najib. 1997. *Democratization and the Islamist Challenge in the Arab World*. Boulder, CO: Westview Press.

Ghannouchi, Rashid al-. 1993. The Participation of Islamists in a Non-Islamic Government. In Azzam Tamimi, ed., pp. 61–3. *Power-Sharing Islam?* London: Liberty for Muslim World Publications.

Gharaybah, Ibrahim. 1997a. The Muslim Brotherhood: Political and Organizational Performance. In Jillian Schwedler, ed., pp. 45–77. *Islamist Movements in Jordan*. Amman: Markaz al-Urdunn al-Jadid.

———. 1997b. *Jama'at al-Ikhwan al-Muslimin fi al-Urdunn, 1946–1996*. Amman: Al-Urdunn al-Jadid.

Gill, Graeme. 2000. *The Dynamics of Democratization: Elites, Civil Society, and the Transition Process*. New York: St. Martin's Press.

Gilsenan, Michael. 1990. *Recognizing Islam: Religion and Society in the Modern Middle East*. London: I. B. Taurus.

Giugni, Marco G., Doug McAdam, and Charles Tilly, eds. 1998. *From Contention to Democracy*. Lanham, MD: Rowman and Littlefield.

Glosemeyer, Iris. 2004. Local Conflict, Global Spin: An Uprising in the Yemeni Highlands. *Middle East Report* 232 (Fall): 44–6.

———. 1993. The First Yemeni Parliamentary Elections in 1993: Practising Democracy. *Orient* 34(3): 439–51.

Goffman, Erving. 1997. Frame Analysis: An Essay on the Organization of Experience. In Charles Lemert and Ann Branaman, eds., pp. 149–66. *The Goffman Reader.* Oxford: Blackwell.

Goldstone, Jack. 1998. Social Movements of Revolutions? On the Evolution and Outcomes of Collective Action. In Marco G. Giugni, Doug McAdam, and Charles Tilly, eds., pp. 125–45. *From Contention to Democracy.* Lanham, MD: Rowman and Littlefield.

Göle, Nilufer. 1995. Authoritarian Secularism and Islamic Participation. In Augustus Richard Norton, ed., *Civil Society in the Middle East,* vol. 1. Leiden: E. J. Brill.

Goodwin, Jeff, and James M. Jasper, eds. 2004. *Rethinking Social Movements: Structure, Meaning, and Emotion.* New York: Rowman and Littlefield.

———. 2003. *The Social Movements Reader: Cases and Concepts.* London: Blackwell.

Gramsci, Antonio. 1995. *Selections from the Prison Notebooks.* Quintin Hoare and Geoffrey Nowell Smith, eds. and trans. New York: International Publishers.

Guazzone, Laura, ed. 1997. *The Middle East in Global Change: The Politics and Economics of Interdependence versus Fragmentation.* New York: St. Martin's Press.

———, ed. 1995. *The Islamist Dilemma: The Political Role of Islamist Movements in the Contemporary Arab World.* Reading, UK: Ithaca Press.

Gutmann, Amy, and Dennis Thompson. 1996. *Democracy and Disagreement.* Cambridge: Belknap Press of Harvard University Press.

Habermas, Jurgen. 1989 [1963]. *The Structural Transformation of the Public Sphere.* Cambridge: MIT Press.

———. 1984. *The Theory of Communicative Action and the Rationalisation of Science.* 2 vols. London: Heinemann.

Hadar, Leon T. 1993. What Green Peril (Fear of Islam)? *Foreign Affairs* 72 (Spring): 27–42.

Haddad, Yvonne. 1983. Sayyid Qutb: Ideologue of Islamic Revival. In John Esposito, ed., pp. 67–89. *Voices of Resurgent Islam.* New York: Oxford University Press.

Hafez, Muhammad. 2003. *Why Muslims Rebel.* Boulder, CO: Lynne Rienner Publishers.

Hall, Catherine. 1995. Histories, Empires and the Post-Colonial Moment. In Iain Chambers and Lidia Curti, eds., *The Post-Colonial Question: Common Skies, Divided Horizons.* London: Routledge.

Halliday, Fred. 1997. The Formation of Yemeni Nationalism: Initial Reflections. In James Jankowski and Israel Gershoni, eds., pp. 26–41. *Rethinking Nationalism in the Arab Middle East.* New York: Columbia University Press.

———. 1996. *Islam and the Myth of Confrontation.* London: I. B. Taurus.

———. 1995. The Third Inter-Yemeni War and Its Consequences. *Asian Affairs* 26(2) (June): 131–40.

———. 1990. *Revolution and Foreign Policy: The Case of South Yemen, 1967–1987.* Cambridge: Cambridge University Press.

———. 1979. *Iran: Dictatorship and Development.* New York: Penguin.

Halliday, Fred, and Hamza Alavi, eds. 1988. *State and Ideology in the Middle East and Pakistan.* New York: Monthly Review Press.

Hamarnah, Mustafa. 1995. *Al-Urdunn.* Cairo: The Ibn Khaldoun Center for Developmental Studies.

Hammad, Waleed. 1997. Islamists and Charitable Work in Jordan: The Muslim Brotherhood as a Model. In Jillian Schwedler, ed., pp. 167–92. *Islamist Movements in Jordan.* Amman: Markaz al-Urdunn al-Jadid.

Hamzeh, A. Nizar. 1998. The Future of Islamic Movements in Lebanon. In Ahmad S. Moussalli, ed., *Islamic Fundamentalism: Myths and Realities.* Reading, UK: Ithaca Press.

———. 1993. Lebanon's Hizbullah: From Islamic Revolution to Parliamentary Accommodation. *Third World Quarterly* 14(2): 321–37.

Haraszti, Miklos. 1999. Decade of Handshake Transition. *East European Politics and Societies* 13(2): 288–92.

Hashmi, Sohail H. 2002. *Islamic Political Ethics: Civil Society, Pluralism, and Conflict.* Princeton: Princeton University Press.

Hawatmeh, George. 1995. *The Role of the Media in a Democracy: The Case of Jordan.* Amman: Center for Strategic Studies.

Hedström, Peter, and Richard Swedberg, eds. 1998. *Social Mechanisms: An Analytical Approach to Social Theory.* New York: Cambridge University Press.

Hefner, Robert. 2000. *Civil Islam: Muslims and Democratization in Indonesia.* Princeton: Princeton University Press.

Held, David, ed. 1992. *Prospects for Democracy: North, South, East, West.* New York: Cambridge University Press.

Hellman, Joel S. 1998. Winners Take All: The Politics of Partial Reform in Postcommunist Transitions. *World Politics* 50 (January): 203–34.

Herb, Michael. 1999. *All in the Family: Absolutism, Revolution, and Democratic Prospects in the Middle Eastern Monarchies.* Albany: State University of New York Press.

Higley, John, and Michael Burton. 1989. The Elite Variable in Democratic Transitions and Breakdowns. *American Sociological Review* 54 (February): 17–32.

Higley, John, Jan Pakulski, and Wlodzimierz Wesolowski. 1998. Introduction: Elite Change and Democratic Regimes in Eastern Europe. In John Higley, Jan Pakulski, and Wlodzimierz Wesolowski, eds., *Postcommunist Elites and Democracy in Eastern Europe.* New York: St. Martin's Press.

Hirshman, Albert O. 1970. *Exit, Voice, and Loyalty: Responses to Decline in Firms, Organizations, and States.* Cambridge: Harvard University Press.

Hofman, Steven Ryan. 2004. Islam and Democracy: Micro-Level Indications of Compatibility. *Comparative Political Studies* 37 (6) (August): 652–76.

Hourani, Hani, ed. 1996. *The Democratic Process in Jordan.* Amman: Markaz al-Urdunn al-Jadid.

Hourani, Hani, and Musa Shteiwi. 1996. *The Civil Society and Public Space in the City of Amman.* Amman: Markaz al-Urdunn al-Jadid.

Hourani, Hani, Taleb Awad, Hamed Dabbas, and Sa'eda Kilani. 1993a. *The Islamic Action Front Party.* Amman: Markaz al-Urdunn al-Jadid.

Hourani, Hani, Hamed Dabbas, and Mark Power-Stevens. 1993b. *Who's Who in the Jordanian Parliament 1993–1997.* Amman: Markaz al-Urdunn al-Jadid.

Hroub, Khalid. 2000. *HAMAS: Political Thought and Practice.* Washington, DC: Institute for Palestine Studies.

Hudson, Michael C. 1995. The Political Culture Approach to Arab Democratization: The Case for Bringing It Back In. In Rex Brynen, et al., eds., pp. 61–76. *Political Liberalization and Democratization in the Arab World, Volume I: Theoretical Perspectives.* Boulder, CO: Lynne Rienner Publishers.

———. 1988. Democratization and the Problem of Legitimacy in Middle East Politics. *Middle East Studies Association Bulletin* 22 (2) (December): 157–71.

———. 1977. *Arab Politics: The Search for Legitimacy.* New Haven, CT: Yale University Press.

Human Rights Watch. 2001. Yemen's *Constitutional Referendum and Local Elections* (February). New York: Human Rights Watch.

Huntington, Samuel P. 1996. *The Clash of Civilizations and the Remaking of World Order.* New York: Touchstone.

———. 1993. The Clash of Civilizations? *Foreign Affairs* 72(3) (Summer): 22–49.

———. 1991. *The Third Wave: Democratization in the Late Twentieth Century.* Norman: University of Oklahoma Press.

———. 1968. *Political Order in Changing Societies.* New Haven, CT: Yale University Press.

Hussein bin Talal bin Abd Allah. 1994. *Selected Speeches by His Majesty King Hussein, The Hashemite Kingdom of Jordan, 1988–1994.* Amman: International Press Office of the Royal Hashemite Court.

Inglehart, Ronald. 1998. The Renaissance of Political Culture. *American Political Science Review* 82(4) (December): 1203–30.

———. 1997. Does Latin America Exist? (And Is There a Confucian Culture?): A Global Analysis of Cross-Cultural Differences. *PS: Political Science and Politics* (March): 34–47.

International Crisis Group (ICG). 2005a. *Jordan's 9/11: Dealing with Jihadi Islamism. Middle East Report* 47 (November 23). Amman/Brussels: International Crisis Group.

———. 2005b. Understanding Islamism. *Middle East/North Africa Report* 37 (March 2). Amman/Brussels: International Crisis Group.

———. 2003. Yemen: Coping with Terrorism and Violence in a Fragile State. *IGC Middle East Report* 8 (January 8). Amman/Brussels: International Crisis Group.

Ismail, Salwa. 2001. The Paradox of Islamist Politics. *Middle East Report* 221 (Winter): 34–9.

———. 1998. Confronting the Other: Identity, Culture, Politics, and Conservative Islamism in Egypt. *International Journal of Middle East Studies* 30(2) (May): 199–225.

———. 1995. Democracy in Contemporary Arab Intellectual Discourse. In Rex Brynen, et al., eds., pp. 93–111. *Political Liberalization and Democratization in the Arab World, Volume I: Theoretical Perspectives.* Boulder, CO: Lynne Rienner Publishers.

Jaber, Hala. 1997. *Hezbollah: Born with a Vengeance.* New York: Columbia University Press.

Jabiri, Muhammad Abid al-. 1990. *Al-'Aql al-islami al-arabi.* Beirut: Markaz Dirasat al-Wahdah al-Arabi.

Joffé, George, ed. 2002. *Jordan in Transition, 1990–2000.* New York: Palgrave.

Johnson, James Turner. 1992. Does Democracy "Travel"? Some Thoughts on Democracy and Its Cultural Context. *Ethics and International Affairs* 6: 41–55.

Kalyvas, Stathis. 2000. Commitment Problems in Emerging Democracies: The Case of Religious Parties. *Comparative Politics* 32(4): 379–98.

———. 1998a. Democracy and Religious Politics: Evidence from Belgium. *Comparative Political Studies* 31(3) (June): 292–320.

———. 1998b. From Pulpit to Party: Party Formation and the Christian Democratic Phenomenon. *Comparative Politics* 30(3) (April): 293–312.

———. 1996. *The Rise of Christian Democracy in Europe.* Ithaca, NY: Cornell University Press.

Karl, Terry Lynn. 1997. *The Paradox of Plenty: Oil Booms and Petro-States.* Berkeley: University of California Press.

———. 1990. Dilemmas of Democratization in Latin America. *Comparative Politics* 23(1) (October): 1–21.

———. 1986. Imposing Consent? Electoralism versus Democratization in El Salvador. In Paul W. Drake and Eduardo Silva, eds., *Elections and Democratization in Latin America.* San Diego: Center for Iberian and Latin American Studies, University of California.

Katz, Kimberly. 2004. *Holy Places and National Spaces: Jerusalem under Jordanian Control.* Austin: University of Texas Press.

Kazem, Ali Abdul. 1997. The Muslim Brotherhood: The Historic Background and the Ideological Origins. In Jillian Schwedler, ed., pp. 11–43. *Islamist Movements in Jordan.* Amman: Markaz al-Urdunn al-Jadid.

Keane, John. 1993. Western Perspectives: Power-Sharing Islam? In Azzam Tamimi, ed., pp. 15–31. *Power-Sharing Islam?* London: Liberty for Muslim World Publications.

Keck, Margaret. 1992. *The Workers Party and Democratization in Brazil.* New Haven, CT: Yale University Press.

Keddie, Nikki R. 1998. The New Religious Politics: Where, When, and Why Do 'Fundamentalisms' Appear? *Comparative Study of Society and History* 40(4) (October): 696–723.

Kepel, Gilles. 2002. *Jihad: The Trail of Political Islam.* Cambridge: Harvard University Press.

————. 1986. *Muslim Extremism in Egypt: The Prophet and Pharaoh*. Berkeley: University of California Press.

Kilani, Musa Zayd al-. 1994. *Al-Harakat al-islamiyyah fi al-Urdunn wa Filistin*. Amman: Dar al-Bashir.

Kilani, Sa'eda. 2002. *Hurriyat al-Sahafa fi al-Urdunn*. Copenhagen: Euro-Mediterranean Human Rights Network.

————. 1997. *Blaming the Press: Jordan's Retreat from Democracy*. London: Article 19.

Kladermans, Bert, Suzanne Staggenborg, and Sidney Tarrow. 2002. Conclusion: Blending Methods and Building Theories in Social Movement Research. In Bert Kladermans and Suzanne Staggenborg, eds., pp. 314–49. *Methods of Social Movement Research*. Minneapolis: University of Minnesota Press.

Kodmani, Bassma. 2005. *The Dangers of Political Exclusion: Egypt's Islamist Problem*. Carnegie Papers 63, Middle East Series, Democracy and the Rule of Law Project (October).

Kohli, Atul, and Vivienne Shue. 1994. State Power and Social Forces: On Political Contention and Accommodation in the Third World. In Joel Migdal, et al., eds., pp. 293–326. *State Power and Social Forces: Domination and Transformation in the Third World*. New York: Cambridge University Press.

Kornbluth, Danishai. 2002. Jordan and the Anti-Normalization Campaign, 1994–2001. *Terrorism and Political Violence* 14(3) (Autumn): 80–108.

Krämer, Gudrun. 1995a. Islam and Pluralism. In Rex Brynen, et al., eds., pp. 113–28. *Political Liberalization and Democratization in the Arab World, Volume I: Theoretical Perspectives*. Boulder, CO: Lynne Rienner Publishers.

————. 1995b. Cross-Links and Double Talk? Islamist Movements in the Political Process. In Laura Guazzone, ed., pp. 39–67. *The Islamist Dilemma*. Reading, UK: Ithaca Press.

————. 1994. The Integration of the Integrists: A Comparative Study of Egypt, Jordan and Tunisia. In Ghassan Salamé, ed., pp. 229–6. *Democracy without Democrats? The Renewal of Politics in the Muslim World*. London: I. B. Taurus.

————. 1993. Islamist Notions of Democracy. *Middle East Report* 183 (July–August): 2–8.

Krasner, Stephen. 1984. Approaches to the State: Alternative Conceptions and Historical Dynamics. *Comparative Politics* 16(2): 223–46.

Kriesi, Hanspeter. 1989. The Political Opportunity Structure of the Dutch Peace Movement. *West European Politics* 12: 295–312.

Kurzman, Charles, ed. 1998. *Liberal Islam: A Sourcebook*. New York: Oxford University Press.

Langohr, Vickie. 2001. Of Islamists and Ballot Boxes: Rethinking the Relationship between Islamists and Electoral Politics. *International Journal of Middle East Studies* 33 (November): 591–610.

Lawrence, Bruce B. 1998. *Shattering the Myth: Islam beyond Violence*. Princeton: Princeton University Press.

Lawson, Stephanie. 1993. Conceptual Issues in the Comparative Study of Regime Change and Democratization. *Comparative Politics* (January): 183–205.

Layne, Linda. 1994. *Home and Homeland: The Dialogics of Tribal and National Identities in Jordan*. Princeton: Princeton University Press.

Lerner, Daniel. 1958. *The Passing of Traditional Society: Modernizing the Middle East*. New York: The Free Press.

Lewis, Bernard. 2003. *The Crisis of Islam: Holy War and Unholy Terror*. New York: Modern Library.

———. 2001. *What Went Wrong? The Clash between Islam and Modernity in the Middle East*. Oxford: Oxford University Press.

———. 1994. *Islam and the West*. Oxford: Oxford University Press.

———. 1992. Rethinking the Middle East. *Foreign Affairs* 71(4) (Fall): 99–119.

Lichbach, Mark Irving. 1995. *The Rebel's Dilemma*. Ann Arbor: University of Michigan Press.

———. 1987. Deterrence or Escalation? The Puzzle of Aggregate Studies of Repression and Dissent. *Journal of Conflict Resolution* 31: 266–97.

Lichbach, Mark, and Alan Zuckerman, eds. 1997. *Comparative Politics*. New York: Cambridge University Press.

Linz, Juan J., and Alfred Stepan. 1996. *Problems of Democratic Transition and Consolidation: Southern Europe, South America, and Post-Communist Europe*. Baltimore: Johns Hopkins University Press.

Lipset, Seymour Martin. 1959. Some Social Requisites of Democracy: Economic Development and Political Legitimacy. *American Political Science Review* 53(1) (March): 69–105.

Lloyd, David, and Paul Thomas. 1998. *Culture and the State*. New York: Routledge.

Lockman, Zachary. 1997. Arab Workers and Arab Nationalism in Palestine: A View from Below. In James Jankowski and Israel Gershoni, eds., pp. 249–72. *Rethinking Nationalism in the Arab Middle East*. New York: Columbia University Press.

Londregan, John B., and Keith T. Poole. 1996. Does High Income Promote Democracy? *World Politics* 49(1) (October): 1–30.

Lowi, Theodore. 1971. *The Politics of Disorder*. New York: Free Press.

Lucas, Russell. 2003. Deliberalization in Jordan. *Journal of Democracy* 14(1) (January): 137–44.

Lynch, Marc. 1999. *State Interests and Public Spheres: The International Politics of Jordan's Identity*. New York: Columbia University Press.

Lust-Okar, Ellen. 2005. *Structuring Conflict in the Arab World: Incumbents, Opponents, and Institutions*. New York: Cambridge University Press.

Lust-Okar, Ellen, and Amaney Ahmad Jamal. 2002. Rulers and Rules: Reassessing the Influence of Regime Type on Electoral Law Formation. *Comparative Political Studies* 35(3) (April): 337–66.

Ma'aytah, Samih. 1994. *Al-Tajrubah al-siyasiyyah li al-harakah al-islamiyyah fi al-Urdunn*. Amman: Dar al-Bashir.

Mainwaring, Scott, Guillermo O'Donnell, and J. Samuel Valenzuela, eds. 1993. *Issues in Democratic Consolidation: The New South American Democracies in Comparative Perspective*. Notre Dame, IN: University of Notre Dame Press.

Mani', Ilham Muhammad. 1994. *Al-Ahzab wa al-tanthimat al-siyasiyyah fi al-Yaman, 1948–1993*. Sana': Kitb al-Thawabit 2.

Mann, Michael. 1984. The Autonomous Power of the State: Its Origins, Mechanisms and Results. *European Journal of Sociology* 25(2) (Spring): 185–213.

Marx, Karl, and Fredrick Engels. 1970 [1846]. *The German Ideology*, C. J. Arthur, ed. New York: International Publishers.

Massad, Joseph Andoni. 2001. *Colonial Effects: The Making of National Identity in Jordan*. New York: Columbia University Press.

Mawdudi, Mawlana. 1982. Political Theory of Islam. In John Donohue and John Esposito, eds. *Islam in Transition*. New York: Oxford University Press.

Mazur, Michael P. 1979. *Economic Growth and Development in Jordan*. Boulder, CO: Westview Press.

McAdam, Doug. 1982. *The Political Process and the Development of Black Insurgency*. Chicago: University of Chicago Press.

McAdam, Doug, John D. McCarthy, and Mayer N. Zald. 1996. Introduction: Opportunities, Mobilizing Structures, and Framing Processes – Toward a Synthetic, Comparative Perspective on Social Movements. In D. McAdam, J. McCarthy, and M. Zald, eds., pp. 1–40. *Comparative Perspectives on Social Movements: Political Opportunities, Mobilizing Structures, and Cultural Framings*. New York: Cambridge University Press.

McAdam, Doug, Sydney Tarrow, and Charles Tilly. 2001. *Dynamics of Contention*. New York: Cambridge University Press.

McCarthy, John D., and Mayer N. Zald. 1987. Resource Mobilization and Social Movements. In J. McCarthy and M. Zald, pp. 15–48. *Social Movements in an Organizational Society*. New Brunswick, NJ: Transaction Publishers.

McCarthy, John D., David Britt, and Mark Wolfson. 1991. The Institutional Channeling of Social Movements by the State in the United States. In Louis Kreisberg, ed., *Research in Social Movements, Conflict, and Change* 13: 45–76.

McFaul, Michael. 2002. The Fourth Wave of Democracy and Dictatorship. *World Politics* 54(2): 212–44.

McGarry, John, and Brendan O'Leary. 1995. *Explaining Northern Ireland: Broken Images*. London: Blackwell Publishers.

Melucci, Alberto. 1985. The Symbolic Challenge of Contemporary Movements. *Social Research* 52(4) (Winter): 789–816.

Menta, Uday. 1990. Liberal Strategies of Exclusion. *Politics and Society* 18(4) (December): 427–54.

Mermier, Franck. 1997. L'Islam politique au Yémen ou 'la Tradition' contre les traditions? *Maghreb Machrek* 155 (January–March): 6–19.

Messara, Antoine. 1993. La regulation étatique de la religion dans le monde arabe: le cas de la Jordanie. *Social Compass* 40 (April): 581–8.

Messick, Brinkley. 1993. *The Calligraphic State: Textual Domination and History in a Muslim Society*. Berkeley: University of California Press.

———. 1988. Kissing Hands and Knees: Hegemony and Hierarchy in Shari'a Discourse. *Law and Society Review* 22(4): 637–59.

Michels, Robert. 1962. *Political Parties*. New York: Collier Books.

Migdal, Joel S. 1994. The State in Society: An Approach to Struggles for Domination. In Joel Migdal et al., eds., pp. 7–34. *State Power and Social Forces: Domination and Transformation in the Third World*. New York: Cambridge University Press.

Migdal, Joel S., Atul Kohli, and Vivienne Shue, eds. 1994. *State Power and Social Forces: Domination and Transformation in the Third World.* New York: Cambridge University Press.

Mill, John Stuart. 1956 [1859]. *On Liberty.* Indianapolis: Bobbs-Merrill.

Milton-Edwards, Beverly. 1996. *Islamic Politics in Palestine.* New York: I. B. Tauris.

———. 1993. Façade Democracy and Jordan. *The British Journal of Middle East Studies* 20(2): 191–203.

———. 1991. A Temporary Alliance with the Crown: The Islamic Response in Jordan. In James Piscatori, ed., *Islamic Fundamentalisms and the Gulf Crisis.* Chicago: American Academy of Arts.

Mitchell, Richard P. 1969. *The Society of the Muslim Brothers.* Oxford: Oxford University Press.

Mitchell, Timothy. 2002a. McJihad: Islam in the U.S. Global Order. *Social Text* 73, 20(4) (Winter): 1–18.

———. 2002b. *Rule of Experts: Egypt, Techno-Politics, Modernity.* Berkeley: University of California Press.

———. 1992. Going beyond the State? Response. *American Political Science Review* 86(4) (December): 1017–20.

———. 1991. Limits of the State: Beyond Statist Approaches and Their Critics. *American Political Science Review* 85(1) (March): 77–96.

Moaddel, Mansoor. 2002. *Jordanian Exceptionalism.* New York: Palgrave Macmillan.

Moaddel, Mansoor, and Kamran Talattof, eds. 2002. *Modernist and Fundamentalist Debates in Islam.* New York: Palgrave Macmillan.

Moore, Pete W. 2004. *Doing Business with the State: Political Reform and Economic Crisis in Jordan and Kuwait.* New York: Cambridge University Press.

Motyl, Alexander. 1998. State, Nation, and Elites in Independent Ukraine. In Taras Kuzio, ed., *Contemporary Ukraine: Dynamics of Post-Soviet Transformation.* Armonk, NY: M. E. Sharpe.

Mouffe, Chantal, ed. 1992. *Dimensions of Radical Democracy: Pluralism, Citizenship, Community.* London: Verso.

Moussalli, Ahmad S. 2001. *The Islamic Quest for Democracy, Pluralism, and Human Rights.* Gainesville: University Press of Florida.

———. 1999. *Moderate and Radical Fundamentalism: The Quest for Modernity, Legitimacy, and the Islamic State.* Gainesville: University Press of Florida.

———. 1994. Hasan al-Turabi's Islamist Discourse on Democracy and Shura. *Middle Eastern Studies* 30 (January): 57–61.

Mufti, Malik. 1999. Elite Bargains and Political Liberalization in Jordan. *Comparative Political Studies* (February): 100–29.

Munck, Gerardo, and Carol Sklalnik Leff. 1997. Modes of Transition and Democratization in Comparative Perspective. *Comparative Politics* 29 (April).

Munson, Henry. 2002. Debate: Between Pipes and Esposito. *ISIM Newsletter* 10 (July): 8.

———. 1996. Intolerable Tolerance: Western Academic and Islamic Fundamentalism. *Contention* 5(3): 99–117.

———. 1993. *Religion and Power in Morocco*. New Haven, CT: Yale University Press.

Mustafa, Nasr Taha. 1996. Al-Harakah al-islamiyyah al-Yamaniyyah: ishrun 'amm min al-musharakah al-siyasiyyah. In Azzam Tamimi, ed., pp. 141–70. *Musharakah Islamiyyah fi al-Sultah*. London: Liberty for Muslim World Publications.

Mutz, Diana. 2002. Cross-cutting Social Networks: Testing Democratic Theory in Practice. *American Political Science Review* 96(1) (March): 111–26.

Nasr, Sayyid Vali Reza. 1994. *Vanguard of the Islamic Revolution: The Jamaat-i Islami of Pakistan*. Berkeley: University of California Press.

Nasr, Vali. 2005. The Rise of "Muslim Democracy." *Journal of Democracy* 16(2) (April): 13–27.

National Democratic Institute for International Affairs (NDI). 1994. *Promoting Participation in Yemen's 1993 Elections*. Washington, DC: National Democratic Institute for International Affairs.

Ndegwa, Stephen N. 1997. Citizenship and Ethnicity: An Examination of Two Transition Moments in Kenyan Politics. *American Political Science Review* 91(3) (September): 599–616.

Nevo, Joseph, and Ilan Pappé, eds. 1994. *Jordan and the Middle East, 1948–1988: The Making of a Pivotal State*. Portland, OR: Frank Cass.

Niblock, Tim, and Emma Murphy, eds. 1993. *Economic and Political Liberalization in the Middle East*. London: British Academic Press.

Nodia, Ghia. 2002. Debating the Transitions Paradigm: The Democratic Path. *Journal of Democracy* 13(3): 13–19.

Norton, Augustus Richard, ed. 1995–6. *Civil Society in the Middle East*, 2 vols. Leiden: E. J. Brill.

———. 1995. The Challenge of Inclusion in the Middle East. *Current History* 94 (January): 1–6.

O'Donnell, Guillermo. 2002. Debating the Transitions Paradigm: In Partial Defense of an Evanescent 'Paradigm'. *Journal of Democracy* 13(3): 6–12.

———. 1996. Illusions about Consolidation. *Journal of Democracy* 7(2) (April): 34–51.

O'Donnell, Guilliermo, and Philippe C. Schmitter. 1996 [1986]. *Tentative Conclusions about Uncertain Democracies*. Baltimore: Johns Hopkins University Press.

O'Donnell, Guilliermo, Philippe C. Schmitter, and Lawrence Whitehead. 1986. *Transitions from Authoritarian Rule*. 4 vols. Washington, DC: The Woodrow Wilson Center for Scholars.

Offé, Claus. 1985. New Social Movements: Challenging the Boundaries of Institutional Politics. *Social Research* 52(4) (Winter): 817–68.

Okruhlik, Gwenn. 2002. Networks of Dissent: Islamism and Reform in Saudi Arabia. *Current History* (January): 22–8.

Okruhlik, Gwenn, and Patrick Conge. 1997. National Autonomy, Labor Migration and Political Crisis: Yemen and Saudi Arabia. *Middle East Journal* 51(4): 554–65.

Owen, Roger. 1992. *State, Power and Politics in the Making of the Modern Middle East*. New York: Routledge.

Pateman, Carole. 1983. Feminist Critiques of the Public/Private Dichotomy. In S. I. Benn and G. F. Gaus, eds., *Public and Private in Social Life*. London: Palgrave Macmillan.

———. 1970. *Participation and Democratic Theory*. New York: Cambridge University Press.

Perthes, Volker. 1994. The Private Sector, Economic Liberalization, and the Prospects for Democratization: The Case of Syria and Some Other Arab Countries. In Ghassan Salamé, ed., pp. 243–69. *Democracy without Democrats? The Renewal of Politics in the Muslim World*. London: I. B. Taurus.

Pettigrew, Thomas F., and Linda R. Tropp. 2003. A Meta-Analytic Test of Intergroup Contact Theory. Unpublished manuscript.

Phillips, Sarah. 2005. Cracks in the Yemeni System. *Middle East Report Online*, July 28.

Piscatori, James. 1983. Ideological Politics in Saudi Arabia. In James Piscatori, ed. *Islam in the Political Process*. New York: Cambridge University Press.

Pitkin, Hanna Fenichel. 1993. *Wittgenstein and Justice: On the Significance of Ludwig Wittgenstein for Social and Political Thought*. Berkeley: University of California Press.

Piven, Frances Fox, and Richard A. Cloward. 1977. *Poor People's Movements: Why They Succeed, How They Fail*. New York: Vintage Books.

Polletta, Francesca. 2002. *Freedom is an Endless Meeting: Democracy in American Social Movements*. Chicago: University of Chicago Press.

Przeworski, Adam. 1998a. Culture and Democracy. pp. 125–46. *World Culture Report: Culture, Creativity, and Markets*. New York: UNESCO.

———. 1998b. Deliberation and Ideological Domination. In Jon Elster, ed., pp. 140–60. *Deliberative Democracy*. Cambridge: Cambridge University Press.

———. 1993. The Games of Transition. In Scott Mainwaring, Guillermo O'Donnell, and J. Samuel Valenzuela, eds., *Issues in Democratic Consolidation: The New South American Democracies in Comparative Perspective*. Notre Dame, IN: University of Notre Dame Press.

———. 1991. *Democracy and the Market: Political and Economic Reforms in Eastern Europe and Latin America*. Cambridge: Cambridge University Press.

———. 1985. *Capitalism and Social Democracy*. New York: Cambridge University Press.

Przeworski, Adam, and John Sprague. 1986. *Paper Stones: A History of Electoral Socialism*. Chicago: University of Chicago Press.

Przeworski, Adam, and Henry Teune. 1982. *The Logic of Comparative Social Inquiry*. Melbourne, FL: Krieger Publishing.

Przeworski, Adam, Michael Alvarez, José Antonio Cheibub, and Fernando Limongi. 1996. *What Makes Democracies Endure? Journal of Democracy* 7(1) (January): 39–55.

Putnam, Robert. 1993. *Making Democracy Work: Civic Traditions in Modern Italy*. Princeton: Princeton University Press.

Quandt, William B. 1998. *Between Ballots and Bullets: Algeria's Transition from Authoritarianism*. Washington, DC: Brookings Institution.

Qutb, Sayyid. 1964. *Ma'alim fi al-Tariq*. Cairo: Maktabat Wahbah.

Rashid, Ahmad. 2000. *Taliban: Militant Islam, Oil, and Fundamentalism in Central Asia*. New Haven: Yale University Press.

Rath, Katherine. 1994. The Process of Democratization in Jordan. *Middle Eastern Studies* 30(3) (July): 530–57.

Rawls, John. 1993. The Domain of the Political and Overlapping Consensus. In David Copp, et al., eds., pp. 245–69. *The Idea of Democracy*. New York: Cambridge University Press.

Ray, James Lee, Donald J. Puchala, and Charles W. Kegley, eds. 1998. *Democracy and International Conflict: An Evaluation of the Democratic Peace Proposition*. Columbia: University of South Carolina Press.

Remmer, Karen L. 1995. New Theoretical Perspectives on Democratization. *Comparative Politics* 28(1) (January): 103–22.

Richards, Alan, and John Waterbury. 1996. *A Political Economy of the Middle East*, 2nd ed. Boulder, CO: Westview Press.

———. 1990. *A Political Economy of the Middle East*, 1st ed. Boulder, CO: Westview Press.

Riedel, Tim. 1993. *Who Is Who in the Jordanian Parliament, 1989–1993*. Amman: Friedrich Ebert Stiftung.

Roberts, Kenneth. 1995. From the Barricades to the Ballot Box: Redemocratization and Political Realignment in the Chilean Left. *Politics and Society* 23(4) (December).

Robins, Philip J. 1991. Politics and the 1986 Electoral Law in Jordan. In Rodney Wilson, ed., pp. 184–207. *Politics and the Economy in Jordan*. London: Routledge.

Robinson, Glenn E. 2004. HAMAS-PFLP Cooperation. Unpublished manuscript.

———. 1998a. Defensive Democratization in Jordan. *International Journal of Middle East Studies* 30(3) (August): 387–410.

———. 1998b. Islamists under Liberalization in Jordan. In Ahmad S. Moussalli, ed., *Islamic Fundamentalism: Myths and Realities*. Reading, UK: Ithaca Press.

———. 1997. Can Islamists Be Democrats? The Case of Jordan. *Middle East Journal* 51(3) (Summer): 373–87.

Robinson, William I. 1996. *Promoting Polyarchy: Globalization, US Intervention, and Hegemony*. New York: Cambridge University Press.

Rose, Richard, William Mishler, and Christian Haerpfer. 1998. *Democracy and its Alternatives: Understanding Post-Communist Societies*. Baltimore: The Johns Hopkins University Press.

———. 2002. *Mobilizing Islam: Religion, Activism, and Political Change in Egypt*. New York: Columbia University Press.

Roy, Olivier. 1994. *The Failure of Political Islam*. Cambridge: Harvard University Press.

Rueschemeyer, Dietrich, Evelyn Huber Stephens, and John D. Stephens. 1992. *Capitalist Development and Democracy*. Chicago: University of Chicago Press.

Russett, Bruce. 1993. *Grasping the Democratic Peace: Principles for a Post-Cold War World*. Princeton: Princeton University Press.

Rustow, Dankwart A. 1970. Transitions to Democracy: Towards a Dynamic Model. *Comparative Politics* 2(2) (April): 337–66.

Ryan, Curtis R. 2002. *Jordan in Transition: From Hussein to Abdullah.* Boulder, CO: Lynne Rienner Publishers.

——. 1998. Jordan and the Rise and Fall of the Arab Cooperation Council. *Middle East Journal* 52(3) (Summer): 386–401.

Ryan, Curtis R., and Jillian Schwedler. 2004. Return to Democratization or New Hybrid Regime? The 2003 Elections in Jordan. *Middle East Policy* XI(2) (Summer): 138–51.

Saad-Ghorayeb, Amal. 2002. *Hizbu'llah: Politics and Religion.* London: Pluto Press.

Sa'id, Abd al-Karim Qasim. 1995. *Al-Ikhwan al-muslimun wa al-harakah al-usuliyyah fi al-Yaman.* Cairo: Maktabah Madbuli al-Qahirah.

Said, Edward W. 1997. *Covering Islam: How the Media and the Experts Determine How We See the Rest of the World,* rev. ed. New York: Vintage.

——. 1978. *Orientalism.* New York: Vintage.

Saif, Ahmed A. 2001. *A Legislature in Transition: The Yemeni Parliament.* Aldershot, UK: Ashgate.

Salamé, Ghassan, ed. 1994. *Democracy without Democrats? The Renewal of Politics in the Muslim World.* London: I. B. Taurus.

Sanchez, Omar. 2003. Beyond Pacted Transitions in Spain and Chile: Elite and Institutional Differences. *Democratization* 10(2) (Summer): 65–86.

Sani, Nasser. 1993. Kuwait. In Azzam Tamimi, ed., pp. 103–8. *Power-Sharing Islam?* London: Liberty for Muslim World Publications.

Saqqaf, Faris al-. 1997. *Al-Islamiyun wa al-sultah fi al-Yaman.* Sana': Markaz Darasat al-Mustaqbal.

Satloff, Robert. 1994. *From Abdullah to Hussein: Jordan in Transition.* Oxford: Oxford University Press.

Schaffer, Frederic C. 1998. *Democracy in Translation: Understanding Politics in an Unfamiliar Culture.* Ithaca, NY: Cornell University Press.

Schmitter, Philippe C., and Terry Lynn Karl. 1994. The Conceptual Travels of Transitologists and Consolidologists: How Far to the East Should They Attempt to Go? *Slavic Review* 53(1) (Spring): 173–85.

——. 1991. Modes of Transition in Latin America, Southern and Eastern Europe. *International Social Science Journal* 128 (May): 269–84.

Schmitz, Charles Paul. 1997. State and Market in South Yemen. Ph.D. diss., University of California, Berkeley.

Schumpeter, Joseph. 1942. *Capitalism, Socialism, and Democracy.* New York: Harper.

Schwedler, Jillian. 2005. Cop Rock: Protest, Identity, and Dancing Riot Police in Jordan. *Social Movement Studies* 4 (2) (September): 155–75.

——. 2003a. The Yemeni Islah Party: Political Opportunities and Coalition Building in a Transitional Polity. In Quintan Wiktorowicz, ed., *Islamist Activism: A Social Movement Theory Approach.* Bloomington: Indiana University Press.

——. 2003b. More than a Mob: The Dynamics of Political Demonstrations in Jordan. *Middle East Report* 226 (Spring): 18–23.

——. 2002. Yemen's Aborted Opening. *Journal of Democracy* 13(4) (October): 48–55.

————. 2001. Islamic Identity: Myth, Menace, or Mobilizer? *SAIS Review* 21(2) (Summer–Fall): 1–21.

————. 1998. A Paradox of Democracy? Islamist Participation in Democratic Elections. *Middle East Report* 209 (Winter 1998–9): 25–9.

————, ed. 1997. *Islamist Movements in Jordan.* Amman: Markaz al-Urdunn al-Jadid.

————. 1995. Civil Society and the Study of Middle East Politics. In Jillian Schwedler, ed., *Toward Civil Society in the Middle East?* Boulder, CO: Lynne Rienner Publishers.

Scott, James C. 1992. *Domination and the Arts of Resistance: Hidden Transcripts.* New Haven, CT: Yale University Press.

————. 1985. *Weapons of the Weak: Everyday Forms of Peasant Resistance.* New Haven, CT: Yale University Press.

Searle, John. 1995. *The Construction of Social Reality.* New York: The Free Press.

Seidman, Steven. 1998. *Contested Knowledge: Social Theory in the Postmodern Age,* 2nd ed. Oxford: Blackwell.

Sewell, William H., Jr. 2001. Space in Contentious Politics. In Ronald R. Aminzade, et al., eds., pp. 51–88. *Silence and Voice in the Study of Contentious Politics.* New York: Cambridge University Press.

————, Jr. 1999. The Concept(s) of Culture. In Victoria E. Bonnell and Lynn Hunt, eds., pp. 35–61. *Beyond the Cultural Turn.* Berkeley: University of California Press.

Shahin, Emad Eldin. 1997. *Political Ascent: Contemporary Islamic Movements in North Africa.* Boulder, CO: Westview Press.

Shanks, Andrew. 1995. *Civil Society, Civil Religion.* Oxford: Blackwell.

Shapiro, Ian. 1999. *Democratic Justice.* New Haven: Yale University Press.

————. 1993. Democratic Innovation: South Africa in Comparative Context. *World Politics* 46(1) (October): 121–50.

Shapiro, Ian, and Grant Reecher, eds. 1988. *Power, Inequality, and Democratic Politics.* Boulder, CO: Westview Press.

Share, Donald. 1987. Transitions to Democracy and Transition through Transaction. *Comparative Political Studies* 19: 525–48.

————. 1985. Two Transitions: Democratization and the Evolution of the Spanish Socialist Left. *West European Politics* 8(1) (January): 82–103.

Share, Donald, and Scott Mainwaring. 1996. Transitions through Transaction: Democratization in Brazil and Spain. In Wayne Selcher, ed., *Political Liberalization in Brazil.* Boulder, CO: Westview Press.

Shils, Edward. 1997. *The Virtue of Civility.* Indianapolis: The Liberty Fund.

Shirabi, Hisham. 1988. *Neopatriarchy: A Theory of Distorted Change in Arab Society.* New York: Oxford University Press.

Shlaim, Avi. 1998. *The Politics of Partition: King Abdullah, the Zionists and Palestine, 1921–1951.* New York: Oxford University Press.

————. 1988. *Collusion across the Jordan: King Abdullah, the Zionist Movement, and the Partition of Palestine.* New York: Columbia University Press.

Shryock, Andrew. 1997. *Nationalism and the Genealogical Imagination: Oral History and Textual Authority in Tribal Jordan.* Berkeley: University of California Press.

Snow, David A., and Robert D. Benford. 1988. Ideology, Frame Resonance, and Participant Mobilization. In Bert Klandermans, et al., eds., pp. 197–217. *From Structure to Action: Social Movement Participation across Cultures.* Greenwich, CT: JAI Press.

Snyder, Richard. 1998. Paths Out of Sultanistic Regimes: Combining Structural and Voluntaristic Perspectives. In H. E. Chehabi and J. Linz, eds., pp. 49–81. *Sultanistic Regimes.* Baltimore: Johns Hopkins University Press.

————. 1992. Explaining Transitions from Neopatrimonial Dictatorships. *Comparative Politics* 24 (October): 379–99.

Somers, Margaret. 1994. The Narrative Constitution of Identity: A Relational and Network Approach. *Theory and Society* 23: 605–49.

Soroush, Abdolkarim. 2000. *Reason, Freedom, and Democracy in Islam.* New York: Oxford University Press.

Stevenson, Thomas B. 1993. Yemeni Workers Come Home: Reabsorbing One Million Migrants. *Middle East Report* 181 (March–April): 15–20.

Stiftl, Ludwig. 1999. The Yemeni Islamists in the Process of Democratization. In Rémy Leveau, Franck Mermier, and Udo Steinbach, eds., pp. 247–66. *Le Yémen contemporain.* Paris.

Stinchcombe, Arthur L. 1991. The Conditions of Fruitfulness of Theorizing about Mechanisms in Social Science. *Philosophy of the Social Sciences* 21(3) (September): 367–87.

Susser, Asher. 2000. *Jordan: Case Study of a Pivotal State.* Washington, DC: The Washington Institute for Near East Policy.

Suwaidi, Jamal S. al-, ed. 1995. *The Yemeni War of 1994.* London: Saqi Books.

Suways, Sulayman. 1990. *Kharitah al-ahzab al-siyasiyyah fi al-Urdunn.* Amman: Al-Urdunn al-Jadid.

Swaminathan, Siddharth. 1999. Time, Power, and Democratic Transitions. *The Journal of Conflict Resolution* 43(2) (April): 178–91.

Swidler, Ann. 1986. Culture in Action: Symbols and Strategies. *American Sociological Review* 51(2): 273–86.

Tal, Lawrence. 1995. Dealing with Radical Islam: The Case of Jordan. *Survival* 37(3) (Autumn): 139–56.

Tamimi, Azzam S. 2001. *Rachid Ghannouchi: A Democrat within Islamism.* New York: Oxford University Press.

————, ed. 1993. *Power-Sharing Islam?* London: Liberty for Muslim World Publications.

Taraki, Lisa. 2003. The Role of Women. In Deborah J. Gerner and Jillian Schwedler, eds., *Understanding the Contemporary Middle East*, 2nd ed. Boulder, CO: Lynne Rienner Publishers.

Tarrow, Sidney. 1996. States and Opportunities: The Political Structuring of Social Movements. In D. McAdam, J. McCarthy, and M. Zald, eds., pp. 41–61. *Comparative Perspectives on Social Movements: Political Opportunities, Mobilizing Structures, and Cultural Framings.* New York: Cambridge.

————. 1995. *Power in Movement: Social Man, Collective Action, and Politics.* Cambridge: Cambridge University Press.

Thompson, John B. 1990. *Ideology and Modern Culture.* New York: Cambridge University Press.

————. 1985. *Studies in the Theory of Ideology*. Los Angeles: University of California Press.

Tibi, Bassam. 1998. *The Challenge of Fundamentalism: Political Islam and the New World Disorder*. Berkeley: University of California Press.

————. 1991. *Islam and the Cultural Accommodation of Social Change*. Boulder, CO: Westview Press.

Tilly, Charles. 2001. Mechanisms in Political Processes. *Annual Review of Political Science* 4: 21–41.

————. 1986. *The Contentious French*. Cambridge, MA: Belknap Press of Harvard University Press.

————. 1978. *From Mobilization to Revolution*. New York: Addison-Wesley.

Traboulsi, Fawwaz. 1991. Les transformations des structures tribales dupuis l'indépendance du Yémen du sud. *Cahiers du Gremamo* 10: 125–43.

'Ubaydi, Awni Jaddu'al-. 1991. *Jama'ah al-Ikhwan al-Muslimin fi al-Urdunn was Filastin, 1945–1970*. Amman.

————. 1990. *Jama'ah al-Ikhwan al-Muslimin wa thawrah al-dustur al-Yamaniyyah 1948*. Amman.

United Nations Development Program (UNDP). 2005. *Human Development Report*. New York: UNDP.

United Nations Education, Scientific, and Cultural Organization (UNESCO). 1998. *Statistical Yearbook*. Paris and Lanham, MD: UNESCO and Bernan Press.

————. 1980. *Statistical Yearbook*. Paris: UNESCO.

Varshney, Ashutosh. 2002. *Ethnic Conflict and Civic Life: Hindus and Muslims in India*. New Haven: Yale University Press.

Vitalis, Robert. 2002. Black Gold, White Crude: An Essay on American Exceptionalism, Hierarchy, and Hegemony in the Gulf. *Diplomatic History* 26(2): 185–213.

————. 1994. The Democratization Industry and the Limits of the New Interventionism. *Middle East Report* 187–8 (March–April/May–June): 46–50.

Vreeland, James. 2003. *The IMF and Economic Development*. New York: Cambridge University Press.

Walters, Delores W. 1987. Perceptions of Social Inequality in the Yemen Arab Republic. Ph.D. diss., New York University.

Wang, Xu. 1999. Mutual Empowerment of State and Society: Its Nature, Conditions, Mechanisms, and Limits. *Comparative Politics* 31(2) (January): 231–49.

Waterbury, John. 1994. Democracy without Democrats? The Potential for Political Liberalization in the Middle East. In Ghassan Salamé, ed., pp. 23–47. *Democracy without Democrats? The Renewal of Politics in the Muslim World*. London: I. B. Taurus.

Watkins, Eric. 1996. Islamism and Tribalism in Yemen. In Abdel Salam Sidahmed and Anoushiravan Ehteshami, eds., pp. 215–25. *Islamic Fundamentalism*. Boulder, CO: Westview Press.

Wedeen, Lisa. 2005. Peripheral Visions: Identifications in Unified Yemen. Unpublished manuscript.

————. 2003. Beyond the Crusades: How Huntington and Bin Laden Are Wrong. *Middle East Policy* 10(2): 54–61.

———. 2002. Conceptualizing Culture: Possibilities for Political Science. *American Political Science Review* 96(4) (December): 713–28.

———. 1999. *Ambiguities of Domination: Politics, Rhetoric, and Symbols in Contemporary Syria.* Chicago: University of Chicago Press.

Weir, Shelagh. 1997. A Clash of Fundamentalisms: Wahhabism in Yemen. *Middle East Report* 204 (Fall): 22–3, 26.

Wenner, Manfred W. 1991. *The Yemen Arab Republic: Development and Change in an Ancient Land.* Boulder, CO: Westview Press.

Werlin, Herbert. 1990. Political Culture and Political Change. *American Political Science Review* 84(1) (March): 249–53.

White, Jenny. 2002. *Islamist Mobilization in Turkey: A Study in Vernacular Politics.* Seattle: University of Washington Press.

Whitehead, Laurence, ed. 2001a. *The International Dimensions of Democratization: Europe and the Americas,* exp. ed. New York: Oxford University Press.

———. 2001b. Democracy by Convergence: Southern Europe. In Laurence Whitehead, ed., pp. 261–84. *The International Dimensions of Democratization: Europe and the Americas,* exp. ed. New York: Oxford University Press.

Whyte, John. 1991. *Interpreting Northern Ireland.* New York: Oxford University Press.

Wickham, Carrie Rosefsky. 2004. The Path to Moderation: Strategy and Learning in the Formation of Egypt's *Wasat* Party. *Comparative Politics* 36 (2) (January): PAGES.

Wiktorowicz, Quintan, ed. 2003. *Islamic Activism: A Social Movement Theory Approach.* Bloomington: Indiana University Press.

———. 2001. *The Management of Islamic Activism: Salafis, the Muslim Brotherhood, and State Power in Jordan.* Albany: SUNY Press.

Williams, Raymond. 1977. *Marxism and Literature.* New York: Oxford University Press.

Williams, Robin. 1947. *The Reduction of Intergroup Tension.* New York: Social Science Research Council.

Wilson, Mary. 1987. *King Abdallah, Britain and the Making of Jordan.* New York: Cambridge University Press.

Wood, Elisabeth Jean. 2000. *Forging Democracy from Below: Insurgent Transitions in South Africa and El Salvador.* New York: Cambridge University Press.

Yavuz, M. Hakan. 1997. Political Islam and the Welfare (Refah) Party in Turkey. *Comparative Politics* 30(1) (October): 63–82.

Young, Iris Marion. 2000. *Inclusion and Democracy.* New York: Oxford University Press.

Zakaria, Fareed. 2003. *The Future of Freedom: Illiberal Democracy at Home and Abroad.* New York: W. W. Norton.

———. 1997. The Rise of Illiberal Democracy. *Foreign Affairs* 76 (November): 22–43.

Zald, Mayer N. 1996. Culture, Ideology, and Strategic Framing. In D. McAdam, J. McCarthy, and M. Zald, eds., pp. 261–74. *Comparative Perspectives on Social Movements: Political Opportunities, Mobilizing Structures, and Cultural Framings.* New York: Cambridge University Press.

Zald, Mayer N., and Roberta Ash Garner. 1987. Social Movement Organization: Growth, Decay, and Change. In Mayer N. Zald and John D. McCarthy, eds., *Social Movements in an Organizational Society*. New Brunswick, NJ: Transaction Books.

Zizek, Slojiv, ed. 1994. *Mapping Ideology*. London: Verso.

———. 1989. *The Sublime Object of Ideology*. London: Verso.

Zubaida, Sami. 2001. Islam and the Politics of Community and Citizenship. *Middle East Report* 221 (Winter): 20–7.

———. 1996. Is Iran an Islamic State? In Joe Stork and Joel Beinin, eds., pp. 103–19. *Political Islam*. Berkeley: University of California Press.

———. 1993. *Islam, the People, and the State: Political Ideas and Movements in the Middle East*. New York: I. B. Taurus.

Index

Printed in the United States
98902LV00005B/196/A

9 780521 040006